THE A

Wong Kiew Kit, popularly known as Sifu Wong, is the fourth generation successor of Venerable Jiang Nan from the famous Shaolin Monastery in China and Grandmaster of Shaolin Wahnam Institute of Kungfu and Qiqong. He received the "Qiqong Master of the Year" Award during the Second World Congress on Qiqong held in San Francisco in 1997.

He is an internationally acclaimed author of books on the Shaolin arts and Buddhism including Introduction to Shaolin Kung Fu (1981), The Art of Qiqong (1993), The Art of Shaolin Kung Fu (1996), The Complete Book of Tai Chi Chuan (1996), Chi Kung for Health and Vitality (1997), The Complete Book of Zen (1998), The Complete Book of Chinese Medicine (2002), The Complete Book of Shaolin (2002), Sukhavati:The Western Paradise (2002) and The Shaolin Arts (2002).

Since 1987, Sifu Wong has spent more time teaching qiqong than kungfu, because he feels that while kungfu serves as an interesting hobby, qiqong serves an urgent public need, particularly in overcoming degenerative and psychiatric illnesses.

Sifu Wong is one of the few masters who have generously introduced the once secretive Shaolin Qiqong to the public, and has helped many people to obtain relieve or overcome so-called "incurable" diseases like hypertension, asthma, rheumatism, arthritis, diabetes, migraine, gastritis, gall stones, kidney failure, depression, anxiety and even cancer.

He stresses the Shaolin philosophy of sharing goodness with all humanity, and is now dedicated to spreading the wonders and benefits of the Shaolin arts to people all over the world irrespective of race, culture and religion.

SUKHAVATI
WESTERN PARADISE
GOING TO HEAVEN AS TAUGHT BY THE BUDDHA

NAMO AMITABHA BUDDHA

WONG KIEW KIT
Author of the bestselling *The Complete Book of Zen*

COSMOS

Published by Cosmos Internet Sdn Bhd
45C (3rd. Floor) Jalan Pengkalan,
Taman Pekan Baru, 08000,
Sungai Petani, Kedah,
Malaysia.

Designed and layout by Saw Seng Aun

Printed in Malaysia by Sun Printers Sdn Bhd

ISBN 983-40879-3-4

CONTENTS

INTRODUCTION

This sutra, taught by Sakyamuni Buddha, is one of the most important sutras in Mahayana Buddhism. It teaches how a person can be reborn in the Western Paradise of Eternal Bliss. In case you think this is too good to be true, remember it is taught by the Buddha himself, and the Buddha stresses that the teaching in the sutra is true, without any tincture of falsehood.

There are three conditions for rebirth in the Western Paradise:

1. Faith that there is a Western Paradise of Eternal Bliss;
2. Vow that you want to be reborn there;
3. Practice that accomplishes your vow.

Buddhist practice can be summed up in Sakyamuni Buddha's own words:

Avoid all evil,
Do good,
Purify the mind.

There are many ways to purify the mind. Probably the easiest is to recite the name of Amitabha Buddha, as taught in this sutra. The school of Buddhism that specially uses this approach to purifying the mind is called the Pure Land School, or Jing Tu Zong (Ching Tu Tsung) in Chinese, also known as the Amitabha School.

There is no hard and fast rule how or where you recite Amitabha's name; but you must recite sincerely, devotedly and regularly. The following are some suggestions taught by masters.

Kneel or sit in a meditation posture before a statue or an image of Amitabha Buddha, or any Buddha or Bodhisattva. If you open your eyes, focus your eyes on the Buddha or Bodhisattva. If you close your eyes, visualize Amitabha Buddha in your mind. Then recite many times "Amitabha Buddha, Amitabha Buddha, ... ", or "Ami Tuo Fo, Ami Tuo fo, ..." in Chinese, softly or aloud or in your heart, alone or in groups. The "many times" may range from tens to thousands. Thus, you see Amitabha in your eyes or mind, recite Amitabha in your mouth or heart, and hear Amitabha in your ears or heart. Many people prefix the term "Namo", which means "pay homage to and take guidance from", to the name Amitabha; and recite in soothing rhythm.

Many people may be surprised and ask, "Is it so simple to go to the Western Paradise of Eternal Bliss?' There are many ways to practice Buddhism, according to a person's needs and aspirations, and some ways are very simple. According to this way as described in the Amitabha Sutra, any person who avoids evil and do good, has faith and has made a vow to be reborn in the Western Paradise, will definitely be reborn in Amitabha's Pure Land if this person sincerely, devotedly and regularly recites the name of Amitabha.

How does the devotee go to the Western Paradise by just reciting Amitabha's name? This is through the grace and great compassion of Amitabha. Many aeons ago, long before our historical Buddha appeared in our world, a king renounced his luxurious life to become a monk. His name was Dharmakara, and he became a Bodhisattva, and later Amitabha Buddha. He made 48 great vows, which include creating out of his miraculous powers a paradise where sentient beings who recite his name will go to, to continue their spiritual cultivation to attain Buddhahood themselves.

Turn to the Amitabha Sutra and learn more about this Western Paradise where you too can go, if you want to.

AMITABHA BUDDHA AND THE WESTERN PARADISE

(Going to Paradise through the Compassion of Amitabha)

Although this method is simple, one must not be mistaken that it is necessarily easy — although it is actually easier than most other methods of spiritual cultivation.

The Western Paradise

Would you like to go to paradise? This is not a joke or play on words. In earnestness, this book explains how you can be reborn in Sukhavati, the Western Paradise of Eternal Bliss, as taught by the Buddha himself! In case you may think this is too ridiculous a suggestion, or too good to be true, please remember that a Buddha never lies.

The Buddha's teachings on the Western Paradise and how to be reborn there is specially recorded in three sutras, namely *Amitabha Sutra*, *Amitayus Sutra* and *Meditation on Amitayus Sutra*. Sutras are records of the teachings spoken by the Buddha. Amitabha, which means "Infinite Light", and Amitayus, which means "Infinite Life", are the two different names of the same Buddha, who attained Buddhahood many aeons before our time.

In his great compassion, Amitabha Buddha (or Amitayus Buddha) vowed that any beings, including those existing in our present aeon, who wish to be reborn in Sukhavati, or the Western Paradise of Eternal Bliss, will have their wish fulfilled with his help.

An aeon, or kalpa, refers to a tremendous length of time in between two calamities that cut off that period from other periods. A great aeon refers to the period of the birth, growth, decay and disintegration of our world, as different from other periods of other worlds. Our aeon is believed to have been in existence for about 12.8 billion years. A small aeon refers to the age of a world civilization, and may vary from thousands to millions of years. According to Buddhist teaching, there were countless world civilizations before our present one.

Amitabha Buddha lived ten aeons before us. We are not told whether these aeons are ten great aeons or ten small aeons, but whatsoever, in our puny human time scale, it means an unimaginable length of time away. How, then, could we know about Amitabha's compassionate vows which can certainly benefit us? This golden opportunity to be reborn in the Western Paradise was revealed to us by another Buddha, Sakyamuni Buddha, who appeared on earth as Siddharta Gautama Sakyamuni from 632 to 543 BCE (Before the Common Era), and who being the Buddha of our aeon in this world, is generally referred to as the Buddha.

There are countless Buddhas in the cosmos — Sakyamuni Buddha and Amitabha Buddha are two of them — and we shall meet some other Buddhas later in this book. A Buddha is a perfectly enlightened being, who has supreme perfect wisdom concerning man and universe.

The school of Buddhism that particularly focuses on this aspect of the Buddha's teaching is the Jing Tu or Pure Land School, so called because the Western Paradise of Eternal Bliss is often referred to as the Pure Land, or Jing Tu in Chinese, in contrast to the defiled Saha world where ordinary people live.

It is sometimes called, especially in Chinese, the Lotus School, which may cause some confusion because another famous Buddhist school, the Tiantai School, is also sometimes referred to, especially in English, as the Lotus School. The Pure Land School is the most popular school of Buddhism today.

Although this Amitabha teaching is Buddhist, followers of other religions may rewardingly use it, perhaps by substituting the name of Amitabha with God, Krishna or any other Deities who have promised after-life in heaven. The famous western scholar, Karl Ludvig Reichelt, claims that "Mahayana's conception of Amitabha was perhaps among those most influenced by the Christian ideas of God.[1]

Another well-known western scholar, August Karl Reischauer, suggested that "it does seem possible, if not probable, that Nestorian Christianity in China strengthened this theistic tendency in Buddhism.[2] Their views are not valid because the Amitabha teaching was already taught by the Buddha a few centuries before Christ, but it shows how universal the Amitabha teaching is.

The Pure Land School

Why is the Pure Land School the most popular form of Buddhism? It is because for most people its explicit aim of attaining rebirth in heaven is more immediate and comprehensible, and its practice of reciting Amitabha's name more easily accomplished than the aim of attaining nirvana and the practice of meditation in most other schools of Buddhism.

The development of the Pure Land School was much influenced by two very important philosophical works in Mahayana Buddhism, namely the *Treatise on Dasabhumi* by Nagajuna and the *Treatise on Rebirth in the Pure Land* by Vasubandhu. Nagajuna explained that spiritual cultivation may be generalized into two categories, namely the hard way and the easy way, and Vasubandhu explained that one can attain enlightenment through self-effort or through another's help.

Historically, Buddhism in India taught that an aspirant had to undergo strenuous developments over countless rebirths before he could attain nirvana or enlightenment. Such a long time is needed because our world, called the Saha world, is beset with "five evil impurities" (to be explained in a later chapter). The Pure Land School teaches an easier and shorter path to nirvana by accepting the gracious help provided by Amitabha Buddha.

Therefore, instead of cultivating in our Saha world, aspirants go to the heaven presided by Amitabha Buddha, where the five evil impurities are absent and where they live blissfully and eternally among spiritual beings, and cultivate with the help of great teachers under the care and love of Amitabha Buddha so that they too will eventually achieve Buddhahood.

It is significant to note that going to heaven, like the Western Paradise of Eternal Bliss, is not the supreme goal of Buddhism, although it is the ultimate of other religions, as well as the desire of most Buddhists who have not reached the spiritual or intellectual level to understand what Buddhahood is.

In 402 CE (Common Era) the famous master Hui Yuan (334-416) initiated the first group of 123 followers who vowed to be reborn in Sukhavati, the Western Paradise, and they recited the name of Amitabha Buddha regularly. This group was called the White Lotus Society and included prominent poets and scholars. Hui Yuan, however, did not actively preach the Amitabha doctrine to the public.

This task of preaching and organizing the Pure Land teaching was carried out by Tan Luan (476-542), who was initially a devoted pursuer after the Taoist elixir of immortality. After his long quest for and finally acquiring the esoteric *Xian Jing* (The Saints' Sutra), which explains the Taoist method to attain immortality, he met the famous Indian Buddhist master, Bodhiruci, who had come to China to spread Buddhism.

Tan Luan was so convinced and impressed by Bodhiruci's explanation of the Amitabha Sutras that he discarded the Taoist Sutra to practice and propagate the Amitabha doctrine. Hence, today, some regard Tan Luan, while others regard Hui Yuan, as the First Patriarch of the Pure Land School.

The Pure Land School became prominent through the efforts of Dao Chuo (562-645), who introduced the use of the rosary in Amitabha recitation, and his disciple Shan Dao (Zendo in Japanese, 613-681), who is regarded especially in Japan as an incarnation of Amitabha himself. Shan Dao expounded five practices for practitioners to be reborn in the Pure Land: reciting the name of Amitabha Buddha, chanting sutras (especially the Amitabha Sutras), meditating on the Buddha, worshipping images of the Buddha, and singing praises to the Buddha.

Another important master is Hui Ri, whom the Tang emperor bestowed the posthumous title of Ci Min (Tz'u Min), meaning "Compassionate and Benevolent". Ci Min (680-748), who received his teachings on Amitabha during his pilgrimage in India from 704 to 716, was the first master who combined the practice of Zen and Amitabha recitation, initiating an excellent way to attain enlightenment.

In Japan, where it is estimated that more than half her population practice the recitation of Amitabha Buddha, or Amida Butsu in Japanese, the Pure Land School is known as the Jodo School, and was established by Honen (1133-1212). His disciple Shinran (1173-1262) founded the Jodo Shin School, which is usually shortened to the Shin School. The Shin School had uniquely abolished all forms of monastic practice, thus making this school solely for lay followers.

The Three Sutras on Amitabha

The three sutras concerning Amitabha — *Amitabha Sutra, Amitayus Sutra* and *Meditation on Amitayus Sutra* — form the basis of the Pure Land School. Hence, this school is also called the Amitabha School.

The *Amitabha Sutra* is the most popular, probably because although it is the shortest, consisting of only about 2000 words in Chinese; it provides the gist of the Pure Land School teaching. It is known as *Sukhavati Vyuha Sutra* in Sanskrit, and *Fo Shuo Omi Tuo Jing* in Chinese, meaning "The Sutra of the Buddha's Teaching on Amitabha". This Sutra was translated from Sanskrit into Chinese by many masters, but the two best known are by the great Kumarajiva in 402, and by the famous pilgrim Xuan Zang in 650. For convenience, we may divide the Sutra into the following three parts:

1. Description of Sukhavati, the Western Paradise of Eternal Bliss, and Amitabha Buddha.
2. The Buddha's exhortation to sentient beings to seek rebirth in Sukhavati and the method to accomplish this.
3. Confirmation by Buddhas of the six directions that this teaching on Sukhavati is true.

Chapters 6 to 10 of this book gives a translation of the *Amitabha Sutra* from the Chinese version by Kumarajiva, a Kuchan prince who denounced a luxurious life to spread Buddhism to China. The translation is provided with a detailed commentary, without which it is difficult even for Buddhists to understand the Sutra, as it was written many centuries ago and contains concepts generally unfamiliar to many people.

The *Amitayus Sutra,* or *Wu Liang Shou Jing* in Chinese, meaning The Sutra on Infinite Life, lays the foundation of the Pure Land School. It describes that many, many aeons ago during the time of Lokesvararadjna Buddha, meaning the Buddha of Supreme Spontaneity, a king renounced his throne to become a monk called Dharmakara.

When he became a Bodhisattva, he made forty-eight great vows in front of Lokesvararadjna Buddha, among which he vowed that he would refuse to become a Buddha if he could not create out of his miraculous powers a paradise where beings could be reborn to continue their spiritual cultivation under the most favorable conditions to gain enlightenment. He vowed that he would help these beings to be reborn in his paradise if they only indicated such a wish by reciting his name.

As he succeeded in fulfilling his vows, he became Amitabha Buddha, and he continues to help sentient beings to be reborn in his Buddha-land. It is interesting to note that Amitabha's creation of Sukhavati in a distant galaxy is conceptually similar to the Christian belief of God's creation of our world system.

This paradise created by Amitabha Buddha, situated millions of light-years to the west of our Saha world, is one of eternal bliss where suffering, which happens to be the prominent characteristic of our own world, is unknown. Astronomers and other scientists may find it illuminating to know that this paradise is actually a world like ours, although there are also many crucial differences which contrast so fundamentally with conditions on our earth that we refer to this Amitabha's world as heaven.

Like our Saha world, as well as all other heavens and hells mentioned in Buddhist philosophy, this paradise exists in the phenomenal — and not in the transcendental — dimension. Hence, as in our and all other phenomenal worlds, the so-called "external reality" is an illusion, a creation of the mind.

In other words, phenomena like fruit flies, people and earthquakes appear to you as such because of the way your eyes are built; your intellect consciousness interprets them, and some other conditions. Another sentient being, like a living cell inside your body, would perceive the "same" phenomena differently. Besides, if you look at a fruit fly under an electron microscope, you would not see a fruit fly; you would see patterns of subatomic particles. Thus the phenomenon perceived by you as a fruit fly or as a pattern of particles is only relative and not ultimate.

Even if scientists were able to land on the star or any form of heavenly body far out in remote space where Sukhavati is situated, they would probably find nothing heavenly about it, because their very gross human senses are unable to perceive the very different vibrations of this world. Even if the star is within the range of their powerful telescopes, the scientists may not see it, if it happens to be in a black hole, or is made up of shadow matter.

Scientists cannot even perceive other sentient beings like ghosts, nature spirits and gods, who actually share the same earth with us, because they operate at frequencies different from those of humans. For similar reasons, what scientists consider in our human paradigm as barren rocks on the moon, or methane ice on Pluto, may actually be what we would call gardens of Eden for their inhabitants still unperceivable to us.

Because "external reality", whether on our earth or in a world millions of light-years away, is a creation of the mind, a human being on earth reborn in the Western Paradise would initially experience the paradise as conditioned by his previous experience on earth. He (or she) would, for example, experience gardens and streams, albeit in celestial light. If he, reminiscent of his earthly desire, suddenly wishes to taste his favorite ice-cream, for example, he merely visualizes it to have his ice-cream materialized to satisfy his appetite!

Hence, in this and other heavens beings can have their heart desires because "matter" in heavenly realms is fine enough for minds to manipulate — a condition not possible on earth where matter is too gross and heavy. On our earth, matter is still shaped by mind, but usually through tools like muscles and machines.

What happens if someone wishes to kill another being in Sukhavati? This simply will not happen, because Amitabha Buddha has so created his Paradise where evil is unknown. Killing may occur on earth because our world is beset with "five evil impurities", but in the Western Paradise there are no "evil impurities". It is as irrelevant for a heavenly being in Sukhavati to think of killing as for a human on earth to think of eating rocks. Killing cannot happen in the Western Paradise because life there is eternal, just as cutting a ray of sunlight is not possible on earth.

The third basic sutra of the Pure Land School is the *Meditation of Amitayus Sutra,* called the *Amitayus Dhyana Sutra* in Sanskrit, and *Guan Wu Liang Shou Jing* in Chinese. It is also known as the *Sutra of Sixteen Meditations,* because it explains sixteen kinds of meditation to reach the Pure Land.

The sixteen kinds of meditation are on (1) the setting sun, (2) water turning into crystals of myriad colors, (3) earth of the Pure Land, (4) the precious trees found in the Pure Land, (5) eight meritorious waters, (6) overall view of Sukhavati, (7) lotus, (8) the Buddha image, (9) Amitabha Buddha, (10) Avalokitesvara Bodhisattva or Guan Shi Yin, (11) Mahasthamaprapta Bodhisattva or Da Shi Zhi, (12) rebirth in the Pure Land by way of the calyx of a lotus, (13) miscellaneous aspects of Sukhavati, (14) highest level of beings, (15) middle level of beings, and (16) lowest level of beings in Sukhavati, the Western Paradise. These are advanced meditation techniques making extensive use of visualization, and they serve well to negate the not infrequent suggestion that in the Pure Land School meditation is insignificant or, at its best, simple.

The last three kinds of meditation describe the three levels of spiritual attainment of the Western Paradise inhabitants. Each level is subdivided into three stages. The highest level consists of Bodhisattvas and highly spiritual beings who understand the higher wisdom of emptiness of Mahayana Buddhism. The "fruit" or expected result of their cultivation is Buddhahood.

The middle level consists of beings of high moral values and discipline who diligently practice spiritual cultivation. Their "fruit" is Arahantship. The lowest level consists of beings who were sinful in their previous lives. Despite their sins, if they repent and accept the very precious offer of Amitabha Buddha, they can enter the stream of spiritual cultivation where they will not retrogress, and eventually will also attain enlightenment.

King Milinda, a Greek ruler in Sagara about 115 BCE, complained to the famous Indian Buddhist master, Nagasena, that it was unfair a sinful man could be saved if he belief in Amitabha Buddha just before the sinner died. Nagasena said that no matter how small a stone was, it would sink in water. But even if a huge rock weighing hundreds of tons were placed in a ship big enough, the rock would not sink. The compassion of Amitabha Buddha is so great, and his miraculous powers infinite, that this Buddha would help even sinners to go to heaven and eventually attain enlightenment.

However, one must not abuse Amitabha's boundless generosity. If a person's karma is so bad, he might not have the chance to learn about the generous offer of Amitabha Buddha, or even if he is told about the offer, he might sacrilegiously ridicule the Buddha. He could not benefit from Amitabha's compassion, not because the Buddha does not accept him, but because his very bad karmic effect prevents him from appreciating genuine help. Hence, anyone who has the very rare opportunity to be born a human, and the rarer opportunity to come across Amitabha's generosity, should not waste this golden chance.

How to be Reborn in Sukhavati

What, then, must you do if you wish to be reborn in Sukhavati, the Western Paradise of Eternal Bliss? There are three conditions for rebirth in this Pure Land:

1. Have faith that there is a Western Paradise of Eternal Bliss;
2. Make a vow that you want to be reborn there;
3. Cultivate the practice that accomplishes your vow.

The practice of Buddhism, which satisfies the third condition above, can be summed up in Sakyamuni Buddha's own words:

Avoid all evil,
Do good,
Purify the mind.

There are many ways to purify the mind. Probably the simplest is to recite the name of Amitabha Buddha, as taught in this sutra, and which is the main method of the Pure Land School. There is no hard and fast rule on how or where you should recite Amitabha's name, except not in such inappropriate times and places like easing in a toilet; but you must recite sincerely, devotedly and regularly. The following are some suggestions taught by masters.

Kneel or sit in a meditation posture before a statue or an image of Amitabha Buddha, or any Buddha or Bodhisattva. If you open your eyes, focus your eyes on the Buddha or Bodhisattva. If you close your eyes, visualize Amitabha Buddha in your mind. Then recite many times softly or aloud or in your heart, alone or in groups:

Amitabha Buddha, Amitabha Buddha, ...
You may recite in any language, such as in Chinese:
Ami Tuo Fo, Ami Tuo Fo, ...

Indeed, the expression "Ami Tuo Fo" has become so popular among Chinese Buddhists that it is often used as a form of greeting and appreciation. When others say "Good day", "How are you?", "Thank you" or "Good-bye", a Chinese Buddhist often says "Omi Tuo Fo", which means "May the blessings of Amitabha Buddha be with you."

Or you may recite in Japanese, Korean or Vietnamese, respectively as follows:

Amida Butsu, Amida Butsu ..... (Japanese)
Amida Pul, Amida Pul .... (Korean)
A Di Da Phat, A Di Da Phat ..... (Vietnamese)

The "many times" that you recite the name of Amitabha Buddha may range from tens to thousands. In this procedure, you see Amitabha in your eyes or mind, recite Amitabha in your mouth or heart, and hear Amitabha in your ears or heart. Aim to attain intensity in the recitation such that you are aware of nothing else except Amitabha. Irrespective of the language used in recitation, many people prefix the term "Namo" — a Sanskrit word meaning "pay homage to and take guidance from" — to the name Amitabha (like Namo Amitabha Buddha, or Namo Ami Tuo Fo); and recite in soothing rhythm, or in a singing manner.

Many people may be surprised and ask, "Is it so simple to go to the Western Paradise of Eternal Bliss?" There are many ways to practice Buddhism, according to a person's needs and aspirations, and some ways are very simple.

According to this way as described in the Amitabha Sutra, any person who avoids evil and do good, has faith and has made a vow to be reborn in the Western Paradise, will definitely be reborn in Amitabha's Pure Land if this person sincerely, devotedly and regularly recites the name of Amitabha.

Although this method is simple, one must not be mistaken that it is necessarily easy — although it is actually easier than most other methods of spiritual cultivation. As the famous Zen master Niao Ke said in the 9th century, although even a three-year old child may understand the moral obligation of avoiding evil and doing good — the prerequisites of spiritual cultivation — an eighty-year old man may not practice it.

How does a devotee go to the Western Paradise by just reciting Amitabha's name? This is through the grace and great compassion of Amitabha. A more philosophical or "scientific" explanation on how this transportation or transformation occurs, will be discussed later. Meanwhile, it is helpful to have a good understanding of Buddhism, which will be described in the next four chapters. If you think that Buddhism is about suffering and extinction, as some people do, or about going to temples and accepting commandments, you will be in for a big surprise.

THE MARVELOUS AND THE FUNDAMENTAL

(Scientific Knowledge and Basic Teaching of Buddhism)

Due to our ignorance and gross sense perception, we mistake the skin as the limiting boundary imprisoning the self; in reality, there is no boundary, and this illusory personal self is the Universal Self.

Countless Buddhas, Countless Worlds

About 2500 years ago, at the age of twenty nine Siddhartha Gautama Sakyamuni (623-543 BCE) made the Great Renunciation, leaving his wife, new-born child and palace, to seek deliverance from suffering for all humanity. At thirty five he attained perfect enlightenment and was henceforth called the Buddha, meaning the Enlightened One. For the remaining forty five years in his physical body on earth, the Buddha selflessly taught the Dharma, meaning the Teaching, which is usually referred to in English as Buddhism.

But Sakyamuni Buddha, or Gautama Buddha as he is sometimes called, is not the founder of Buddhism, as is commonly misunderstood. There were countless Buddhas before him, and there will be countless Buddhas in the future. Even at this very moment, there are countless Buddhas in other worlds in the billions of stars in the universe.

Sakyamuni Buddha is the Buddha of our aeon in our world, known as the Saha world, which also includes besides the familiar realms of humans and animals, the realms of hell inhabitants, hungry ghosts, asuras (titans), devas and brahmas (heavenly beings who stay in more than twenty different heavens in our Saha world), sravakas, pratyeka buddhas and bodhisattvas, who are enlightened beings of the first, second and third degree, and who may choose to exist in any of the six lower realms if they wish.

For example, out of great compassion Ksitigarbha Bodhisattva, or the Earth-Store Bodhisattva, chooses to go to the lowest realm, i.e the realm of hell inhabitants, to help suffering beings there.

The Buddha of the previous aeon in our Saha world was Kasyapa Buddha, and that of the next aeon will be Maitreya Buddha. Maitreya, known as Ajita Bodhisattva, was a disciple of Sakyamuni Buddha in the human realm, and is now in Tushita Heaven waiting for the appropriate time to be reborn as the next Buddha. It is heart warming to note that while the prominent characteristic of the human realm in this aeon is suffering, that in the next aeon under Maitreya Buddha will be laughter.

Millions of light-years from our Saha world is another world called Sukhavati, or the Western Paradise of Eternal Bliss, under the care of Amitabha Buddha. Amitabha became a Buddha ten aeons ago, but he has presided, and will continue to preside over Sukhavati eternally as he has vowed to do so due to his boundless compassion. The prominent feature of Sukhavati is bliss; suffering is unknown in Amitabha's world.

Buddhist Wisdom and Modern Science

Many people would be surprised to find out that the ability of our senses to perceive physical reality is infinitesimally limited. For example, the range of the electromagnetic spectrum visible to our eyes is only from 0.4 to 0.8 micron (i.e. 0.0004 to 0.0008 mm), whereas the range of the electromagnetic spectrum presently known to science is from 0.000000047 micron to over 30 kilometres!

In other words, there is an incredibly enormous amount of physical entities in the external world that both our scientists and we are unaware of. As most of the realms of existence fall outside the extremely limited range of electromagnetic waves visible to humans, it is understandable that we normally cannot see ghosts, asuras, devas and other "astral" beings.

This fact should remind us to be open-minded when reading materials beyond what many people would consider "normal", and not simply relegate it as superstitions. Neither should we accept any information blindly. The Buddha himself and Buddhist masters have repeatedly advised their followers not to accept any Buddhist teaching on faith alone, not even on the authority of the Buddha, but to assess the teaching according to the best of their understanding and experience.

In their typical arrogance, most mediocre scientists decree that what they cannot perceive and measure do not exist, despite the fact they know how limited their perception and measurement are. Understandably, only a few great scientists have been farsighted and brave enough to put forward revolutionary concepts that have turned out to be valid, like our earth is not the center of the universe, there are unimaginably more stars than what our eyes can see, matter is energy, contact over immense distance without discernable physical connection is possible, the implicate order of reality, the presence of shadow matter, and the existence of multi-dimension universes where only the one that is observed is manifested.

Interestingly, all these exciting scientific discoveries have been discussed in Buddhism for centuries, and have been recorded in numerous sutras. The following are just two random examples. The first example is from the Anguttara Nikaya, a collection of fundamental Theravada sutras, and the second from the Mahayana Lankavatara Sutra.

As far as these suns and moons revolve, shining and shedding their light in space, that far extends the thousand-fold world system. There are thousands of suns, thousands of moons.

The knowledge of an objective world does not come from objects, nor from the senses; nor is it a mere accident; nor is it an illusion. A combination of the several conditions or factors is necessary to produce the knowledge. But mere combination is not enough. This combination must take place in the originally pure, bright, illumination Essence, which is the source of knowledge. When this is realized, all the worlds in the ten quarters including one's own existence are perceived as so many particles of dust, floating, rising, and disappearing like form, in the vast emptiness of space which the one illuminative Mind-essence eternally pervades.

The refinement as well as "modernity" of Buddhist wisdom is even more astounding if we compare it with what leading western philosophers taught more than ten centuries later. For example, the famous English philosopher, John Locke, writing in 1690 on human understanding confessed that:

Sensations convinces us, that there are solid, extended substances; and reflection, that there are thinking ones: experience assures us of the existence of such beings; and that one had a power to move body by impulse, the other by thought; this we cannot doubt of. Experience, I say, every moment furnishes us with the clear idea both of the one and the other. But beyond these ideas, as received from their proper sources, our faculties will not reach. ... So that, in short, the idea we have of spirit, compared with the idea we have of body, stands thus: The substance of spirit is unknown to us; and so is the substance of body equally unknown to us.

How, then, did the Buddha and Buddhist masters have access to such fantastic knowledge and wisdom? They acquired them through direct experience! Indeed, virtually all the teachings in Buddhism are based on direct experience.

Unlike in western philosophy where concepts and principles are usually the result of intellectual speculation, all Buddhist knowledge and wisdom are gathered from deep meditation, where the Buddha and masters experience and perceive reality as it really is. For example, the Buddha could know of Amitabha's forty-eight great vows in the past, and the present conditions of the Western Paradise millions of light-years away, because of his miraculous power of perception that transcends time and space.

The Buddha's Teaching on Cosmic Reality

For various reasons, current western knowledge on Buddhism is unbalanced because it comes mainly from merely one source, the Theravada tradition, which Mahayana and Vajrayana Buddhists consider as only the preparatory stage of Buddhism. Theravada, Mahayana and Vajrayana are the three principal traditions of Buddhism. Hence, readers who are familiar with only Theravada Buddhism, and who are under the misconception that Buddhism is just a way of moral living with little concern for after-life and metaphysics, will be much surprised at what the Buddha has taught.

Immediately after his perfect enlightenment, when he was still sitting motionlessly in his *anuttara-samyak-sambodhi,* or the meditation of the supreme perfect wisdom, Sakyamuni Buddha gave a majestic sermon on the mystery of the universe, mainly to gods, dragon kings and heavenly beings. The Buddha taught that phenomenally everything in the universe is simultaneously arising and mutually penetrating; transcendentally everything is tranquil and undifferentiated. Very few beings could understand this marvelous but profound teaching, which becomes comprehensible to scientists only after their discovery of relativity and quantum mechanics. This teaching is recorded in the *Avatamsaka Sutra,* or *Hua Yen Jing* in Chinese, meaning the Flower Adornment Sutra. The following are some lines from this splendid sutra:

The bodies of all the buddhas
Are just this one body.
The Dharma body can enter the smallest particle,
And in the whole are the characteristics of that particle.
Through the effort and the motive power arising from their happiness

And from their actions, people see
That the dharma nature is not separate though separately made.
When you know that the mind, the Buddha and living beings
Are not three separate entities,
Then you will instantly see the Buddha.

The Buddha's Dharma nature body is without obstruction;
It appears at every place in the universe
And like a light and a shadow it penetrates all lands.
The Dharma nature is ultimately non-origination:
When the Buddha assumes the body of the Dharma nature, of
Suchness,
Without moving, he eternally purifies all of the lands in the ten
directions.

To comprehend the above two passages, it is necessary to understand that the Buddha is manifested in three bodies, namely the Spiritual Body (Dharmakaya), the reward body (sambhogakaya) and the transformational body (nirmanakaya). An example of the transformational body of the Buddha is the physical body he appears on earth as Siddhartha Gautama Sakyamuni. Even when the physical body of Siddhartha had been cremated after he had completed his earthly life, the Buddha exists in his reward body or bodies in some astral realms; spiritually advanced people may meet the Buddha in his reward body on earth. His Spiritual Body, on the other hand, is omnipresent and omniscient; it is the infinite, eternal cosmos.

The gist of the above teaching is that the Buddha, manifested in his Spiritual Body, "can enter the smallest particle"; at the other scale, "it appears at every place in the universe." In modern scientific language, it means that the "stuff" that constitutes a subatomic particle, is the same as the "stuff" that constitutes the whole universe, because a subatomic particle does not have any definite boundary that delineates where the "inside" of the particle ends, and where its "outside" starts. This particle "exists" because we define and conceptualize it. And that "stuff", whether in the particle or in the universe, is the Spiritual Body of the Buddha.

The great physicist, Max Planck, expressed the same cosmic truth when he said:

It is impossible to obtain an adequate version of the laws for which we are looking, unless the physical system is regarded as a whole.

According to modern mechanics [field theory], each individual particle of the system, in a certain sense, at any one time, exists simultaneously in every part of the space occupied by the system. This simultaneous existence applies not merely to the field of force with which it is surrounded, but also its mass and its charge.

Similarly, going up from the subatomic to the human scale, the "stuff" that makes up our body is the same as the "stuff" that makes up the universe, because our skin is in reality only a linear concentration of subatomic particles constantly in motion. Due to our ignorance and gross sense perception, we mistake the skin as the limiting boundary imprisoning the self; in reality, there is no boundary, and this illusory personal self is the Universal Self. In Buddhist terms, everyone is a Buddha, and the ultimate aim of Buddhism is to see this Buddha, i.e. actualize the Buddha that is intrinsically in us. "When you know that the mind, the Buddha and living beings are not three separate entities, then you will instantly see the Buddha."

This period of the Buddha's teaching on cosmic reality, which lasted only a week while he was still in meditation, is called the Avatamsaka Period, because the main teachings are recorded in the Avatamsaka Sutra. The school of Buddhism that emphasizes this aspect of the Buddha's teaching, with its brilliant doctrine of totality where all phenomena are simultaneously arising and mutually interpenetrating, is called respectively in Sanskrit, Chinese and Japanese, the Avatamsaka, Hua Yen and Kegon School, named logically after its prominent sutra.

Noble Truths and Middle Way

The majestic teaching about the Supreme Reality in the Avatamsaka Sutra is too profound for most people. Thus, for about the first ten years after coming out of his anuttara-samyak-sambodhi, the Buddha preached the basic teaching on moral purity as a preparatory stage for higher wisdom later on. This basic teaching, which can be summarized in the Four Noble Truths and the Noble Eightfold Path, is recorded in the four *Agama Sutras* in Mahayana and Vajrayana Buddhism, which correspond to the five *Nikayas* in Theravada Buddhism. The period of about ten years when the Buddha focused on this teaching is therefore called the Agama Period.

The Four Noble Truths state that (1) living is suffering, (2) the cause of suffering is desire, (3) to eliminate suffering it is necessary to eliminate desire, and (4) the way to accomplish this is the Noble Eightfold Path.

Shallow understanding of the First Noble Truth and the Second Noble Truth can easily mislead a person to think that Buddhism is pessimistic and negative. What the teaching actually means is that if a person continues his endless cycle of birth and rebirth, known in Buddhist terminology as *samsara*, he will deny himself the opportunity of enlightenment, or *nirvana*. Hence, living in samsara is suffering, compared to eternal bliss in nirvana. The First Noble Truth does not suggest that there is no joy in living; indeed, Buddhists are generally joyful people.

The driving force of the endless cycle of birth and rebirth is karma, which means the action of cause and effect. Karma is operated through desire. In other words, the desire of a person causes him to act, resulting in effect which in turn becomes the cause of other actions, thus generating continuous chains of actions and reactions, or karma. Karma does not stop at the person's death. His karma determines the nature and conditions of his next rebirth: whether he will be reborn well or badly into his next life, in the human or other spheres of existence, depends on whether he has good or bad karma. The Second Noble Truth expresses this concept of desire generating karma and perpetuating samsara, which is suffering compared to bliss in nirvana.

Therefore, if a person attains equanimity, he eliminates desire, particularly evil desire, leading to the cessation of karma, samsara and suffering. This is accomplished by following the Noble Eightfold Path, which consists of right understanding, right thought, right speech, right action, right livelihood, right effort, right mindfulness and right concentration.

The Noble Eightfold Path is also known as the Middle Way, because it avoids the two extremes of sensual indulgence and ascetic practice. The Buddha says:

There are these two extremes (*anta*), O Bhikkhus, which should be avoided by one who has renounced (*pabbajitena*):

(i) Indulgence in sensual pleasures — this is base, vulgar, worldly, ignoble and profitless; and
(ii) Addiction to self-mortification — this is painful, ignoble and profitless.

Abandoning both these extremes the Tathagata has comprehended the Middle Path (*Majjhima Patipada*) which promotes sight (*cakkhu*) and knowledge (*nana*), and which tends to peace (*vupasamaya*), higher wisdom (*abhinnaya*), enlightenment (*sambodhaya*), and Nibbana.

Nibbana is the Pali word for the Sanskrit *nirvana*, which means "enlightenment". In Chinese it is transcribed as *nie pan*. This period of the Buddha's preaching, which emphasized on moral purity, is known as the Agama Period, because the main teachings are recorded in the Agama Sutras.

All schools of Buddhism accept the teaching described in this section as the Buddha's basic teaching, except the Theravada which postulates that only this is the original teaching of Sakyamuni Buddha, usually called Gautama Buddha in Theravada, and all other Buddhist teachings described in other sections of this chapter and the next three chapters are later adulteration.

Historically, the Theravada was one of the many schools following the Hinayana tradition, but is now generally used to refer to all Hinayana schools. The teachings that mark the transition from Hinayana to Mahayana, which reveal the majestic grandeur of Buddhism are explained in the next chapter.

MAJESTIC GRANDEUR OF BUDDHISM

(The Compassion and Wisdom of Mahayana)

When we recite a sutra, we assume an exceedingly privileged and honored position — we act as a medium for the Buddha or the highly spiritual being speaking in the sutra.

The Compassion of the Bodhisattvas

After having laid the foundation of his basic teaching the Buddha spent the next eight years preaching what is known as "popular teaching on expedient means to help the masses". The prominent feature of the teaching of this period is compassion. This teaching is recorded in a group of sutras called the *Vaipulya Sutras,* which means Sutras of Development. Some examples are the three sutras on Amitabha, *Vimalakirti Nirdesa Sutra, Lankavatara Sutra* and *Surangama Sutra.*

This Vaipulya Period marked the transition from Hinayana to Mahayana philosophy, with the change of onus from self-cultivation to helping others in their salvation. The ideal of the Hinayana, meaning the Small Vehicle, is the Arahant, or the Worthy One. He is worthy because he has overcome lust, hatred and suffering, and has attained nirvana. An Arahant is usually not concerned with others' cultivation, not because he is selfish, but because he believes everyone has to work for his own salvation.

On the other hand, the ideal of the Mahayana, meaning the Great Vehicle, is the Bodhisattva, or the Sentient Being with Great Wisdom. His most remarkable characteristic is his great compassion. Bodhisattvas have vowed that they will provide help whenever it is asked of them, and the extent they would sacrifice to help others is simply awe-inspiring. If a being needs a fish to survive, for example, a Bodhisattva would become a fish to let him eat!

The different approaches to cultivation employed by the Hinayana and Mahayana traditions also indicate their philosophical inclination. The Hinayanist Arahant uses the Noble Eightfold Path, whereas the Mahayanist

Bodhisattva uses the Six Paramitas, which are the perfection of charity, discipline, tolerance, effort, meditation and wisdom. All the eight tenets of right practice in the Eightfold Path concern personal development; whereas in the Bodhisattva's cultivation, the first three paramitas benefit others, and the latter three improve oneself.

"Ask and you will be answered" is the motto of the Bodhisattvas. How do we ask assistance from Bodhisattvas who may exist in temporal and spatial dimensions different form us?

One effective way to call a Bodhisattva for help is to recite his or her name. For example, if we wish to seek the help of Bodhisattva Guan Shi Yin, we recite her name many times, like the example in the Chinese language below, then earnestly entreat her to help us solve our problem:

Namo Guan Shi Yin Pusa, Namo Guan Shi Yin Pusa, Namo Guan Shi Yin Pusa .....

Bodhisattva Guan Shi Yin, which means the Bodhisattva who listens to the cries of suffering beings for help, is the most popular Bodhisattva in Chinese Buddhism. Her name is often shortened to Guan Yin. In Japanese, she is known as Kanzeon or Kannon, and in Tibetan as Chen-re-zig.

In Indian Buddhism, this Bodhisattva of Great Compassion appears as Bodhisattva Avalokitesvara, who is masculine. In case you may wonder why the masculine Avalokitesvara in India becomes the feminine Guan Yin in China, Japan, Tibet and other countries, it is because in the higher realms of existence, there is no differentiation of sex. Thus, the Bodhisattva may choose to appear on earth in either sex. At still higher levels, there is not even form. So, a being in such a high realm does not need have a body; the being exists as consciousness. If you find this odd, it is because you are used to the gross characteristics in our human realm, which of course represents only an infinitesimally puny part of the known universe.

Those who suffer from deep depression, suicidal tendency or some psychiatric problems, inflictions not uncommon in modern societies, will find it helpful to call this Bodhisattva of Great Compassion for help. The procedure is simple, but it needs devotion and sincerity. Kneel before an image of the Bodhisattva, if available, or if you are not humble enough to kneel, as I once was, you may stand, sit or assume any comfortable position, and recite silently, softly or aloud the following "appeal" many times daily for a few weeks or until you are relieved of your psychiatric problems:

Bodhisattva Guan Yin, please give me peace of mind.

Bodhisattva is pronounced as "Bod-dhi-satt-tuo" (not ...satt-va). You do not even have to be a Buddhist to benefit from the Bodhisattva's help.

Another effective way to call a Bodhisattva is to use his mantra, which is usually in Sanskrit. A Bodhisattva is a very highly spiritual being, and is extremely powerful. He does not need to be near (in your scale) to hear you; he may be at a far corner of our world, or in another galaxy, but if you call sincerely, he will come to your aid instantaneously. The famous mantra of Bodhisattva Guan Yin, which is frequently used in Vajrayana Buddhism, and is sometimes known as the Mantra of Universal Protection, is:

Om Mani Padme Hum

This Guan Yin mantra means "Homage to the Jewel in the Lotus". How does chanting a mantra enable a sincere seeker to obtain help? Let us say you are very powerful, rich and compassionate. To help others, you promise that whoever in need of help will receive it if he communicates a password to you. To ensure that other people would not utter the password by accident and be mistaken by you as a cry for help, you make the password extraordinary, perhaps in some exotic sounds like "yuan yiqie zhongsheng pinan" (which actually means "May all sentient beings be safe" in Chinese). So, to keep your promise, whenever you receive the exotic password you dispatch the necessary help to the seeker.

In a similar way, a mantra is a password of a Bodhisattva who has vowed to relieve suffering. Of course, a Bodhisattva is infinitely more powerful than a mere mortal. In situations where another mortal could not help much, though he would like to, like someone being caught in a storm at sea, inflicted with a disease that doctors say to be incurable, or tormented by evil spirits in nightmares, seeking the help of a Bodhisattva through a mantra often proves to be very effective.

To show due reverence, the seeker should kneel before an image of the Bodhisattva when chanting a mantra; but in situations like when he is fast falling down a dangerous ravine, he may have neither time nor facilities, but if he has the presence of mind to chant a mantra, his friends may later tell him what a miraculous escape he had.

The Great Compassion Heart Dharani

A third way to seek help is to recite, or chant in a melodious way, the Bodhisattva's *dharani*, which is like a very long mantra. Unlike a mantra which is often used for immediate, expedient needs, such as escape from some dangerous situations like a fire or an accident, a dharani is usually employed for seeking long-term assistance, like recovery from an illness, minimizing the effects of previous bad karma, and requesting spiritual protection for people or places.

The most famous dharani is the Great Compassion Heart Dharani of Bodhisattva Guan Yin, popularly known in Chinese as *Da Bei Zhou*. The following is the Chinese transcription of the dharani, chanted daily by tens of thousands of Mahayana Buddhists:

Na mo he luo dan na tuo luo ye ye.
Na mo e li ye. Po lu jie di shou bo luo ye.
Pu ti sa duo po ye. Mo he sa duo po ye.
Mo he jia lu ni jia ye.
An. Sa pan luo fa xie. Shu dan na dan xie.
Na mo shi ji li duo yi meng a li ye.
Po lu ji di shi fo luo leng tuo po.
Na mo li na jin chi. Xi li mo he pan duo sha mi.
Sa po e tuo dou shu peng. E shi yun.
Sa po sa duo na mo po sa duo na mo po qie.
Mo fa te dou. Dan zhi tuo. An. E po lu xi.
Lu jia di. Jia lu di. Yi si li.
Mo he pu ti sa duo. Sa po sa po. Mu luo mu luo.
Mo xi mo xi li tuo yun. Ju lu ju lu jia meng.
Du lu du lu fa she ye di. Mo he fa she ye di.
Tuo luo tuo luo. Di li ni. Shi fo luo ye.
Zhe luo zhe luo. Mo mo fa mo luo. Mu di li.
Yi li yi li. Shi nuo shi nuo.
E uo san fo luo she li. Fa she fa san.
Fo luo she ye. Hu lu hu lu mo luo.
Hu lu hu lu xi li. Suo luo suo luo.
Xi li xi li. Su lu su lu.
Pu ti ye pu ti ye. Pu tuo ye pu tuo ye.
Mi di li ye. Nuo luo jin chi. Di li se ni nuo.
Po ye mo nuo. Suo po he. Xi tuo ye. Suo po he.
Mo he xi tuo ye. Suo po he.

Xi tuo yu yi. Shi pan luo ye. Suo po he.
Nuo luo jin chi. Suo po he.
Mo luo nuo luo. Suo po he.
Xi luo seng e mo qu ye. Suo po he.
Suo po mo he e xi tuo ye. Suo po he.
Zhe ji luo e xi tuo ye. Suo po he.
Bo tuo mo jie xi tuo ye. Suo po he.
Nuo luo jin chi pan qie luo ye. Suo po he.
Mo po li sheng jie luo ye. Suo po he.
Na mo he luo dan nuo duo luo ye ye.
Na mo e li ye. Po lu ji di.
Shuo pan luo ye. Suo po he.
An xi dian du. Man duo luo.
Ba tuo ye. Suo po he.

Do not be discouraged if you find the above words bewildering. Most Buddhists (including those who know Chinese) who faithfully chant these words daily do not know its meaning; like most magic formulae, what is important is the sounds of the words, and the sincerity in the chanting. Actually, of the eighty five expressions in the dharani, the first is an adoration to the Triple Gem (Buddha, Dharma and Sangha), and the remaining eighty four are adorations to eighty four divine beings like gods and Bodhisattvas.

English readers will probably find it easier to learn and chant the original Sanskrit version of the Great Compassion Heart Dharani given below.

Namo Ratnatrayaya. Namo Arya Avalokitesvaraya.
Bodhisattvaya. Mahasattvaya. Mahakarunikaya.
Om. Sarva Abhayah Sunadhasya.
Namo Sukrtvemama Arya Avalokitesvara Garbha.
Namo Nilakantha Siri Maha Bhadra Shrame.
Sarvathasubham Ajeyam Sarvasattva Namavarga
Mahadhatu. Tadyatha Om Avalokelokite Kalate.
Hari Mahabodhisattva. Sarva Sarva Mala Mala.
Masi Mahahrdayam. Kuru Kuru Karmam.
Kuru Kuru Vijayati Mahavijayati.
Dhara Dhara Dharim Suraya.
Chala Chala Mama Bhramara Muktir.
Ehi Ehi Chinda Chinda Harsham Prachali.
Basha Basham Presaya Hulu Hulu Mala.

Hulu Hulu Hilo Sara Sara Siri Siri Suru Suru.
Bodhiya Bodhiya Bodhaya Bodhaya.
Maitreya Nilakantha Dharshinina.
Payamama Svaha. Siddhaya Svaha.
Mahasiddhaya Svaha. Siddhayo Geshvaraya Svaha.
Nilakantha Svaha. Vara Hananaya Svaha.
Simha Shira Mukhaya Svaha.
Sarva Mahasiddhaya Svaha. Chakra Siddhaya Svaha.
Padma Hastya Svaha. Nilakantha Vikaraya Svaha.
Maha Sishankaraya Svaha. Namo Ratnatrayaya.
Namo Arya Avalokitesvaraya Svaha.
Om Siddhayantu Mantra Padaya Svaha.

One can understand why this Great Compassion Heart Dharani is so popular after knowing what this dharani can do. Commenting on the Venerable Hsuan Hua's book, *The Dharani Sutra,* which provides an excellent commentary on this dharani, the great western scholar of eastern religions, John Blofeld, says:

Skeptics and philosophers who disdain what strikes them as magical practice would be well advised to give this book a miss; whereas those who deem that Western civilization is the poorer for having abandoned magic in favor of treating the universe like a piece of clockwork, as Newton did, may find it intriguing; and those who quite seriously desire to gain a Bodhisattva-like Bodhi-mind or 'Heart of Great Compassion' may be encouraged to try putting the dharani to actual mantric use.

Some of the benefits a person can get by reciting the dharani sincerely include protection against evil influences, avoiding calamities, recovering from illness, enjoying longevity, experiencing inner peace, and commanding ghosts, spirits and even heavenly kings to do one's biding! The Venerable Hsuan Hua, for example, could summon the relevant forces to prevent earthquakes or produce rain. Needless to say, the dharani must always be used for good, and never be used for any evil purposes.

Miraculous Powers of Sutras

Still another way how a Bodhisattva can help us, and how we may in turn help other beings, is to recite a sutra, or part of a sutra, which has some special significance to the Bodhisattva. For example, the famous *Prajna Paramita Hrdaya Sutra,* or the Heart Sutra, is a description of Bodhisattva Guan Yin's enlightenment experience. Thus, by reciting and understanding this sutra, we benefit from the Bodhisattva's experience, and derive both inspiration and guidance for our own spiritual cultivation. Other beings, including the non-human who may be around us although we cannot see them due to the limitation of our eyes, will similarly benefit from hearing our recitation of the sutra, and as a bonus we reap the merits that will contribute to our good karma.

This accumulation of merits is particularly relevant when we recite a sutra like the Amitabha Sutra. Souls who are lost — and there are plenty of them around — will derive inspiration and guidance on hearing our recitation of the Amitabha Sutra, and if they follow the advice recommended by the Buddha in the Sutra, they may eventually arrive at Sukhavati, the Western Paradise. Language is not a serious barrier when reciting or chanting a sutra. When you recite in English, so long as your recitation is sincere, beings who may not know English may still pick up your meaning from your mental vibrations.

One of the best services any person can perform for a close family member, relative, friend or even a stranger who has just died, is to recite the Amitabha Sutra for him or her. In this function it is similar to the Tibetan *Bar-do'i-Thos-grol,* which means the "Great Liberation through Hearing in the Bardo", but is popularly though wrongly translated as the "Tibetan Book of the Dead."

During the crucial forty nine days after his death, when his soul is bewildered by the new environment and undecided as what to do, the Amitabha Sutra may provide him with the most invaluable information guiding him to the Western Paradise.

His (or her) chance of going to the Western Paradise is even better if the sutra is recited and explained to him before he died. It will give him inspiration or assurance that death is nothing to be afraid of, for viewing from the other side, it is birth into another sphere, and unless he has been extremely evil whereby he would be reborn in hell, the chances are the other sphere of existence is better than our suffering world.

If you have ever wished to save someone from going to hell, this will be a good chance, for even if this dying person has been evil, if he only has access to the information of the Amitabha Sutra and is able to grasp the golden opportunity offered therein, he may be saved by the grace of Amitabha Buddha. Anyone who has ever observed a friend or family member dying, would appreciate the meaning of compassion this great Buddha so excellently exemplifies.

Even if a dying person cannot go to the Western Paradise, he will still derive great benefit from hearing a sutra or part of a sutra. Zhuming, the Devil King in charge of life and death, respectfully told Sakyamuni Buddha:

> Honored of the World, if all dying persons have an opportunity of hearing only the name of one Buddha or one Bodhisattva, or the chanting of the Sutra, or even the chanting of one sentence or one poem of any Sutra, I can assure you that these dying persons will be kept away from the five Avici Hells. If a dying person has committed only small evil deeds which will cause him to be cast into the evil State for punishment, he will be relieved upon hearing the name of the Buddha or Bodhisattva or even the chanting of the Sutra.

Devil Kings are deities controlling devils, ghosts and hell inhabitants. They spend part of their time in heavens, and those who cultivate later become Brahma gods and Bodhisattvas. The Buddha explains that although Devil Kings look fierce and are a terror to sinners and devils, they are compassionate at heart; and says that 170 aeons later Devil King Zhuming will become Nirlaksana Buddha in the world known as Pure Abode.

Another Devil King, Edu, who is in charge of "fierce evilness" promised Sakyamuni Buddha:

> We promise you that whenever we come across a male or a female in any part of the world who though seen practicing only a small fraction of good or making any kind of offerings to images of Buddhas or Bodhisattvas or be heard chanting a sentence or poem of the Sutras, my followers and I shall treat such persons respectfully as if we pay homage to the Buddhas of the preset, past and the future. We shall instruct our followers and the spirits from different places to protect such virtuous beings. We shall never allow any unhappy occasions, disease or any undesirable events from happening, not only to their homes, but also in places close to their residences.

Hence, whenever we recite a sutra, we assume an exceedingly privileged and honored position — we act as a medium for the Buddha or the highly spiritual being speaking in the sutra; whenever we recite a sutra, we are repeating for the benefit of others and ourselves the teaching of the Buddha.

Recitation of sutras and mantras is a regular feature in all schools of Buddhism, though the Theravada School places little emphasis on seeking a Bodhisattva's help through such recitation. The school that specializes on the chanting of Amitabha Buddha is the Pure Land School, which is probably the most popular of all Buddhist schools today. The school that places great importance on the power of mantras is the Mantra School, which is known as Zhen Yen School and Shingon School in Chinese and Japanese respectively.

Lay Followers and Non-Duality

Another significant feature of this Vaipulya Period was the emergence of lay followers. Unlike the monks who had left family life to follow the Buddha, lay followers were still householders who carried on their normal lives. Do not be mistaken to think that the spiritual attainment of lay followers must be far behind that of the monks. Even Manjusri and Sariputra, reputed to be the wisest among the Bodhisattvas and Arahants, felt themselves inadequate when discussing the Buddha's teaching with Vimalakirti, the most distinguished of the Buddha's lay disciples.

The Buddha's teaching discussed by Vimalakirti and thirty three Bodhisattvas is recorded in the *Vimalakirti Nirdesa Sutra,* which exemplifies two significant features in Buddhism. One, while the Hinayana tradition represents the withdrawal of aspirants from society to pursue spiritual cultivation in quietude, the Mahayana tradition as symbolized here by Vimalakirti represents bringing spiritual cultivation into society despite its hustle and bustle. Two, while Hinayana monks practice the vehicle of the Arahant with emphasis on self-development, lay followers practice the vehicle of the Bodhisattva with emphasis on helping others.

Vimalakirti, who was wealthy, cultured, philosophical, and married with wife and children, is an excellent model of a lay follower. This represents an important aspect in the Mahayana and the Vajrayana traditions: while becoming a monk is certainly a great advantage in spiritual cultivation, it is not essential; enlightenment can be attained by lay followers without having to leave their families.

One of the main themes discussed in the *Vimalakirti Nirdesa Sutra* is non-duality. The great master Fa Zang, more popularly known by the imperial title "Yen Shou" meaning "The Foremost Among the Wise" bestowed on him by a Tang emperor, explained:

> Absolute reality is marvelously tranquil, without characteristics; it is undifferentiated suchness where all separateness has disappeared; thus it is called non-duality.

Before the emergence of the new physics, many people might have thought the master was dabbling in metaphysical riddles. Now, of course, we are amazed at his profound insight, many centuries ahead of modern science.

Vimalakirti asked the Bodhisattvas who had gathered in his house what non-duality was and how to enter into it. They explained that duality is caused by polarity, and the entry into non-duality is to tear down the illusory polarities, such as perception and non-perception, defilement and purity, action and thought, characteristics and non-characteristics, sin and blessing, conditioned and unconditioned, causation and non-causation, form and non-form, self and non-self, mundane and supramundane, samsara and nirvana, ignorance and enlightenment.

The Bodhisattvas then asked Manjusri, considered to be the wisest of them all, what his view on non-duality was. Bodhisattva Manjusri replied:

> According to my opinion, for all phenomena and selves, there is no language, no verbalization, no explanation, no self-consciousness, away from all questions and answers; this is the entry into non-duality.

Bodhisattva Manjusri's answer was superior to the other answers because all the others involved *self-consciousness or personal mind,* and therefore they had not attained the non-duality of *cosmic consciousness or universal mind.* For example, the fact that they had to discard perception and non-perception, or defilement and purity, or any other polarities, meant the presence of self-consciousness and differentiation. In other words, there was the presence of a separate self-conscious of the difference between perception and non-perception, or other polarities.

Manjusri transcended these polarities. Without language and without verbalization indicate that non-duality is inexplicable; without explanation and without self-consciousness indicate that non-duality is beyond thought.

Away from questions and answers indicates that non-duality is beyond intellectual comprehension; it has to be experienced to be comprehended.

Beyond Words and Beyond Thoughts

To say that non-duality is inexplicable does not mean that we cannot describe it in words: we can, but our description at its best is only provisional, and the listeners or readers will interpret it according to their limited experience. To say that non-duality is beyond thought does not mean we cannot think about it, but the act of thinking itself results in duality. Beyond intellectual comprehension does not mean we cannot intellectualize on it, but intellectualization, even if it is correctly done, is only an imitation of reality, which has to be experienced directly.

Finally Manjusri on behalf of the Bodhisattvas asked Vimalakirti for his comment on non-duality.

Vimalakirti remained silent.

On which, Manjusri exclaimed, "Excellent! Excellent! This entry without language and without verbalization is the real entry into non-duality." Earlier, Manjusri used language to show the inapplicability of language in describing non-duality — as soon as language was used, there was differentiation that was in contradiction to non-duality. Vimalakirti was more direct; he showed the inapplicability of language by *not* using language. His silence is often described as a "thundering silence".

It is understandable that some readers may find the above explanation on non-duality puzzling. Some may wonder how one can enter into non-duality by tearing down polarities — whatsoever that may mean; or, more puzzling still, how keeping a "thundering silence" leads to non-duality.

One must remember that the above encounter was amongst very advanced beings with great wisdom, who could comprehend from just a little hint. But for us, ordinary people, a provisional use of language despite its imperfection is necessary to help us in our path towards enlightenment. Thus, in the next period of his teaching, to be described in the next chapter, the Buddha used words to explain the concept of emptiness, which incorporates non-duality.

THE BUDDHA'S TEACHING ON EMPTINESS

(Why is the World an Illusion)

As the concepts to be discussed here are unfamiliar to most readers, the explanation will be presented step by step; readers are therefore requested to exercise some patience — they will be rewarded by understanding some of the deepest and greatest teachings the world has ever been exposed to.

The Wisdom of Emptiness

Many people are aware of the Buddhist teaching that the world we normally see, is an illusion, but not many understand why it is so. This chapter will explain this very important philosophy of the Buddha's teaching.

When the Buddha first explained the nature of cosmic reality, most people as well as other beings could not understand because of its profundity; therefore he spent the first ten years laying the foundation for spiritual cultivation by emphasizing moral purity and teaching the ways to eliminate suffering (please see Chapter 2). Then, as he found that some of his followers were concerned only with their own salvation, the Buddha emphasized the Bodhisattva philosophy of compassion and helping others (Chapter 3). Having helped his followers to cultivate moral purity for themselves and compassion for others, the Buddha taught them the higher wisdom concerning emptiness so that they could understand the great truth about cosmic reality and so attain enlightenment.

This period of the teaching on emptiness is the longest period of the Buddha's teaching, lasting about twenty years, and is known as the Prajna Period. Prajna, which is the Sanskrit word for higher wisdom, refers particularly to the spiritual awareness of emptiness or *sunyata,* which includes non-duality. Here emptiness or void does not mean nothingness; it means emptied or devoid of phenomena as we ordinarily see them. The term "phenomena", it is significant to note, comes from the Greek word meaning "appearances".

This concept of emptiness is crucial to understanding Mahayana Buddhism. Bodhisattva Nagarjuna, regarded by many as the Second Buddha, said that anyone who does not attain *prajna* or this higher wisdom on emptiness, misses the essence of Mahayana Buddhism. The huge collection of sutras on higher wisdom is called the *Prajna Sutras,* or the Wisdom Sutras, which include the famous *Heart Sutra* and *Diamond Sutra.*

In emptiness, there is no duality. In other words, when a person attains enlightenment, all forms of duality disappear. As the concepts to be discussed here are unfamiliar to most readers, the explanation will be presented step by step; readers are therefore requested to exercise some patience — they will be rewarded by understanding some of the deepest and greatest teachings the world has ever been exposed to. Needless to say, these teachings are not mine; they are the Buddha's! I merely report in a language and vocabulary western readers will find comprehensible.

Emptiness and Non-duality

First of all, what is duality? We may better appreciate what duality is, not by attempting a definition but by examining some examples, such as man and woman, good and bad, joy and suffering, purity and defilement, form and non-form. If we differentiate a man from a woman, or form from non-form — as we normally do because we normally live in the phenomenal world — then we exist in a world of duality. This, of course, does not necessarily mean that if we cannot or do not differentiate a man from a woman, or form from non-form, we exist in a world of non-duality. This jumping into a conclusion — such as: if A is non-B, and as C is not B, therefore C must be A — is in fact an example of dualistic thinking.

The examples we have chosen (man and woman, etc) are also examples of polarities. While polarity is a useful way to illustrate duality, it is not the only way. If we differentiate a man from a boy, or a man from another man, we also exist in duality. Similarly, when we say that our mind is pure, or believe that cheating is bad, we are dualistic. It is significant to note that the issue at hand is one of duality, not one of morality: we are not concerned here with whether 'cheating is bad' is a morally valid statement.

That is why, in a famous Zen story, when Emperor Han Wu Di asked Bodhidharma what the first law of holiness was, the great Indian master replied that there is only Emptiness, no holiness. Again, we must guard against the dualistic or polaristic thinking that the above two statements infer 'cheating is good' and 'emptiness and holiness are exclusive'.

Hence, in non-duality there is no differentiation. As soon as we differentiate one object from another, or one object from nothingness, in fact, as soon as the concept 'we' arises, or any concept arises, there is duality. In emptiness or non-duality, there is no difference whatsoever between the knower and the known, between the subject and the object.

If some readers think that this is mere philosophy, just a play of words without any real meaning, let us remember that in Buddhism, 'philosophy' means 'love and search for truth', and not as many modern philosophers have practiced it as 'intellectual speculation or reasoning'. All Buddhist teachings are based on direct experience. When the Buddha and other Buddhist masters taught that in attaining emptiness, there is no difference between the knower and the known, they were teaching from their experience, not from speculation or reasoning.

Interestingly, the latest science provides both the conceptual framework to explain as well as the empirical evidence to confirm this Buddhist wisdom on emptiness — albeit imperfectly, because science explains only matter, which is just one of the many aspects of reality, whereas Buddhism also explains the other aspects of perception, thought, processes and consciousness. Even an elementary understanding of science tells us that everything in the universe, from the chair you are sitting on to the distant star that our telescope has not reached, is composed of atoms — a concept which no scientist has disputed; and the atoms are made of subatomic particles like protons, electrons and the numerous ions — the empirical evidence of which scientists have seen on electromagnetic plates or worked out in universally accepted mathematical tables.

Yet when scientists try to measure or define an electron or any subatomic particle, they find it most elusive. For example, if they set up their apparatus to measure an electron as a particle, it turns out to be a particle; if they want to measure it as a wave, it turns out to be a wave! It is more elusive when they try to define its boundary — they find it has none! The well-known scientist Robert Oppenheimer says:

> If we ask, for instance, whether the position of the electron remains the same, we must say 'no'; if we ask whether the electron's position changes with time, we must say 'no'; if we ask whether the electron is at rest, we must say 'no'; if we ask whether it is in motion, we must say 'no'.[1]

Reporting on the 'Copenhagen Interpretation', which holds the most influential opinion on the topic in question, the Cambridge professor Alastair Rae says:

It is not meaningful to think of the electron as 'really' possessing a particular position or momentum unless these have been measured; and if its momentum, say, has been measured it is then meaningless to say that it is in any particular place.[2]

Thus, scientists have found that subatomic particles, the "stuff" that makes up the so-called external world, have no definite boundary or location. In other words, what we think or see as a particle, actually is everywhere; it assumes a particular form and position only when we measure or define it. This is why scientists say that the result of an experiment is directly related to the thought of the experimenter: there is no such thing as an objective world!

What applies to an electron as mentioned above, also applies to you or any other person or object. If you look at your body through the wisdom-eye of an enlightened person, or through a gigantic, powerful electron microscope (which, unfortunately, is yet to be invented), you will find that you have no body! What you have regarded as your body is now a concentration of subatomic particles. You cannot even tell which particles are "inside" you because they are not only constantly moving "in" and "out" at great speed, but also constantly disintegrating into energy or nothingness, into what scientists call anti-particles.

You will find that the usual objects you used to see with your naked eyes — like people and trees, houses and cars, and all phenomena or appearances — are no longer there: you will only find patterns of subatomic particles. If you can further transcend this level —the level Hinayana Buddhists stop at because they consider "dharmas" or "subatomic particles and forces" as ultimately real; and the level scientists are now trying to transcend to accomplish the unified field theory — you will not even perceive subatomic particles; you will attain emptiness or nirvana. "You" too will disappear — you will be emancipated from the imaginary prison of "your" illusory body and actualize the Universal Self or Buddhahood.

Devoid of Characteristics

There are many terms to describe the attaining of emptiness, such as enlightenment, nirvana, becoming a Buddha, achieving bodhi, and, as commonly mentioned in Zen Buddhism, realizing your original face, or seeing the Buddha nature. It is called emptiness because all characteristics, all phenomena have disappeared.

The following quotation from the Diamond Sutra, which explains the Buddha's teaching on emptiness, provides a good example on the detachment of characteristics. However, it may not be easily comprehended by the uninitiated.

Why is it that these beings can easily recognize the true teaching? It is because they do not fall back on ego characteristics, personality characteristics, sentient being characteristics, and life characteristics. They also do not cherish characteristics of dharmas, and of non-dharmas.

Why is it so? It is because if the minds of these sentient beings are tarnished by any characteristics, these beings will become attached to ego, personality, sentient beings, and life.

If they cherish any characteristics of dharma, they will also be attached to ego, personality, sentient beings, and life.

Further, if they cherish any characteristics of non-dharma, they too will be attached to ego, personality, sentient beings, and life.

The Buddha teaches that enlightened beings can perceive reality as it ultimately and absolutely is, because they are free from the four characteristics of ego, of personality, of sentient beings and of life, and the two characteristics of dharma and of non-dharma. In other words, if a being realizes and directly experiences that ego, personality, sentient beings, life, dharma and non-dharma are not ultimate or absolute, but relative and illusory, then he attains emptiness or enlightenment.

But if he clings to the characteristics of ego, of personality, of sentient being and of life, he will be deluded into thinking of himself as an individual self, separated from all other individual selves and objects. If he clings to the characteristics of dharma and of non-dharma, he will be deluded into thinking that phenomena are ultimately real, each phenomenon differentiated from all other phenomena and selves. Thus, because he is deluded into perceiving that selves and phenomena are separated and differentiated, he lives in the world of duality, loosing sight of the great cosmic truth that in reality he and the universe and everything in it IS actually one organic whole, unseparated and undifferentiated.

For example, if he perceives just any one of the characteristics of his ego — like his name, his hand, his particular mannerism, or his wife — he would remind himself as an individual with an ego, separated and different from other individuals and phenomena. This is an illusion. If he frees himself from all these characteristics, he attains emptiness, which is ultimate, absolute reality.

Similarly if he perceives just one of the characteristics of personality — like somebody's name, somebody's hand, other people's mannerism, or other people's spouses — he too would remind himself as an individual, which again is an illusion. In the same way, if he perceives just one characteristic of sentient being — like an ant, a whale, a bacterium or a ghost; or if he perceives one characteristic of life — like the process of breathing, feeling of joy and sorrow, growth and decay, or the cycle of reincarnation — he is deluded into thinking of himself as an individual, separated and differentiated from other individuals and other phenomena. If he can free himself from the delusion, by freeing himself from the attachment of these characteristics (as well as the characteristics of dharma and non-dharma explained in the next paragraph), he realizes emptiness or nirvana.

The attachment to the above characteristics of ego, of personality, of sentient beings and of life results in the illusion of self. Similarly the attachment to the characteristics of dharma and of non-dharma results in the illusion of phenomena. For example, if he attaches himself to any one characteristic of dharma — such as a house or an electron; or of non-dharma — such as space or intellectualization, he reminds himself of phenomena, which are an illusion. By freeing himself from these characteristics of dharma and of non-dharma, he frees himself from the illusion of phenomena. When an aspirant achieves emancipation from the illusion of phenomena and self, he attains emptiness or enlightenment. He actualizes his innate Buddha nature, or the Supreme Reality. Are there other endeavors, which is greater or nobler?

Coming back to the analogy from science, suppose you look through a gigantic, powerful electron microscope at your hand, or at someone's hand, at an ant, at the process of breathing, at a house, or at space, or at any characteristics of self or phenomena, you will not see your hand, someone's hand, etc, but you will see patterns of subatomic particles.

If the microscope is more powerful, like the wisdom-eye of an enlightened being, you will not even see subatomic particles; you will perceive a tranquil, undifferentiated spread of cosmic consciousness, emptied of all selves and phenomena that we normally see in our ordinary but deluded self-consciousness. This is emptiness — and a direct experience of this emptiness, this transcendental infinite cosmic reality in eternal bliss, is nirvana or enlightenment.

The most representative school of Buddhism that draws its inspiration from the Buddha's teaching on emptiness, and aims to attain enlightenment in an instant, is Chan, or Zen in Japanese. On the other hand, viewing from the other perspective, i.e. from the phenomenal rather than the transcendental perspective taken by the Zen School, the most representative is the Ideation School, called *Vijnaptimatra* (formerly *Yogacara*) in Sanskrit, *Fa Xiang* in Chinese, and *Hosso* in Japanese. Modern psychologists can benefit much if they care to study the profound philosophy of the Ideation School on why the external world is a creation of the mind.

Does the Soul Exist?

Mahayanists and Vajrayanists, out of deep concern for their Theravadin brothers, and certainly not out of self-glorification, expounds that the Theravada tradition has not understood this concept of emptiness sufficiently. Due to this inadequate understanding, Theravadins face many contradictions, which they seek to avoid, perhaps unwittingly, with the excuse that such understanding is not necessary for the attainment of nirvana, although they know the Buddha had stressed that his teaching should be accepted only on the basis of understanding and experience.

Hence, while Mahayanists and Vajrayanists believe in the existence of souls (in the phenomenal dimension), Theravadins cling tenaciously to the doctrine of non-soul, despite obvious contradictions like the involvement of the soul, or self or call it whatever you like, in the progress of a Theravadin cultivator from the first stage of "entering the stream" to the fourth and final stage of Arahantship over countless lifetimes. If the cultivator does not have a soul, or any identity connected to a continuity of self, it would not be possible for him (or her) to progress from one stage to the next over different lives.

Thailand and Burma, two prominent Theravada countries, are well known for cases of village children remembering clearly particulars of their previous lives. If these cannot be taken as examples of souls or selves migrating from one life to another, what can?

The classic attempt of Theravadins to explain this phenomenon by saying it is a transference of karmic force, but not souls or selves, giving the example of the transference of the flame of a lighted candle to an unlighted one, is unsatisfactory. Theravadins argue that when a lighted candle transfers its flame to an unlighted one, only the force is transferred; the first candle did not become the second candle, illustrating that the self of one person did not become the self of another. This argument is not valid because the crucial point is the flame, which symbolizes the soul, and not the candles, which symbolize the physical bodies.

In fact, more than fifteen centuries ago in China when Confucians attacked the Buddhist belief in the in destructivity of the soul, Chinese Buddhists used this same transfer of flame (which actually is not a good analogy) to illustrate that souls migrate from one body to another. When one candle transfers its flame to another, the first candle may be burnt out, but the second candle continues burning, illustrating that when the physical body dies (represented by the burnt out first candle), the soul (the flame) continues its existence in another body (the second candle). The second body is able to live due to the migration of the soul, without which the physical body is dead, just as the second candle is lighted because of the transferred flame, without which the candle is without light.

Theravadins fail to appreciate that the doctrine of non-soul is an expedient means to help aspirants attain the Cosmic Soul or nirvana, and not a rigid dogma claiming souls do not exist, just as the doctrine of suffering is an expedient means to help aspirants achieve eternal joy, not a dogma insisting that joy is lacking. When they have attained the transcendental level of emptiness, when they have overcome the illusion of the so-called external world, the soul or anything else (be it their physical self, heaven, hell, a stone or a distant galaxy) does not exist.

HEAVEN AND ENLIGHTENMENT

(Various Aspects of the Buddha's Extensive Teaching)

A person becomes a Buddhist by practicing the Buddha's teaching, like disciplining oneself in moral purity, showing loving-kindness to all beings, and cultivating wisdom for spiritual development.

The Marvelous Teaching of the Lotus

If we are asked to condense the meaning and purpose of practicing Buddhism as explained in thousands of volumes of Buddhist scriptures into one short phrase, a good choice is "attaining the Buddha's cosmic experience". In his last seven years of teaching, the Buddha concentrated on helping his followers actualize this phrase, i.e. to attain Buddhahood. This advanced teaching, which is the accumulation of all previous teachings, is recorded in the *Saddharma Pundarika Sutra,* or Lotus Sutra, and the *Nirvana Sutra,* or Enlightenment Sutra.

The Buddha explained that because most people were initially not ready to accept the higher wisdom of his teaching, he set up an expedient way to prepare them for subsequent profound teaching:

These men are hard to save.
For this reason, Sariputra,
I set up an expedient for them,
Proclaiming a Way to end suffering,
Revealing it as Nirvana.
Yet, though I proclaim Nirvana,
It is not real extinction;
All things from the beginning
Are ever of Nirvana nature.
When a Buddha-son fulfills his course,
In the world to come he becomes Buddha.
It is because of my adaptability
That I tell of a Three-Vehicle Law,
But truly the World-Honored Ones
Preach the One-Vehicle Way.[1]

Nirvana means enlightenment, but because the Theravada School interprets nirvana in a narrow sense, implying it to be total extinction, Mahayanists often use other terms instead of nirvana to indicate enlightenment, such as bodhi, anuttara-samyak-sambodhi, and Buddhahood. Thus, the term "Nirvana" in the quotation above refers to the narrow concept of nirvana commonly suggested in the Theravada tradition.

The quotation illustrates that the teaching concerning the way to end suffering as emphasized in the Four Noble Truths and Eightfold Path, is a preparatory stage towards later, more profound teaching in the Buddha Vehicle. The three other vehicles — the Sravaka Vehicle, the Pratyekabuddha Vehicle, and the Bodhisattva Vehicle — are expedient means; the ultimate path, the one taught by all Buddhas, is the Buddha Vehicle.

Sravakas, literally meaning "hearers", are disciples who attain nirvana through hearing and practicing the Buddha's teaching, especially the teaching of the Agama period. The Sravaka Vehicle is based on the Four Noble Truths and Eightfold Path, helping aspirants to eliminate lust, hatred and suffering.

Pratyekabuddhas, literally meaning "enlightened alone", refer to those who attain nirvana through their own efforts, and who are not concerned with the enlightenment of other people. Pratyekabuddhas may or may not use the Buddhist way in their cultivation. This illustrates another admirable aspect of the liberal attitude of Buddhism, which recognizes that non-Buddhist methods too can lead to enlightenment.

The onus of the Pratyekabuddha training is to meditate deeper and deeper into the nature of phenomena until finally ultimate reality is reached. In Buddhism, the Pratyekabuddha Vehicle focuses on the Doctrine of Dependent Origination, which explains how the originally undifferentiated cosmic reality is gradually transformed into differentiated phenomenal worlds.

The two vehicles of Sravakas and of Pratyekabuddha lead to Arahantship, attaining nirvana in a narrow, Hinayanist sense, because although Arahants have freed themselves from the illusion of self, they have not freed themselves from the illusion of dharmas, for they believe that dharmas are ultimately real though existing only momentarily.

The Bodhisattva Vehicle is of the Mahayana tradition, with emphasis on compassion and helping others, in contrast to the Hinayana tradition of self-development. The Bodhisattva mode of cultivation is the Six Paramitas, which lead to the Buddha Vehicle, where the emphasis is on emptiness and attaining Buddhahood.

In striking contrast to the Theravadin belief that the highest level any being in this aeon can ever attain is to become an Arahant (and never a Buddha), because Sakyamuni Buddha is the only Buddha in our aeon, Mahayanists and Vajrayanists belief that not only every being is a potential Buddha, but every being is originally a Buddha. This concept becomes clear if we understand the concept of emptiness, where the Spiritual Body of the Buddha penetrates the infinitesimal particles as well as fills all the infinite galaxies. Moreover, the Buddha says:

> Know, O Sariputra!
> Of yore I made a vow,
> In desire to cause all creatures
> To rank equally with me.[2]

In this advanced stage of Mahayana teaching, the term "Buddha" frequently refers to the Spiritual Body of the Buddha, rather than his transformational body. In other words, when Mahayanists and Vajrayanists mention "Buddha", they often mean the transcendental cosmos or the Supreme Reality, rather than the person of Siddhartha Gautama Sakyamuni.

The school which specializes on the Lotus Sutra, and which represents a synthesis of the characteristic philosophies of various Buddhist schools is the Tian Tai School, which is named after a famous mountain in China where this school developed. The Tian Tai School is also called the Lotus School in English. But the term "Lotus School" is almost never used in the Chinese language for the Tian Tai School; if it is used in Chinese, the Lotus School usually refers to the Pure Land School.

The Tian Tai School (Tendai in Japan) provides some excellent examples of the Chinese contribution to Buddhist philosophy. Again, it should be noted that in Buddhism, the term philosophy never means "speculative intellectualization"; it always means "love and search for truth".

Buddhist masters have always insisted that the intellect, while highly regarded in Buddhism too, is subordinate to direct experience. All Buddhist teachings are not arrived at through logical or speculative reasoning; they are the result of direct experience. When a master teaches, for example, that by practicing the Noble Eightfold Path or the Six Paramitas, one can attain enlightenment, this teaching is acquired not through rigorous reasoning, but through his and other masters' personal practice.

One of the fundamental doctrines of the Tian Tai School is poetically described as "One Thought, Three Thousand Worlds". "Three Thousand" here is a figurative term meaning "myriad". This Tian Tai doctrine postulates that all the myriad worlds in the cosmos, including heavens and hells, are created by thought!

Again, we are amazed at not just how much earlier, but how much more profound were the Buddhist masters than modern quantum physicists in discovering that external reality exists only if we perceive it. Professor David Mermin exclaims that, "We now know that the moon is demonstratively not there when no body looks", and he wants us to take his bold declaration literally.[3] At present quantum physicists deals only with matter and at the subatomic level on our earth (despite this quotation about the moon); but Buddhist wisdom deals with matter, perception, thought, activity (or processes), and consciousness, ranging from the micro-world of a mote of dust to the countless worlds of the infinite cosmos.

Closer to the Original Teaching

Theravadins in general, as well as some scholars, including Professor Soothill from whose work the above quotations from the Lotus Sutra are taken, postulate that the Lotus Sutra and other Mahayana sutras were not taught by the Buddha, but were developed by later Buddhist masters.

Even if we presume that these sutras were not taught by Siddhartha Gautama Sakyamuni — though Mahayanists and Vajrayanists sincerely belief they were, and have a stronger case to belief that their teaching is closer to his original teaching, as will be shown presently — a true Buddhist could still use them if they help him to attain the highest enlightenment. Sakyamuni Buddha himself has likened his teaching to a raft that could be discarded after it has ferried sentient beings from samsara to nirvana, clearly indicating that the onus is on arriving at the destination, and not on squabbling over the type of raft.

Moreover, as there are countless other Buddhas in the universe — a fact also shared by Theravadins — it is highly possible that some of them might have chosen to be reborn on earth to add their teaching to help us. Vimalakirti, for example, is thought to be an incarnation of Jinli Buddha, and Shan Dao an incarnation of Amitabha Buddha.

More significantly, the Mahayana sutras are probably closer to the Buddha's original teaching than the Theravada sutras. The Buddha's teaching was initially transmitted orally from masters to disciples, and was only written down as sutras about the first century BCE, a few hundred years after his parinirvana, because it was a tradition then that only personal transmission was worthy enough for the highest teaching. The Buddha's teaching was taught, and later written down, in many languages, but the two most important languages in India at that time were Sanskrit and Pali.

The Sanskrit sutras had been translated into Chinese since the second century CE, generally in a most meticulous manner under imperial order. The great translator Kumarajiva, for example, with 800 of the best minds the emperor could provide to help him, worked for a few years to translate and revise a sutra.

Sanskrit continued to flourish in India until the Muslim conquest in the 13th century, but by that time all the important Buddhist texts had long been translated into Chinese. So when Sanskrit became obsolete, Chinese succeeded it as the main language that recorded the Buddhist Canon. It is important to note that the transmission and preservation of the sutras in the Chinese Canon have been continuous.

In Sri Lanka, on the other hand, the Buddhist Canon was first written down in Pali in the first century BCE at Aluvihara. Soon, "war and famine had depopulated the country and the oral transmission of the Pitakas was in danger. The holy language of the Canon was Pali, whereas the Commentaries were in Sinhalese."[4] Because of social and political reasons, Pali also became obsolete.

Only in about 400 CE a few sutras written in Pali were found in Sri Lanka. For the first time they were translated into Sinhalese, the main language of Sri Lanka. It is significant that at this same time in Sri Lanka, Mahayana Buddhism was also widely practiced; for example in Abhayagiri Vihara, one of its principal monasteries, Mahayana doctrines and sutras were incorporated into the Theravada tradition and practiced in the monastery.[5]

It is therefore incompatible to say that Mahayana teaching was a later adulteration, when it was being practiced in a prominent Theravada monastery at the time when the Theravada sutras, which the Theravada School claims to contain the original teaching of the Buddha, were first translated into Sinhalese.

Moreover some Mahayanist teaching, such as the Bodhisattva concept, is still found in Theravada texts today, like mentioning that the Buddha-to-be cultivated for many lifetimes as a Bodhisattva before he was finally reborn as Siddhartha.

However, Theravada became the principal tradition in Sri Lanka when a council at Anuradhapura in 1160 ended the dissensions between the Mahavihara, a prominent Theravada monastery, and its rivals by suppressing them. Earlier in the previous century Theravada had spread to Burma, where Mahayana was also practiced; and in the 14th century Sri Lankan Theravada was established in Thailand, which has continued to today as a stronghold of Theravada. However, beginning in the 16th century, the Portuguese persecuted Theravadins in Sri Lanka, forcing many of them to become Roman Catholics.

The Theravada tradition in Sri Lanka was so severely affected that its sangha died out and monks had to be repeatedly imported from Burma and Thailand in the 17th, 18th and 19th centuries. Revival began about 1880, first stimulated by the Theosophical Society, then under the impulse of awakening nationalism.[6] Today Sri Lanka has restored its position as the foremost champion of the Theravada tradition.

There were two significant breaks in the transmission of the Theravada tradition. The first break lasted about 400 years, starting in the first century BCE when the Buddha's teaching was first recorded in Pali, and then Pali became obsolete due to social and political reasons. Only a few Pali sutras were discovered about 400 CE, when they were for the first time translated into Sinhalese. The second break lasted about 300 years in the 17th, 18th and 19th centuries, when the Theravada sangha in Sri Lanka died out, and its revival began about 1880. Thus the revived Theravada tradition in Sri Lanka today is only slightly more than a hundred years old.

On the other hand, the Mahayana tradition has been continuous in China for almost two thousand years. Sanskrit and Pali, in which the teachings of the Mahayana and the Theravada traditions were originally written, are now obsolete. The obsolescence of Pali about first century BC affected the Theravada tradition severely, because it occurred soon after the start of recording sutras, with the result that only a few Pali sutras were available around 400 CE for translation to Sinhalese, the language of Sri Lanka today.

Later, Pali revived for some time, but this revival could not recover the Pali sutras lost earlier. On the other hand, the obsolescence of Sanskrit about the 13th century had little effect on the Mahayana tradition, because long before that, by the 6th century, virtually all Mahayana sutras had been translated from Sanskrit to Chinese. There were also many translations after the 6th century, but they were improvement or revision over earlier versions.

Thus, with this historical background, it is sensible to ask whether those Mahayana sutras that are found in the Chinese Canon but not in the Pali Canon, are the result of their being lost in the Pali Canon, rather than their being added by later writers to the Chinese Canon. It is also significant to note that most of these Mahayana sutras in Chinese are also found in the Vajrayana tradition in the Tibetan Canon, which were mostly translated directly from Sanskrit.

There are also other reasons to suggest that the Mahayana tradition is closer than the Theravada tradition is, to the original teaching of the Buddha. During the Buddha's time, the Indian mind was already among the finest in the world, and the Indian people were highly philosophical and spiritual. Would such a people, keenly involved in seeking the mystery of man and the universe, and deeply trained in mystical experience, readily accept a religion that merely taught moral living on this earth, with little or no concern with metaphysics and the after-life? It is reasonable to postulate that it was the Mahayana tradition, with its majestic grandeur of cosmic reality, rather than the Theravada tradition, with its stress on suffering and extinction, that had inspired kings to sacrifice the throne and men to sacrifice family life, to seek the ultimate truth.

Different Periods of the Buddha's Teaching

The Buddha taught for forty five years, from the time of his enlightenment at thirty five years of age to his parinirvana at eighty.[7] He was an excellent teacher, always teaching according to the needs and levels of understanding of his disciples. Even an ordinary good teacher, teaching for any substantial length of time, would improve his methods and increase the amount of knowledge to be taught, as his students progress.

Do you think an excellent, selfless teacher like the Buddha, whose knowledge and wisdom is without any doubt unimaginably enormous, would continue teaching just the Four Noble Truth, the Noble Eightfold Path, and the three doctrines of suffering (*dukkha*), impermanence (*anicca*), and non-soul (*anatta*) — which he taught in the very first two sermons to humans in the Deer Park — throughout his forty five years? Mahayanists and Vajrayanists believe that these form only his basic teaching for the first ten years in the Agama Period. The Buddha's teaching can be divided into the following five periods with their respective emphasis:

1. The Avatamsaka (Flower Adornment) Period — first seven days, emphasis on cosmic reality, recorded in the Avatamsaka or Hua Yen Sutra.

2. The Agama (Transmission) Period — first ten years, emphasis on moral purity and elimination of suffering, recorded in the Agama Sutras (or the Nikayas in the Theravada tradition).
3. The Vaipulya (Development) Period — next eight years, emphasis on compassion and the development of the Bodhisattva doctrine, recorded in sutras like Amitabha Sutras, Lankatavara Sutra, Surangama Sutra and Vimalakirti Nirdesa Sutra.
4. The Prajna (Wisdom) Period — next twenty years, emphasis on emptiness, recorded in the Wisdom Sutras.
5. The Pundarika (Lotus) Period — last seven years, emphasis on attaining Buddhahood, recorded in the Lotus Sutra and the Nirvana Sutra.

Because of their different emphasis on the teaching of the Buddha, the Mahayana tradition is different from the Theravada tradition. Theravadins adhere to the Four Noble Truths and the Noble Eightfold Path; and nirvana, which Theravadins consider as ontologically different from samsara, is generally regarded as the extinction of lust, hatred and suffering.

Mahayanists use many expedient means according to the needs and abilities of the followers, believing that there are many paths to the same goal. These expedient means include recitation of mantras and sutras, devotional worship of the Buddha and Bodhisattvas, transference of merits, moral discipline, practice of charity, meditation, and cultivation of wisdom.

Many Mahayanists aim to go to heaven, which is comparatively easy if they accumulate good karma, because while there is only one heaven in most other religions, in Buddhism even in our Saha world system alone there are more than twenty heavens, before taking into account the countless heavens in other star systems, of which Amitabha Buddha's Western Paradise is only one of them. The Theravada School also believes in these heavens, but they are not emphasized, with the result that many Theravada followers may be denied a heavenly rebirth, as they may not be aware of the numerous heavens in Buddhism.

A more difficult and the most noble goal is nirvana or enlightenment, which can be attained in any realms of existence. Nevertheless, it is most difficult, but not impossible, to attain enlightenment in hell because conditions there are most unfavorable; it is almost equally difficult in heaven (with some exceptions like the Western Paradise, as will be explained in subsequent chapters) because conditions there are so joyful that heavenly beings have little incentive to cultivate.

Hence, the Buddha and Buddhist masters have frequently reminded human beings to make full use of their opportunity, for their conditions for attaining enlightenment are most favorable. Enlightenment in the Mahayana tradition, or more commonly referred to as Buddhahood, is the actualization of transcendental cosmic reality. In other words, if you become a Buddha, you are awakened to the fact that you are actually the Supreme Reality. Can you think of a greater or more glorious attainment?

From Awakening to Enlightenment

In Mahayana philosophy, samsara and nirvana are not ontologically different; the difference is one of spiritual perspective. What is samsara to an ordinary person, is nirvana to an enlightened being. When he is unenlightened, he sees reality as the phenomenal world; he sees, for example, birds and people, streams and mountains as separated and differentiated. When he is enlightened, he sees reality as emptiness, where all duality, all separateness and differentiation cease.

Thus, in the Mahayanist view, nirvana is not extinction, for there is nothing to be extinguished. There is no extinction of birds and people, streams and mountains, because they were not there in the first place. Their appearance was an illusion, created by the mind. Another unenlightened being operating under different sets of conditions from us, such as a bacterium or a fairy, would have perceived the "same" phenomena differently.

What applies to the Mahayana tradition is generally applicable to the Vajrayana tradition too, because Vajrayana Buddhism is a development of Mahayana Buddhism, incorporating various prominent features from Tantricism and the Tibetan native Bon religion. Yet, because of this incorporation, there are some noticeable differences between these two traditions.

The Mahayana teaching is open, but much of Vajrayana teaching is secretive, taught only to initiated disciples, which is a legacy of Tantricism. Mahayanists cultivate to go to heaven or to attain enlightenment, but while these are also the main aims of Vajrayanists, some Vajrayanists are also concerned with developing magical powers for more immediate purposes like curing illnesses, obtaining material wealth, exorcising evil spirits, and causing terror in an enemy, which are legacies of Tantricism as well as the Bon religion.

It should be pointed out that Mahayana, Vajrayana and Theravada are not three different Buddhisms; they are three Buddhist traditions representing different developments and emphasis of the same religion. Needless to say, the Mahayanist claim that Theravada Buddhism is only a preparatory stage, is made in good faith and sincerity, and is never meant as a slight to Theravadins. Mahayanists are also aware of the very meritorious work Theravadins have been doing in spreading Buddhism.

Just as Mahayanist masters have impartially examined how valid the Theravadin claim is, that the Mahayana teaching is a later adulteration, it is hoped that for their own and their followers' sake, Theravadin masters would honestly examine whether the Mahayana teaching is really the Buddha's advanced teaching, so that they too can confidently look forward to experience nirvana in all its glory and magnificence, instead of being undecided whether it is total extinction.

It is also heartening to note that the supreme aim of Buddhism, especially as expressed in the Mahayana tradition, is similar to that of all the other world religions, despite their superficial, ritualistic difference. As William James mentioned in his classic *The Varieties of Religious Experiences,* "the overcoming of all usual barriers between the individual self and the Absolute is the great mystic achievement. In mystic states we both become one with the Absolute and we become aware of our oneness. This is the everlasting and triumphant mystical tradition, hardly altered by differences of clime or creed."[8]

The Buddhist attainment is even deeper and more lasting. There are many levels of enlightenment; and a mystic glimpse of transcendental cosmic reality, like the one described above, is of an earlier level, known in Zen Buddhism as an awakening, or *wu* in Chinese, and *satori* or *kensho* in Japanese. At the ultimate level of perfect enlightenment, which is quite some distance from the earlier level of awakening, the spiritual fulfillment is not just a cosmic glimpse, but a total, unobstructed becoming of the Supreme Reality, known as *bodhi* or Buddhahood.

The similarity between Buddhism and other religions in their spiritual aims and accomplishments, like going to heaven in an after-life, or awakening to transcendental cosmic reality here and now, is one of several reasons why Buddhists genuinely respect all other religions.

Although it is probably the religion with the most followers in the world today, and has never once in history resort to force nor said a harsh word against any other religion, it has not attempted any active conversion of followers. Except for monks who literally have to beg to be admitted into the Sangha or Buddhist monastic order, one becomes a Buddhist in a most unofficial and unobtrusive way, often being unaware of the process itself. A person becomes a Buddhist by practicing the Buddha's teaching, like disciplining oneself in moral purity, showing loving-kindness to all beings, and cultivating wisdom for spiritual development.

VARIOUS FORMS OF HEAVENLY BLISS

(Why is the Paradise called Eternal Bliss)

Because people are so used to conditions on earth, they may find these heavenly conditions unbelievable, just as a primitive society constantly living in hunger and hardship may not believe in the rich and luxurious living of an affluent society.

Getting to Know the Heavens

If you wish to go to heaven one day, practicing Buddhism is a very good way to make your dream come true. Many people, including some Buddhists themselves, are unaware that there is not just one, but literally countless heavens in Buddhism! Even in our world system which is known as the Saha world, there are twenty two main heavens. According to the Buddha's teaching, the Saha world is merely one of millions of worlds in our galaxy, and there are millions of galaxies. Each of the countless world system in the myriad galaxies is teeming with life, and has its own heavens.

This, incidentally, is a major difference between Buddhist wisdom and modern science, whose "official" view at present is that life is found only on our earth, although a few eminent scientists belief in extraterrestrial life. Perhaps future scientists may be astonished at how egoistic and geocentric their 20th century colleagues were, just as present scientists are astonished at their former colleagues claiming the earth to be the center of the universe barely four centuries ago.

The requirement for being reborn in heaven is having good karma, which can be generalized in the Buddha's advice of "avoiding evil, and doing good." A person who has bad karma because of his evil deeds will be reborn in a lower station in his next human life, or in one of the "evil realms" of animals, ghosts, asuras (titans) and hells. The Buddha explains that an evil deed is one that brings harm to oneself or others, like being prone to anger, stealing someone's spouse, and killing; whereas a good deed brings benefits, like being peaceful, helping others, and saving lives.

The characteristic of heaven is happiness, and heavenly beings enjoy exceedingly long lives by our human standard. For example in the lowest heaven in our Saha system called *Catumaharajika,* or the Heaven of Four Great Kings — the realm just above our human realm — the average life-span of a heavenly being there is 500 Catumaharajika years, which works out to be about 9,124,000 human years.

In the highest heaven known as *Akanittha,* or the Heaven of Form Perfection —the realm just below the four formless realms, and twenty two realms above our physical human world — the average life-span of a heavenly being there is 16,000 aeons, which in term of human years is a figure beyond the imagination of most people. Thus, for practical purpose, we say life in heaven is "everlasting"; but in reality, when his previous good karma is spent, a heavenly being under-goes reincarnation according to his current karma.

The heaven of Amitabha Buddha's Sukhavati is different in some crucial aspects. It is situated not in our Saha world system, but millions of galaxies away. Life in Sukhavati is eternal; beings here do not have to undergo further reincarnation unless they wish to, like wishing to be reborn in another world to help other beings. Even humans and other beings who have bad karma, who would not be reborn in any of the heavens in the Saha system, could still go to Sukhavati if they seize the opportunity in time. This is possible by the grace of the great Amitabha Buddha.

Perhaps the most important difference is that while heavenly beings in all the heavens in our Saha system are usually too preoccupied with enjoying heavenly bliss that they neglect to cultivate, heavenly beings in the Sukhavati continue to cultivate under the guidance of Amitabha and other great teachers towards enlightenment or Buddhahood. Moreover, beings in Sukhavati are free to visit other heavens whenever they wish.

However, one should remember that going to heaven, including Sukhavati, is not the highest attainment in Buddhism; the highest attainment is the actualization of the Supreme Reality here or in heaven. Nevertheless, for most people who are not yet developed spiritually for perfect enlightenment, going to heaven is certainly the best and most practical choice.

Starting below and continuing for five chapters, the Amitabha Sutra is translated from the Chinese in suitable passages, and explained in each accompanying commentary. The passages are numbered for easy reference. The Chinese version was translated from the original Sanskrit by the great Kumarajiva about 402 under imperial patronage and assisted by eight hundred monks and scholars in Chang-an, the capital of the then Yao-Qin Dynasty.

As a sutra records the sacred words of the Buddha, we should handle a sutra, or any scripture of any religion, with reverence. We should take care, for example, not to sit on or step over any holy book, or to leave it at any place that someone may unwittingly desecrate it. We do so not because we are afraid of any retribution (if there is any retribution, it is definitely from the Buddha or any divine beings), but because of our respect for holiness.

The Buddha's Disciples

Translation

Thus have I heard. Once, the Buddha was at Anathapindika Park of Jeta Grove in the country of Sravasti, with a great following of 1,250 monks, who were all great Arahants, known and recognized by the public. Among them were the Venerable Sariputra, Maudgalyayana, Mahakasyapa, Mahakatyayana, Mahakaustila, Revata, Suddhipanthaka, Nanda, Ananda, Rahula, Gavampati, Pindola-Bharahaga, Kalodayi, Mahakapphina, Vakkula, Aniruddha, and other great disciples; and great Bodhisattvas and Mahasattvas, such as Manjusri, the Prince of the Dharma, Bodhisattva Ajita, Bodhisattva Gandhahasti, Bodhisattva Nityodyukta, and other great Bodhisattvas; and also Sakradeva Indra and countless heavenly beings.

Commentary

This is the preface of the Sutra, stating the time, the place and the beings present. "Thus have I heard" is the conventional start of almost all sutras. The "I" here is Ananda, who, being the Buddha's personal attendant, had heard most of the Buddha's teaching. Ananda also had the power of miraculous memory, being able to remember everything he had heard. In the first Great Council held in Rajagrha a few months after the Buddha's parinirvana (final nirvana), five hundred disciples gathered to rehearse and compiled the Buddha's teaching. Ananda recited what the Buddha had taught, and the Council verified it.

Those present to hear this Sutra included both human and heavenly beings. Some names were mentioned and the following is a brief description of them.

Sariputra was the Buddha's chief disciple, and the foremost among the Arahants in wisdom. Maudgalyayana was the foremost in miraculous powers. His filial effort to save his mother from hell initiated the Ullambana festival, where merits made in offerings to monks are transferred to one's dead parents. Mahakasyapa was a hundred and sixty years old when he became the Buddha's disciple. He is still around in our world system, and will accomplish his task of handing the Buddha's bowl to Maitreya when the latter comes to our world as the Buddha of the next aeon.

Mahakatyayana was the foremost in debate. Once a believer of anihilationism asked, "If the doctrine of rebirth is correct, why hasn't any person come back from hell?" Mahakatyayana said, "Before I answer your question, please tell me whether a prisoner jailed for a crime can come home at his convenience?" "Of course not!" "It is even less free in hell," added Mahakatyayana.

"Then what about those reborn in heaven? Why don't they return to visit their families?" "If you have left a place of suffering, and reach a new place of happiness, would you return to your old place to suffer?" "Of course not!" the anihilationist replied. "So it is the same with those reborn in heaven. Moreover, there is the question of time. A day in the Heaven of Thirty Three, for example, is equivalent to a hundred years in the human world. So, by the time a new arrival settles down at that heaven and thinks about visiting his family back in the human world, his family is no longer there." (The Heaven of Thirty Three, or Trayastrimsa Heaven, is just above the Heaven of Four Great Kings. There are thirty three heavens in this heavenly realm.)

Mahakausthila was Sariputra's maternal uncle, and had very long nails. Revata was foremost in being calm and clear-minded. One night in his sleep he saw two ghosts eating his body. On awaking, he went round asking people whether he had a body. Everyone thought he was mad until he met two Arahants, who told him that his body was actually an illusion of five aggregates.

Suddhipanthaka is an inspiration for all of us. He was so stupid that he could not remember even a line of the Buddha's teaching. His elder brother, Mahapathaka, who was also a monk, told him he was not fit to be in the monastic order. Suddhipanthaka wept profusely for he really wanted to cultivate as a monk.

The Buddha advised him that his brother was his brother, and he was he, so if his brother said he was not fit to be a monk, it did not necessarily have to be so. The Buddha taught him just one word — sweep — to be recited whenever he swept the temple floor, which he did very often.

After some time there was nothing in his mind except this word "sweep". He then asked the Buddha what did "sweep" mean. "It means sweep away all defilements from your mind," the Buddha explained. The Buddha then taught him how to meditate on his breathing, and Suddhipanthaka soon attained enlightenment. All the Buddha's teaching suddenly became very clear to him. If a person reckoned to be stupid could attain enlightenment, most people could do so more readily if they are serious and dedicated.

The Buddha's disciples came from the noble and rich as well as the humble and poor. Nanda was a cowherd, but was a king in a former reincarnation. Such Buddhist knowledge reminds us to treat all people respectfully, irrespective of their present social or economical position. Once the Buddha asked Nanda to preach to 500 nuns, who attained Arahantship after hearing his sermon. The nuns, interestingly enough, were his concubines in their former lives.

Ananda was the Buddha's cousin and personal attendant. He had the miraculous power of not forgetting anything he had heard even once; hence he recited and compiled all the Buddha's teachings into sutras after the Buddha's parinirvana.

Rahula was the Buddha's son; he was foremost in practice, being able to attain samadhi anywhere. As retribution for insulting a monk in a past life, Gavampati became a cow for five hundred reincarnations; but after enlightenment as a Arahant, he lived in heaven and was the foremost in receiving offerings from gods. Arahants and Bodhisattvas are many levels above gods and goddesses.

Pindola-Bharahaga is believed to be still in the Saha world, blessing those who make offerings to the Triple Gem, i.e. the Buddha, the Dharma (Teaching) and the Sangha (Monastic Order). Kalodayin was foremost in teaching the Dharma on behalf of the Buddha. Mahakapphina was foremost in astrology. Vakkula did not cry but smiled when he was born. Aniruddha, who was the Buddha's cousin, had the miraculous power of "heavenly eyes", being able to see countless other worlds.

Bodhisattva Manjusri is often called the Prince of the Dharma. When he was born, ten auspicious signs were manifested: bright light filled his room, sweet dew filled all vessels, seven jewels rained from the sky, gods opened buried treasures, hens gave birth to phoenixes, pigs gave birth to dragons, horses gave birth to unicorns, cows gave birth to mystical oxen, grains turned to gold, and elephants with six tasks appeared.

Bodhisattva Ajita will appear in our world in the next aeon as Maitreya Buddha, the Laughing Buddha. Our world in the present aeon is characterized by suffering; the next aeon will be characterized by laughter. "Gandhahasti" means "never resting", and "Nityodyukta" means "ever vigorous". These two Bodhisattvas complemented each other in their spiritual cultivation.

Actually, the number of heavenly beings taught by the Buddha was greater than that of men. Sakradeva Indra, the ruler of the Trayastrimsa Heaven, led countless heavenly beings to hear the Buddha's sermon.

Heaven in a Distant Galaxy

Translation

At that time the Buddha told the Venerable Sariputra: passing over ten thousand billions of Buddha-lands to our west is a world known as Sukhavati, where a Buddha called Amitabha teaches the Dharma.

Commentary

It is a convention in Buddhist sutras for the Buddha to name one disciple, although the Buddha is actually speaking to countless beings. As in many other sutras, the Buddha addresses Sariputra, the wisest of the Arahants. But unlike other sutras which are often the Buddha's responses to questions asked by his disciples, in this sutra the Buddha teaches from his own initiative, without any prior inquiry, thus illustrating the great importance of this teaching for the people.

It is indeed astounding that at a time when almost all other religious teachers and philosophers were thinking of a geocentric cosmology comprising of only earth, hell and heaven, and twenty centuries before Copernicus suggested that the sun and not the earth was the center of the universe, the Buddha already taught of a world separated from us by billions of other worlds! The Buddha explained that millions of "small-worlds", figuratively described as specks of dust in the cosmos, make up a "middle-world", and millions of "middle-worlds" make up a "great-world", and there are millions of "great-worlds". Translated into modern terms it reads millions of stars make up a galaxy, and millions of galaxies make up a universe, and there are millions of universes.

This world in a distant galaxy where another Buddha, Amitabha Buddha, is teaching the Dharma, is the Western Paradise of Eternal Bliss, or *Sukhavati* in Sanskrit, and *Jile Shijie* (pronounced as "jit-lerk-shi-jie") in Chinese. It is so called because suffering, which unfortunately is the characteristic of our own world, is unknown here and its inhabitants experience boundless bliss.

It is significant to note that what Amitabha teaches in the Western Paradise is called the Dharma, which is translated as the Teaching, and sometimes translated as the Law. It is not described as Buddhism as we know it in our world. Dharma, in its wide sense as used here, refers to the teaching of an Enlightened One who leads sentient beings to enlightenment. Hence, even on our puny earth, Dharma may refer to the teaching of any other religions besides Buddhism as taught by Sakyamuni Buddha. This illustrates the liberal attitude of the Buddha's teaching.

Worldly Suffering and Heavenly Bliss

Translation

Sariputra, why is this world called Sukhavati or Eternal Bliss? It is because the inhabitants of this world not only have no suffering, but also have boundless bliss. Thus, it is named Sukhavati or Eternal Bliss.

Commentary

Our human realm in the Saha world is characterized by suffering. This does not mean that there is no joy in the human realm, but it means that there is comparatively more suffering than joy. This comparison may be made between joy and suffering in the human realm itself, or between the human realm and heavenly realms. Of course, if the human realm is compared with the lower realms of animals, asuras, ghosts and hell inhabitants, our human realm is full of joy.

Suffering may be classified into three main categories:

(1) "bitter-suffering" (*ku-ku,* pronounced as "kh'u kh'u") or suffering due to desires;
(2) "destructive-suffering" (*huai-ku*) or suffering due to the impermanence of form;
(3) "samsaric-suffering" (*xing-ku*) or suffering due to samsara.

Beings existing in the realms of desire, like humans, are subjected to all the three categories of suffering; beings existing in the realms of form, like Brahma-gods, are subjected to only the latter two categories; and beings existing in the formless realms, like Sravakas and Prateyakabuddhas, are subjected to only samsaric suffering.

Suffering due to desires is classified into eight types, namely suffering due to:

(a) birth;
(b) age;
(c) sickness;
(d) death;
(e) failure to satisfy needs;
(f) parting of loved ones;
(g) meeting of persons who hate each other;
(h) illusion of the five skandhas (aggregates of form, perception, thought, activity and consciousness) that make up a person.

Brahma-gods, who exist in the realms of form above the realms of desires, are free from suffering due to desires, but as they still have form, they suffer from the impermanence of their form. Sravakas and Prateyakabuddhas, who are very advanced beings existing as pure consciousness in the formless realms above the realms of form, still have some traces of samsaric suffering because they have not attained Buddhahood.

Sukhavati, the Western Paradise of Eternal Bliss is free from all suffering. Beings in this Pure Land of Amitabha enjoy three categories of bliss:

(1) the bliss of purity and tranquillity, i.e. the heavenly beings are free from defilement and carving, thus eliminating suffering due to desires;
(2) the bliss of everlasting life, i.e. the beings do not die and the Paradise is eternal, thus eliminating suffering due to impermanent form;
(3) the bliss of nirvanic stability, i.e. the beings are not subjected to further rebirth, thus eliminating suffering due to samsara.

In contrast with the eight types of human suffering, beings in Sukhavati enjoy the bliss of:

(a) transformation by way of the lotus to the Pure Land, thus overcoming suffering due to human birth;

(b) magnificent body, which does not grow old, thus overcoming suffering due to old age;

(c) spontaneous purity, which has spontaneous harmony of "earth", "fire", "water" and "wind" (the four fundamentals of the universe), thus overcoming suffering due to sickness;

(d) boundless longevity, thus overcoming suffering due to death;

(e) materialization according to wish, which enables the beings to materialize whatever they need by thought, thus overcoming suffering due to failure to satisfy needs;

(f) sea of beings, where the heavenly beings can meet whoever they wish at any time, thus overcoming suffering due to parting of loved ones;

(g) meeting of goodness, where hatred is absent in the Paradise, thus overcoming suffering due to meeting hated persons;

(h) tranquillity, where the existence of the heavenly beings is due not to karma but to the grace of Amitabha Buddha, thus overcoming suffering due to five skandhas which come together because of various karmic conditions.

Because people are so used to conditions on earth, they may find these heavenly conditions unbelievable, just as a primitive society constantly living in hunger and hardship may not believe in the rich and luxurious living of an affluent society. What is the main cause for the difference between our world and the Western Paradise? It is the mind of the inhabitants — the mind of humans is defiled, whereas that of beings in the Pure Land is purified. The Western Paradise and our own world, as well as all other phenomenal realms of existence, are a creation of the mind!

DESCRIPTION OF WESTERN PARADISE

(What Life is Like in Paradise)

So if the working of your good karma has led you to read this book,
you would not be so unwise as to brush aside the golden opportunity lightly.

After explaining why the Western Paradise of Eternal Bliss is so called, as described in the previous chapter, the Buddha continues to relate its environment and heavenly beings.

What does Heaven Look Like?

Translation

Then, Sariputra, this Paradise of Eternal Bliss is surrounded by seven tiers of ornamental railings, seven curtains of netted tapestries, and seven rows of tress. All these are made of four treasures. Thus, this world is called Eternal Bliss.

Sariputra, in this Paradise of Eternal Bliss there are ponds of seven treasures, filled with waters of eight merits. The bottoms of the ponds are purely covered with gold sand. On all sides the walks are made of gold, silver, lapis-lazuli and crystal. Above are built towers and pavilions, adorned with gold, silver, lapis-lazuli, crystal, beryl, red pearls and carnelian.

In the ponds are lotus flowers as large as carriage wheels — green-colored with green radiance, yellow-colored with yellow radiance, red-colored with red radiance, white-colored with white radiance, subtle, wonderful, fragrant and pure. Oh Sariputra, thus is the Paradise of Eternal Bliss, brought to such a glorious state of magnificence through the merits of Amitabha Buddha.

Commentary

Descriptions of heaven in most religions or cultures are usually vague or reminiscent of scenes on earth. In some religions or cultures, heaven resembles some sort of empyrean battlefields where heroes go to, in others a celestial representation of palaces complete with ministers similar to earthly ones, and in most an idyllic scene of streams and trees. The description of heaven in Buddhism, like the Western Paradise of Eternal Bliss described in this Amitabha Sutra, is most detailed and specific.

The ornamental railings, curtains of tapestries, and rows of tress in the Western Paradise are different from those found on earth; they are all made of the four treasures of gold, silver, lapis-lazuli and crystal in different combinations. For example, some trees may have gold fruit and crystal leaves, while the trunks of others may be of silver and leaves of lapis-lazuli.

The number seven, which has been repeatedly used in the description, reminds of the seven weeks of the Buddha's intensive meditation just before his perfect enlightenment, the seven days of sitting in meditation after the enlightenment preaching the Avatamsaka teaching on cosmic reality to heavenly beings, and the seven sections of the "thirty seven doctrines of spiritual training", which are as follows:

(1) Four focuses of meditation to develop wisdom:
   (a) at the body, viewing the body as defiled, which needs purification to attain tranquillity;
   (b) at perception, realizing that samsaric perception results in suffering, which needs transcending to attain bliss;
   (c) at the mind, realizing personal mind is impermanent, thus cultivating to attain Universal Mind, that is eternal;
   (d) at phenomena, realizing that phenomena are absent of self-nature, thus overcoming illusion to experience ultimate reality.
(2) Four Proper Activities to enhance effort:
   (a) Terminate all evil thoughts that have arisen;
   (b) Prevent the emergence of evil thoughts that have not arisen;
   (c) Generate good thoughts that have not arisen;
   (d) Develop good thoughts that have arisen.
(3) Four States of Mind to cultivate meditation:
   (a) intention to cultivate the mind;
   (b) effort to cultivate the mind;
   (c) tranquillity in meditation;
   (d) insight in meditation.

(4) Five Roots to develop spirituality:
   (a) Faith;
   (b) Effort;
   (c) Understanding;
   (d) Mental Concentration;
   (e) Wisdom.
(5) Five Powers to enter spirituality:
   (a) Power of faith;
   (b) Power of effort;
   (c) Power of thought;
   (d) Power of mental concentration;
   (e) Power of wisdom.
(6) Seven Branches of Bodhi to lead ordinary people to bodhi or enlightenment:
   (a) Right explanation of bodhi;
   (b) Effort to practice bodhi;
   (c) Joy to practice bodhi;
   (d) Determination to eliminate perverse views so as to attain bodhi;
   (e) Readiness to sacrifice whatever is irrelevant to bodhi;
   (f) Concentration on bodhi;
   (g) Mindfulness of bodhi.
(7) Eightfold Path:
   (a) Right understanding;
   (b) Right thought;
   (c) Right speech;
   (d) Right action;
   (e) Right livelihood;
   (f) Right effort;
   (g) Right concentration.
   (h) Right contemplation.

The water in the ponds possesses the eight merits of being spontaneously pure, fresh, sweet, soft, nourishing, calming, quenching hunger and thirst, and promoting good spiritual roots. You may, for example, take a bath in the pond, yet the water will not be soiled, because it is spontaneously pure; your friend drinking the water next to you will not be angry at your having a bath because the water spontaneously calms him. If someone laughs at these occurrences as impossible, he is using his limited earthly standards to judge heavenly conditions — comparable to someone unfamiliar with the thermostat thinking it impossible for you to have just the temperature you want in your air-conditioned room despite changing weather conditions.

The lotus in the Pure Land has a special significance. When a person in the Saha world makes a vow to be reborn in the Pure Land, and earnestly recites the name of Amitabha Buddha, a new lotus flower will bloom in the Paradise. When that person dies in the Saha world, he will be reborn in Sukhavati, the Western Paradise, from the lotus, not as a baby but at the same age as he is in the Saha world.

Heavenly Music and Inter-Galaxy Travel

Translation

Sariputra, celestial music is always heard in the air. Day and night for six times heavenly mandarava flowers with exquisite fragrance rain from the sky onto the ground of gold. Often at dawn the heavenly beings of this Pure Land receive with their robes these marvelous, beautiful mandarava flowers, and present them in reverence to ten million billion Buddhas of other worlds. At meal times, these heavenly beings return to the Western Paradise for their meals. Sariputra, such is this world, brought to so glorious a state of excellence through the merits of Amitabha Buddha.

Commentary

During the Buddha's time, day and night are divided into six periods, namely early day, middle day, late day, early night, middle night, and late night. Thus the term "six times" mentioned in the Sutra in classical Chinese, which is a very concise language, may be interpreted as "for six times during the day and night", or "throughout the six time-periods of the day and night".

It has been known since ancient times in Buddhism that there are billions of other worlds in the universe besides our own world, each with its own Buddha. The heavenly beings in Sukhavati pay reverence to the billions of Buddhas with the marvelous mandarava flowers, and return before meal-time at noon. If you are in heaven, you do not have to worry about working for a living, or finding your meals; you merely think of whatever you want to materialize it!

Some readers may wonder how is it possible for these beings to travel to distant galaxies to pay homage to other Buddhas and return in the same morning. The problem only arises when we try to view it from our limited human knowledge and ability. As an analogy, a butterfly in Asia depending on its butterfly knowledge and ability will not be able to reach America, even if it may have heard of the distant continent; but if it is placed in an aeroplane, for example, it will be able to do so.

Heavenly beings, not subjected to our human limitations — such as our being imprisoned in a comparatively massive body of matter, and the inability to travel faster than the speed of light — have transcended space and time, which are actually not absolute truths but merely human constructs. Even on earth, I can confidently predict Einstein's axiom that nothing can travel faster than light, which necessarily confines us to a puny space in the infinite cosmos, will become outdated in the near future, just as Galileo's courageous proposition that the sun and not the earth was the center of the universe became outdated in the past, and Newton's laws which led to scientific determinism has become outdated at present.

Indeed in 1982 Alain Aspect, Jean Dalibard and Gerard Roger unequivocally confirmed Bell's Theorem, which provides a brilliant mathematical proof to explain instantaneous action at a distance. Surprisingly, many scientists choose to ignore such outstanding discoveries.

Cultivating for Enlightenment

Translation

Next, Sariputra, in the Western Paradise there are marvelous, multi-colored birds, like white cranes, peacocks, parrots, swans, jiva-jivas and the kala-vindas. These birds sing six times days and night in melodious voices to proclaim doctrines like Five Roots, Five Powers, Seven Branches of bodhi, and Eightfold Path. When the heavenly beings hear these voices, they will spontaneously think of the Buddha, the Dharma and the Sangha.

Sariputra, do not be mistaken that these birds are reborn here in the animal realm as the result of their sinful karma in their previous lives. Why is this so? There are no three evil realms of existence in this Pure Land. Sariputra, even the names of the evil realms are unknown here; how can there be products of the evil realms. These various birds are the creation of Amitabha Buddha as a means to dissipate the sounds of the Dharma so that the heavenly beings will cultivate towards enlightenment.

Sariputra, when breeze blows through the Western Paradise, the rows of precious trees and curtains of tapestries send out subtle, wondrous music, as if hundreds and thousands of heavenly orchestras are playing. When the beings hear the heavenly music, they spontaneously think of the Buddha, the Dharma and the Sangha. Sariputra, such is this Buddha-land, brought to so glorious a state of excellence through the merits of Amitabha Buddha.

Commentary

Jiva-jivas and kalavindas are rare birds believed to be found in our world in the past. The voices of jiva-jivas are exceedingly melodious. Kalavindas have two heads in one body.

Five Roots, Five Powers, Seven Branches of bodhi, and Eightfold Path are twenty five of the seven groups of thirty seven doctrines to attain bodhi or enlightenment, which are mentioned in the commentary of Passage 4. The other twelve doctrines are Four Meditation Focuses, Four Proper Activities and Four States of Mind.

The Buddha, the Dharma and the Sangha are collectively known as the Triple Gem. The Buddha is the Enlightened One. The Dharma is the Teaching of the Buddha. The Sangha is the monastic communities dedicated to seeking enlightenment.

There are six realms of existence where sentient beings usually reincarnate in, namely the realms of:

1. devas, or heavenly beings;
2. humans;
3. asuras, or titans — female asuras are very beautiful, but male asuras are fierce and always fighting among themselves because they are very jealous of one another;
4. animals;
5. ghosts, who are always hungry;
6. hell inhabitants, who suffer for their evil deeds.

The lower three realms are known as the three evil realms because beings are reborn there because of their evil karma.

The heavenly beings in the Western Paradise, unlike heavenly beings in other heavens, need not undergo reincarnation. Here, they are all spiritually awakened and cultivate under the guidance of Amitabha Buddha and other teachers until they attain perfect enlightenment.

One should remember that going to heaven is not the same as perfect enlightenment, which is the highest spiritual fulfillment. One can attain perfect enlightenment here and now in our human world. Some schools, like Zen and Vajrayana Buddhism, which are meant for those with strong spiritual roots, are dedicated to this objective. As for others, whose spiritual roots are weak, will naturally find attaining enlightenment an exceedingly difficult task. For them, rebirths in the Western Paradise where they can cultivate in most favorable conditions, not only assure them of eventual enlightenment, but also once and for all relieve them of samsaric suffering.

This does not necessarily imply that rebirth in the Western Paradise is meant for those of inferior spiritual roots, as it is sometimes alleged. Even Bodhisattva Manjusri, reputed to be the wisest of the Bodhisattvas, indicated his wish to be reborn in the Western Paradise.

What actually is perfect enlightenment? Perfect enlightenment or Buddhahood is the actualization of cosmic reality. When a being is perfectly enlightened, i.e. when he becomes a Buddha, he liberates himself from the illusory separation between himself and everything else in the infinite, eternal universe, and realizes that he is actually the infinite, eternal universe, the omnipresent, omniscient Cosmic Being, the Supreme Reality, or God. Once we understand this great cosmic truth, we realize how naive the following claim is: mine is a religion of God, yours (referring to Buddhists') is a religion of humans, for Siddhartha Gautama himself was a human.

Boundless Light and Boundless Life

Translation

Sariputra, what is you opinion? Why is this Buddha called Amitabha? Sariputra, the radiant light of this Buddha is boundless, illuminating all the lands of ten directions without any obstruction. Thus he is called Amitabha. Also, Sariputra, the lifespan of this Buddha as well as of the inhabitants of his Buddha-land is boundless, lasting for assamkhyeyas kalpas. So he is called Amitabha.

Sariputra, Amitabha Buddha has become a Buddha for ten kalpas. Besides, Sariputra, this Buddha has countless, limitless Sravaka-disciples, who are all Arahants, and their number is beyond computation. In the same way, there are countless, limitless Bodhisattvas. Thus, Sariputra, is this Buddha-land, brought to so glorious a state of excellence through the merits of Amitabha Buddha.

Next, Sariputra, all the sentient beings in this Western Paradise of Eternal Bliss are Avarvartyas, among them are numerous Ekajati-Pratibuddhas. There are so many of them that their number is beyond computation, but may be described as immeasurable, limitless assamkhyeyas kalpas.

Commentary

Amitabha means boundless light. He is also known as Amitayus, which means boundless life. The lifespan of Amitabha and the beings in Western Paradise is limitless, lasting for assamkhyeyas kalpas, which means infinite aeons.

It should be noted that Amitabha is here referred to in his *sambhogakaya* or reward body. A Buddha may manifest in three bodies, namely *dharmakaya, sambhogakaya* and *nirmanakaya*. The *dharmakaya* or Spiritual Body of the Buddha is the infinite, eternal cosmos, similar in concept to the omnipresent, omniscient Almighty God. The *sambhogakaya* or reward body is the astral body seen by heavenly beings, and sometimes by highly spiritual human beings; it is similar to the concept of God as a Fatherly Figure. The *nirmanakaya* or transformational body is his physical manifestation, such as his human body as Bodhisattva Dharmakara before he became a Buddha; it is similar to the concept of Jesus Christ.

Amitabha Buddha has become a Buddha for ten kalpas. A kalpa or an aeon refers to a cycle of birth, growth, decay and extinction of a world system. For us in our Saha system, a kalpa is about 12.8 billion years. Hence, since Bodhisattva Dharmakara became Amitabha Buddha, our world system has come into being then become extinct, and come into being again, for ten times. Historians who believe civilization began only a few thousand years ago, archaeologists who believe Homo sapiens appeared a million years hence, and astronomers who believe the earth is about four billion years old, will have some material to argue about.

Amitabha Buddha has countless Sravaka-disciples who have become Arahants, and Mahayanist disciples who have become Bodhisattvas. A Sravaka is one who learns mainly through hearing the Buddha's teaching. He is Hinayanist because he believes that everyone has to work for his own salvation, and his highest attainment before becoming a Buddha himself is Arahantship.

On the other hand, a Mahayanist believes in working for his as well as others' salvation. His highest attainment, before becoming a Buddha, is becoming a Bodhisattva, who is a very advanced being of great compassion. Many Bodhisattvas actually have attained Buddhahood, but they return to the phenomenal dimension so as to help others. The two greatest Bodhisattvas of Sukhavati, the Western Paradise, who usually appear on the left and right of Amitabha Buddha, are Bodhisattva Avalokitesvara or Guan Shi Yin, and Bodhisattva Mahasthamaprapta or Da Shi Zhi. Bodhisattva Guan Shi Yin, usually called Guan Yin Bodh Satt in Chinese, is the most popular Bodhisattva in Chinese Buddhism.

All the beings in the Western Paradise, including the less spiritual ones, are Avarvartyas, which means they will never retrogress in their spiritual path. Some people with bad karma may still win rebirth in the Western Paradise if they are opportune enough to accept the grace of Amitabha Buddha. This illustrates the great compassion shown in Buddhism — that of accepting even sinners to heaven so that they can improve themselves.

The great majority of the beings in the Western Paradise are reborn there because of their good karma, and they are highly spiritual. Many of them are Ekajati-Pratibuddhas, i.e. Buddhas-elect who will attain Buddhahood in only one more lifetime in any realm of existence. Actually in the Western Paradise, all beings will attain Buddhahood in one more lifetime, because they are not subjected to reincarnation; those of a lower spiritual level will of course take a much longer time.

One should note that not many people actually have the blessing to learn about the grace of Amitabha Buddha and the opportunity to be reborn in the Western Paradise. Some people, because of the burden of their bad karma, may not belief in it even though they are aware of the rare opportunity. In Buddhist philosophy, nothing happens by chance: nevertheless, this does not mean that everything is predetermined. (Scientists puzzled at the seemingly random combination of the XX or XY factors in determining the sex of a baby, or the random integration and disintegration of energy and particles, may draw some inspiration from this Buddhist philosophy for future research.) So if the working of your good karma has led you to read this book, you would not be so unwise as to brush aside the golden opportunity lightly.

WINNING REBIRTH IN THE WESTERN PARADISE

(Conditions and Procedure for Going to Heaven)

The Western Paradise is definitely as real as the physical world you exist in now.

After describing the Western Paradise and its inhabitants, as narrated in the previous two chapters, in this chapter the Buddha explains the second and, for many of us, the most significant part of the Amitabha Sutra, i.e. how we can be reborn in the Western Paradise.

Spiritual Roots and Blessings

Translation

Sariputra, sentient beings who have heard about this teaching, should make a vow, vow to be reborn in this Western Paradise. Wherefore? To be in the company of advanced, virtuous beings. Sariputra, in order to be born there, one must not lack good spiritual roots and blessings from good karma.

Commentary

The Buddha explains that we must have good spiritual roots and blessings from good karma if we wish to be reborn in Sukhavati, the Western Paradise of Eternal Bliss. Having good spiritual roots means possessing the wisdom concerning cosmic reality. Having blessings means possessing good karmic effect due to meritorious deeds performed in the past.

In Mahayana Buddhism, both cultivating for blessings and cultivating for wisdom are essential. This is one of the reasons why Mahayanists consider helping others in their spiritual development as important as attaining their own enlightenment.

The following anecdote illustrates the cultivation of blessings and of wisdom. There was once a monk who begged for his daily meal, but frequently he was hungry because he could not get any food. Each day on his return to his temple he passed by an elephant which was well fed and lavishly looked after by a rich man, and which had some inexplicable mutual affinity with him.

The hungry monk thought sadly to himself, "Despite my knowledge of the Four Noble Truths and the Eightfold Path, my life is not even comparable to this lucky elephant!" So he asked his master why was he in such a miserable condition.

The master, who had the miraculous power of looking into past lives, told him, "Actually you and the elephant were dharma classmates in your past reincarnations. You spent all your time studying the sutras but did not bother to help others; he was lazy and did not study the sutras as he should, but he compensated for this setback by serving other people. Hence, as a result of your karma, you have a hard time in this life although you possess much spiritual wisdom, whereas your classmate the elephant is comfortable although he is still spiritually ignorant."

"Master, please advise me."

"Spend some time to cultivate blessing, like doing more charity."

"I don't even have enough to feed myself; how do I do charity?

"As a monk you hardly have any material possessions, but you are rich in many ways. Recite some sutras at night, for example, so that ghosts and nature spirits may also benefit from the Buddha's teaching. In this way you will acquire a lot of blessings."

If spiritual roots and blessings are necessary conditions for rebirth in the Western Paradise, why, then, are sinners able to be reborn there if they sincerely recite the name of Amitabha Buddha? The fact that they can accept the teaching and be humble enough to recite the Buddha's name sincerely shows they have good spiritual roots. The fact that they have the opportunity to know of this teaching shows they have sufficient blessings. Although they have sinned, they must have acquired good roots and blessings in their former lives, or in earlier parts of their present lives. The typical Buddhist attitude towards sinners is not to contempt them but to help them redeem themselves.

If sinners are also found in the Western Paradise, why is it said that anyone reborn there finds himself in the company of advanced, virtuous company. This is because all the inhabitants of the Western Paradise are Avarvartyas, i.e. they will never retrogress in their spiritual path. A sinner who has repented himself and who will never sin again but steadfastly progresses in his spiritual training is more admirable than someone, irrespective of his initial spiritual level, who makes no effort in spiritual cultivation and thus may retrogress.

Rebirth in Western Paradise

Translation

Sariputra, if a virtuous man or a virtuous woman, hearing this teaching about Amitabha Buddha, recites the Buddha's name for one day, or two days, or three days, or four days, or five days, or six days, or seven days, recites whole-heartedly without any other thoughts, when this person is about to pass away in his or her physical life, Amitabha Buddha and other holy beings will appear before him or her. At the time of death, if his or her mind is free from mundane distraction, this person will be reborn in Amitabha's Paradise of Eternal Bliss.

Commentary

The mention of reciting the Buddha's name for one day to seven days, may be interpreted in the following two ways. If some readers are disturbed that a scripture can be interpreted in more than one way, they can be comforted by the fact that the Buddha's teaching is never dictatorial. It does not, as is common in some other religions, adopt the attitude of telling its followers: Do this... Do this... ; Do not do that...

The Buddha's approach has always been like one who having found the way, points it out to others so that they too may share its rewards, and constantly reminds them that they should assess the way to the best of their own understanding and experience. Secondly, it should be remembered both the original Sanskrit, and classical Chinese into which the Sutra was translated more than 15 centuries ago, are exceedingly concise languages.

Reciting Amitabha Buddha's name whole-heartedly without any other thoughts is expressed poetically in the famous Chinese phrase as yi xin bu luan, which becomes quite prosaic in the literal translation of "one-heart, no disturbance".

Many people may not be able to attain *yi xin bu luan,* or a one-pointed mind, on the first day of practice. On the second day, their mental concentration should improve, and they may achieve a one-pointed mind on the third day. If not, they may accomplish it on the fourth day, or the fifth, or even the sixth. By the seventh day, usually everyone who has put in some effort can accomplish *yi xin bu luan,* but if anyone still cannot do so, he only has to keep trying the next day until he succeeds. This is the first interpretation.

In the second interpretation, the devotee after having attained a one-pointed mind or *yi xin bu luan* in the recitation of Amitabha Buddha's name continues to do so the second day. If he succeeds, he continues the third day, and so on until he can recite the Buddha's name whole-heartedly without any mental distraction for a continuous stretch of seven days. If on any day he fails to attain a one-pointed mind, he starts from scratch the next day.

The important question is not which interpretation was the one originally intended by the Buddha, but which interpretation will better help you to achieve you spiritual goal. Very likely, the Buddha himself would have given different answers to different people because of their different nature and different needs.

Many people choose the first interpretation, not because it is easier, but because it is the logical first step. When they can attain a one-pointed mind reciting Amitabha Buddha's name, they then proceed to do so for two consecutive days, then three, then four and so on. Usually if they can do so for seven consecutive days, they can do so for any reasonable number of days.

Most people are not unduly worried about either interpretation; they just concentrate on reciting Amitabha Buddha's name with all their soul, to the exclusion of everything else. Nevertheless, their progress is still similar to adopting the first and then the second interpretation. Many Buddhists, especially followers of the Pure Land School, recite the name of Amitabha Buddha for life.

In each recitation session, how long or how many times should we recite the name of Amitabha Buddha? In the *Amitayus Sutra,* Amitabha Buddha himself when he was the Bodhisattva Dharmakara said in the 18th of his 48 great vows that:

When I become a Buddha, if sentient beings of the ten directions — with the exception of those who commit the five monstrous crimes and those who blaspheme the True Teaching — in their great faith to seek happiness, are desirous to be reborn in my Buddha-land, have recited my name ten times, but are not reborn there, I do not accept Buddhahood.

Thus, according to Amitabha Buddha Himself, except those who have committed the five monstrous crimes and those who blaspheme the True Teaching, anyone desirous to be reborn in the Western Paradise could do so if he has recited His name at least ten times. The five monstrous crimes are killing a Buddha, killing one's father, killing one's mother, killing one's teacher, and killing a Bodhisattva, an Arahant or a holy member of the monastic order.

Does this mean that those who have committed a monstrous crime or blasphemed the True Teaching will never have the chance to go to the Western Paradise? Not necessary so. They will not have a chance in their current life, and they will also suffer for their bad karma in their next life. But if they earnestly repent, and cultivate good roots and blessings, they will have the opportunity of rebirth in the Western Paradise in future lives.

If ten times is the minimum requirement of recitation, can a person wait till his end is near to do so? He can, but it is certainly very unwise, as there are so many factors in operation that can nullify his intention. A person who is not bothered about spiritual cultivation is not likely to be blessed with a peaceful death; thus he may, for example, be too busy struggling for life to remember reciting Amitabha Buddha's name.

Most devotees recite many more times than the minimum ten — usually in the regions of hundreds or thousands, not just once but regularly — not because they are worried Amitabha Buddha may not have heard them, but because they enjoy the recitation, especially when the recitation has led them into a deep meditative state.

Sentient beings in countless world systems in the universe can be reborn in the Western Paradise if they so desire and whole-heartedly recite Amitabha Buddha's name. Why is this possible? It is because of the grace of Amitabha Buddha. Some readers may not be satisfied with this spiritual answer. A philosophical or "scientific" explanation is as follows.

All phenomenal realms, including Sukhavati and our Saha world, are creations of the mind. This great cosmic truth, which has been taught by many Buddhist as well as non-Buddhist teachers since ancient times, and which the public usually held in suspicion if not in downright disbelief, is now an established scientific fact, although common people may still be unaware of it. Professor Michael Talbot says:

Even the world we know may not be composed of objects. We may only be sensing mechanisms moving through a vibration dance of frequencies. Pribram suggests that the reason we translate this vibrating dance of frequencies into the solidity and objectivity of the universe as we know it is that our brains operate on the same holographic like principles as the dance of frequencies and is able to convert them into a picture much the same as a television converts the frequencies it receives into a more coherent image.

What we regard as the so-called external objective world is actually an illusion caused by our senses. In scientific language, what we think are objects and processes are fundamentally random patterns of particles and energy, constantly disintegrating and coalescing — meaningful to scientists only in the form of mathematical equations.

Whether "reality" appears as particles or as energy depends on how our mind chooses to interpret it. If, for example, a scientist sets up an experiment to measure particles, electrons will appear as particles; if he sets up an experiment to measure energy, the "same" electrons will appear as waves! Alastair Rae, a well-known physicist, reports:

> We now have two models to describe the nature of light depending on the way we observe it: if we perform an interference experiment light behaves as a wave, but if we examine the photoelectric effect light behaves like a stream of particles.

A research scientist, Anjam Khursheed, expresses the same truth:

> We are forced nowadays to acknowledge that measurements of time and space are relative to frames of reference and to admit that certain of our measurements must affect the very reality we are measuring.

A popular physicist, John Gribbin, who emphasizes that quantum mechanics is the greatest scientific achievement in the twentieth century, expresses this truth directly:

> For what quantum mechanics says is that nothing is real and we cannot say anything about what things are doing when we are not looking at them.

We often take for granted that what we perceive is also what other creatures perceive. For example, we presume that what appears to us as a house is also what appears as a house to a cow. This presumption is not necessarily valid. Just as a cow is unlikely to understand the substratum of particles and energy, because (to the best of our knowledge) it does not know mathematics, we are unlikely to understand what a cow perceives because we do not know cow-sense.

Indeed, scientists have circumstantial evidence that a bird's eye-view or a fish's eye-view of the same scene is different from the human's. The so-called external objective world is therefore illusory as well as relative — illusory because it is not ultimately real, and relative because the illusion varies among different sentient beings.

Although scientists are now aware that the phenomena we perceive are creations of our minds, they are still puzzled as to why everyone has create the same phenomena. For example, why does the collection of subatomic forces and particles (called *dharmas* in Buddhist philosophy) that you interpret as water, is also interpreted as water by your friends and all other human beings, although they may call it by other names?

Buddhism has long provided an illuminating answer. It is because, besides the similar sets of sense organs and mode of intellectualization, you, your friends and all other human beings have the same alaya consciousness, or collective consciousness.

This alaya consciousness, which is the 8th consciousness in Buddhist psychology, is the result of thousands or millions of years of collective human experience. Other beings having different alaya consciousness (and other conditions), will interpret the same collection of subatomic forces and particles differently. For example, what is water to us, is crystal to devas or gods, but fire to ghosts and hell inhabitants. This is one reason why priests of almost every religion use holy water for consecration and exorcism.

Hence, what we think, is extremely important, as it directly affects what we will become, and the effects often extend into future lives. If our thoughts are noble, we become noble; if our thoughts are evil, we become evil. This cosmic truth can be expressed so simply, but its operation may not be easy to comprehend. Hence many people may not believe in it. A person whose mind is constantly full of beautiful, kind thoughts will go to heaven or to a beautiful, kind rebirth in the human realm; a person whose mind is constantly full of hideous, wicked thoughts will go to hell or to some evil realms.

If a person whole-heartedly recites the name of Amitabha Buddha and steadfastly visualizes the Western Paradise, he would have created a lasting blueprint in his mind. When his physical body dies, his mind, which is formless, lives on. When he reincarnates into the realm of form again, the blueprint in his mind decides what kind of form will be manifested. Hence, a devotee whose mind is highly charged with the cosmic vibration of Amitabha Buddha and the Western Paradise to the exclusion of all other thoughts, when he dies in this Saha world, he will be reborn in Amitabha Buddha's Western Paradise of Eternal Bliss.

Interestingly, this cosmic truth, albeit in the study of earthly birth, is now discovered in the life sciences, although many biologists, reminiscent of their predecessors in their attempt to be objective in order to emulate Newtonian physics, still talk about the mechanistic nervous system instead of the subjective mind.

Nevertheless, eminent biologists now base the definition of life not on any substance or even on energy, but on a measure of pure information, which is passed from one birth to another deciding on the form of life to be born. Professor Edmund Jack Ambrose says:

> The matter in life has no permanence; only the pattern according to which it is arranged or organized has permanence. Life is basically a pattern of organic activity taking place within a liquid. This liquid is water; freeze or remove the water and only a state of suspended animation can be produced in simple organisms. But not only is the pattern preserved throughout the life of the individual cell or organism while matter flows steadily through it, but the organism is also capable of implanting its pattern on other matter and so reproducing itself. The pattern of reproduction can be almost unbelievably stable provided there is no gross change in the environment in which the organism lives.

Hence, information is imprinted onto the consciousness of an organism, and this imprint not only decides the form of the organism, although its substance has been changed (like all the cells of the organism have been replaced), but also decides the form of its reproduction. It is amazing how similar in principle is this biological concept with the Buddhist concept of reincarnation.

As the Western Paradise, like all other phenomenal realms of heavens, worlds and hells, is a creation of mind, then, is it real? The Western Paradise is definitely as real as the physical world you exist in now. The heavenly music, the exquisite fragrance of the mandarava flowers, and the pleasant company of heavenly beings in the Western Paradise are as real as the objects and people you meet in this world.

Yet, at the highest spiritual level, both the Western Paradise and this physical world are not the ultimate, absolute reality. Experiencing the ultimate, absolute reality is nirvana or Buddhahood, and can be attained in the Western Paradise, or here and now in this world. But for most people, who have not yet developed to a very high spiritual level, it is understandably difficult to attain Buddhahood here; gaining rebirth in the Western Paradise not only ensures an eternal blissful life, but also guarantees eventual Buddhahood.

Making a Vow

Translation

Sariputra, as I see the great benefit of this teaching, I therefore preach it. If sentient beings hear of this teaching, they should make a vow to be reborn in this Western Paradise.

Commentary

The fact that you have the opportunity to know this Amitabha Sutra shows you have acquired a lot of blessings in your former lives, because you possess five rare achievements, namely:

1. the rarity of being born a human;
2. the rarity of being born in a civilized place;
3. the rarity of being born with all the sense organs and senses functioning normally;
4. the rarity of being encouraged by friends or teachers to develop spiritually (most people are only concerned with worldly things);
5. the rarity of being exposed to the Buddha's teaching.

Being blessed with such rare achievements and yet not making use of the opportunity is indeed very unwise. Therefore, in his great compassion, the Buddha once again exhorts sentient beings to make a vow to be reborn in the Western Paradise.

The procedure for winning rebirth in the Western Paradise of Eternal Bliss is as follows:

1. Believe that the Western Paradise exists.
2. Make a vow that you will be reborn in the Western Paradise.
3. Cultivate to fulfill your vow. The simplest way is to recite the name of Amitabha Buddha whole-heartedly.

A vow can be made informally in any suitable way you like, or formally such as in front of an image of Amitabha Buddha, or any Buddha or Bodhisattva, alone by yourself or witnessed by other people. Burn a joss stick or present some flowers as an offering to the Buddha or Bodhisattva, and say your vow in your heart or aloud. The same vow, expressed in the same or different words, can be, and often is repeated many times to be reinforced.

There are other ways of cultivation to win rebirth in the Western Paradise, such as the various types of meditation described in the Amitayus Dhyana Sutra mentioned in Chapter 1. The simplest and most popular method is reciting Amitabha Buddha's name. More details of the recitation as well as examples of vows in verse and prose are given in Chapter 17.

BUDDHAS OF OTHER WORLDS

(Meeting Buddhas in All Directions)

May all sentient beings have faith in this Sutra which glorifies the incredible merits of Amitabha Buddha, and which is guarded and meditated by all Buddhas.

After describing the Western Paradise and its heavenly beings, and explaining how we can be reborn in this Pure Land, as set forth in the previous three chapters, Sakyamuni Buddha gives an account of numerous other Buddhas who also praise Amitabha Buddha for his incredible merits.

Buddhas of the East

Translation

Sariputra, as I now praise and appreciate the incredible merits of Amitabha Buddha, and the benefits of winning rebirth in his Pure Land, in the East there are Akshobhya Buddha, Merudhavaju Buddha, Mahameru Buddha, Meruprabhasa Buddha, Manjudhvaja Buddha, and other Buddhas as immeasurable as the sands of the River Ganges, each in their respective Buddha-land, revealing the characteristics of their long, wide tongue, spreading the teaching over the countless worlds in the myriad galaxies, proclaiming truthfully thus: May all sentient beings have faith in this Sutra which glorifies the incredible merits of Amitabha Buddha, and which is guarded and meditated by all Buddhas.

Commentary

Ahead of our modern astronomers by many centuries, Buddhist masters have taught that there are countless worlds in the myriad galaxies. In each world system there is a presiding Buddha; hence there are countless Buddhas in the universe.

Our Buddha, Sakyamuni Buddha, explains that countless Buddhas in other world systems also praise Amitabha Buddha, and extol all sentient beings to have faith in this Amitabha Sutra. He cites the names of some Buddhas.

Having a long, wide tongue is one of the characteristics of a Buddha. This is the result of speaking only the truth in his numerous past lives as a Bodhisattva. It is said that if a Buddha puts out his tongue, it can cover his whole face.

As the names of all the Buddhas mentioned here are in Sanskrit, some readers may wonder (mistakenly) why all the Buddhas are Indian. Can people of other races become Buddhas? They certainly can, and actually have become Buddhas. Many Chinese and Japanese Zen masters, for example, have become Buddhas, or Enlightened Ones. But there is only one presiding Buddha in any world system, and in our Saha world system, he is Sakyamuni Buddha, or the Noble-Warrior Buddha.

A Buddha transcends his race. No non-Indian Buddhists in the whole world would honor or love Sakyamuni Buddha any bit less because he was Indian. The Buddhas mentioned above are from other world systems, some of which are in other galaxies. Their names are given in Sanskrit (or Pali and other Indian languages) because they were first revealed to us by Sakyamuni Buddha in India.

In the Chinese version of the Amitabha Sutra from which this English translation is derived, these Buddha's names are given in Chinese (or in Chinese transliteration), but I rendered them back into Sanskrit for the convenience of English readers.

Akshobhya Buddha is called A-Zhong-Bi Fo in Chinese. Akshobhya means No-Motion, illustrating that in perfect enlightenment there is no life or death. Askhobhya Buddha is the presiding Buddha of the Eastern Paradise of Happiness in a distant galaxy.

Merudhavaju Buddha (Xu-Mi-Xiang Fo) means Characteristics-of-Mount-Meru Buddha. Mount Meru is the sacred central mountain of four continents in Buddhist cosmology.

Mahameru Buddha (Da-Xu-Mi Fo) means Great-Meru Buddha, whose merit is great like a mountain.

Meruprabhasa Buddha (Xu-Mi-Guang Fo) is Meru-Light Buddha, who appears like a mountain of light.

Manjudhvaja Buddha (Miao-Yi Fo) is Wondrous-Sound Buddha, who has seven types of wondrous sound, namely sound that is exceedingly melodious, gentle, harmonious, sonorous, conveying wisdom, non-effeminate, non-confusing, and non-harsh.

All these Buddhas are presiding Buddhas in galaxies to the east of our Saha system. East, of course, is relative; in outer space, compass directions become irrelevant.

Mount Meru, or Mount Sumeru, refers to the great mountain in the center of our Saha world in Buddhist cosmology. It is used here figuratively to describe the greatness of the various Buddhas as manifested in their reward or celestial bodies appearing in the phenomenal dimension. If we refer to the Spiritual Body of the Buddha, which is the Supreme Reality in the transcendental dimension, Mount Meru is just like an insignificant grain of sand in a gigantic desert.

Since these celestial Buddhas are in other worlds or other galaxies, why is the term Meru, which is in our Saha world, used to designate their names? This is for the benefit of our comprehension. Except for highly advanced beings who can project their minds to distant galaxies and lucky beings who have an opportunity to view these distant worlds through the revelation of the highly advanced beings, sentient beings here on earth will not have any concept of these distant worlds. Because of their lack of direct experience, sentient beings on earth will not understand, even if the Buddha were to use the languages of the distant world, presuming that they too use languages like we do. Hence, a provisional use of our language and imagery is necessary, but we must remember that such verbalization is an expedient means, and the concepts we obtain from this verbalization may be very different from the actual situations in the distant worlds.

Buddhas of the South, West and North

Translation

Sariputra, in world systems in the South there are Chandra-Suryapradipa Buddha, Yasahprabha Buddha, Maharchiskandha Buddha, Merupradipa Buddha, Anantavirya Buddha, and other Buddhas as immeasurable as the sands of the River Ganges, each in their respective Buddha-land, revealing the characteristics of their long, wide tongue, spreading the teaching over countless worlds in the myriad galaxies, proclaiming truthfully thus: May all sentient beings have faith in this Sutra which glorifies the incredible merits of Amitabha Buddha, and which is guarded and meditated by all Buddhas.

In world systems in the West, there are Amitabha Buddha, Amitaskandha Buddha, Amitadhvaja Buddha, Mahaprabha Buddha,

Mahnyata Buddha, Maharatnaketu Buddha, Suddharasmiprahba Buddha, and other Buddhas as immeasurable as the sands of the River Ganges, each in their respective Buddha-land, revealing the characteristics of their long, wide tongue, spreading the teaching over countless worlds in the myriad galaxies, proclaiming truthfully thus: May all sentient beings have faith in this Sutra which glorifies the incredible merits of Amitabha Buddha, and which is guarded and meditated by all Buddhas.

In world systems in the North, there are Archiskandha Buddha, Vaisvanaranirghosa Buddha, Dushpradharsha Buddha, Adityasambhava Buddha, Jalenipradha Buddha, and other Buddhas as immeasurable as the sands of the River Ganges, each in their respective Buddha-land, revealing the characteristics of their long, wide tongue, spreading the teaching over countless worlds in the myriad galaxies, proclaiming truthfully thus: May all sentient beings have faith in this Sutra which glorifies the incredible merits of Amitabha Buddha, and which is guarded and meditated by all Buddhas.

Commentary

The Buddha taught by preaching. The sutras, which are records of the Buddha's spoken words, were recited, and followers learnt by hearing. Hence, it is common that important parts of sutras are repeated.

The Amitayus Buddha mentioned in the example above is not the same as Amitabha Buddha of Sukhavati, who is also known as Amitayus Buddha. As there are countless Buddhas, many Buddhas have the same name; on the other hand, a Buddha may also have more than one name.

Further, we must realize that a particular Buddha may be known by a different name in his own world among his people. For example, even in our own world, our Buddha is usually known as Sakyamuni Buddha to Mahayanist and Vajrayanist Buddhists, but as Gautama Buddha to Theravadin Buddhists. To Chinese who do not know English or Sanskrit, our Buddha is generally known as Shi-Jia-Mou-Ni Fo.

Chandra-Suryapradipa Buddha (Ri-Yue-Deng Fo) means Lamp-of-Sun-and-Moon Buddha, suggesting that the wisdom-light of this Buddha is like the lamp of the sun and moon in dispersing darkness.

Yasahprabha Buddha (Ming-Wen-Guang Fo) means Name-Renown-Light Buddha, suggesting that his teaching is like light dispelling the ignorance of sentient beings.

Maharchiskandha Buddha (Da-Yan-Jian Fo) means Great Flaming-Shoulders Buddha, whose outstanding wisdom and expedient means bear the burden of ignorant beings.

Merupradipa Buddha (Xu-Mi-Deng Fo) means Meru-Lamp Buddha, who is like a mountain of light.

Anantavirya Buddha (Wu-Liang-Jing-Jin Fo) means Infinite-Effort Buddha, who works tirelessly for others' salvation.

Amitayus Buddha (Wu-Liang-Shou Fo) means Infinite-Life Buddha, whose existence in his reward body for the benefit of sentient beings to see is eternal.

Amitaskandha Buddha (Wu-Liang-Xiang Fo) is Infinite-Characteristics Buddha, who may appear in countless manifestations to help others.

Amitadhvaja Buddha (Wu-Liang-Chuang Fo) means Infinite-Pillars Buddha, acting like righteous supports for an infinite number of beings.

Mahaprabha Buddha (Da-Guang Fo) means Great-Light Buddha, illuminating the ten directions.

Mahanyata Buddha (Da-Ming Fo) means Great-Brightness Buddha, whose wisdom disperses darkness of the world.

Maharatnaketu Buddha (Bao-Xiang Fo) is Precious-Characteristics Buddha, who could convert his followers through his excellent characteristics.

Suddharasmiprahba Buddha (Jing-Guang Fo) is Pure-Light Buddha, whose light purifies his Buddha-land.

Archiskandha Buddha (Yan-Jian Fo) means Flaming-Shoulders Buddha, whose shoulders are figuratively aflame with wisdom and expedient means to save others.

Vaisvanaranirghosa Buddha (Zui-Sheng-Yin Fo) means Superb Voice Buddha, whose voice is not only melodious and comforting, but also can simultaneously enable beings of different natures and abilities to comprehend whatever is said according to their needs and levels.

Dushpradharsha Buddha (Nan-Ju Fo) is the Invincible Buddha, meaning nothing can obstruct his own enlightenment as well as his effort to help others to be enlightened.

Adityasambhava Buddha (Ri-Sheng Fo) is Sun-Born Buddha, meaning that his teaching is like sunlight dispersing everybody's ignorance without any discrimination in any aspect.

Jalenipradha Buddha (Wang-Ming Fo) Radiant-Net Buddha, whose teaching radiates to all directions.

Buddhas of the Nadir and the Zenith

Translation

Sariputra, in the Nadir there are Simha Buddha, Yasas Buddha, Yasasprabhava Buddha, Dharma Buddha, Dharmadhvaja Buddha, Dharmadhara Buddha, and other Buddhas as immeasurable as the sands of the River Ganges, each in their respective Buddha-land, revealing the characteristics of their long, wide tongue, spreading the teaching over countless worlds in the myriad galaxies, proclaiming truthfully thus: May all sentient beings have faith in this Sutra which glorifies the incredible merits of Amitabha Buddha, and which is guarded and meditated by all Buddhas.

Sariputra, in the Zenith there are Brahmaghosha Buddha, Nakshatraraja Buddha, Gandhatama Buddha, Grandhaprabhasa Buddha, Maharchiskandha Buddha, Ratnakusumasampushpitagtra Buddha, Salendraraja Buddha, Ratnapalasri Buddha, Saruarthadarsa Buddha, Semerukalpa Buddha, and other Buddhas as immeasurable as the sands of the River Ganges, each in their respective Buddha-land, revealing the characteristics of their long, wide tongue, spreading the teaching over countless worlds in the myriad galaxies, proclaiming truthfully thus: May all sentient beings have faith in this Sutra which glorifies the incredible merits of Amitabha Buddha, and which is guarded and meditated by all Buddhas.

Commentary

Simha Buddha (Shi-Zi Fo) is the Lion Buddha, suggesting the magnificence of the lion, and destroying greed, anger and delusion of his followers.

Yasas Buddha (Ming-Wen Fo) means Name-Renown Buddha, whose name is known over all directions because of his teaching.

Yasasprabhava Buddha (Ming-Guang Fo) means Name-Light Buddha, whose name and teaching is spread like sunlight over all the worlds.

Dharma Buddha (Da-Mo Fo) is True-Teaching Buddha, who attained enlightenment because of the true teaching, and now diffuses the true teaching to others.

Dharmadhvaja Buddha (Fa-Chuang Fo) means Teaching-Pillar Buddha, whose teaching acts like pillars to support the followers.

Dharmadhara Buddha (Chi-Fa Fo) means Upholding-the-Teaching Buddha, who promotes the true teaching for eternity.

Brahmaghosha Buddha (Fan-Yin Fo) means Pure-Sound Buddha, who helps others to attain enlightenment through audio means.

Nakshatraraja Buddha (Xu-Wang Fo) means Star-King Buddha, whose radiance is like the brightest star.

Gandhatama Buddha (Xiang-Shang Fo) means Supreme-Fragrance Buddha, whose preaching is not in the form of sounds or written words, but in the form of fragrance. He has five forms of marvelous fragrance, namely the fragrance of discipline, meditation, wisdom, emancipation, and enlightenment.

Grandhaprabhasa Buddha (Xiang-Guang Fo) is the Fragrance-Radiance Buddha, who uses both the senses of smell and sight in his teaching.

Maharchiskandha Buddha (Da-Yan-Jian Fo) is Great Flaming-Shoulders Buddha, who has the same name as another Buddha to the South mentioned earlier.

Ratnakusumasampushpitagtra Buddha (Za-Se-Bao-Hua-Yen-Shen Fo) means Multi-Colored-Precious-Jewels-Adorning-the-Body Buddha, who has performed so many, many good deeds in his numerous previous lives that the boundless merits manifest in his having a superbly magnificent body as if he is adorned with multicolored precious jewels.

Salendraraja Buddha (Suo-Luo-Shu-Wang Fo) means Ironwood-King Buddha, who is strong and protective like the best ironwood tree.

Ratnapalasri Buddha (Bao-Hua-De Fo) is Precious-Beautiful-Virtuous Buddha, whose virtues illustrate great beauty.

Saruarthadarsa Buddha (Jian-Yi-Qie-Yi Fo) means Seeing-All-Meaning Buddha, implying that this Buddha has completely understood the universe.

Semerukalpa Buddha (Ru-Xu-Mi-Shan Fo) is the Like-Sumeru-Mountain Buddha, whose spiritual accomplishment is figuratively compared to the highest mountain of the Saha world.

A Sutra Endorsed by All Buddhas

Translation

Sariputra, why do you think this Sutra is named "The Sutra that is Protected and meditated by all Buddhas"?

Sariputra, it is because if there are virtuous men and virtuous women who hear this Sutra, accept its teaching and practice it, and hear the names of the Buddhas just mentioned, they will be protected and remembered by the Buddhas, and will never retreat from attaining Anuttara-Samyak-Sambodhi, or the supreme perfect wisdom.

Commentary

The original title of this Sutra is "Praising the Incredible Merits of the Sutra that is Protected and Meditated by All Celestial Buddhas". When the great Kumarajiva translated this Sutra, he shortened the title to "The Buddha Explains the Amitabha Sutra", which has become popular, and which is often further shortened to "The Amitabha Sutra".

It is so called, the Buddha explains, because if virtuous men or women hear this Sutra, accept it and practice it, and hear the names of the various Buddhas, these virtuous men and women will be protected and remembered by the Buddhas, and they will never retrogress in their spiritual path. In other words, they are assured that they will one day acquire Anuttara-Samyak-Sambodhi, i.e. the wisdom concerning ultimate reality which will emancipate them from their illusory selves so as to actualize their universal self. Such a certainty of inevitable enlightenment is indeed incredible.

How is it that by hearing the names of the celestial Buddhas, one gain protection and remembrance from them?

Buddhas appear in the phenomenal realms for only one reason:

All the Buddhas take the one vow:
The Buddha-way which I walk,
I will universally cause all the living
To attain this same Way with me.

When a person hears the name of a Buddha, he imprints in his mind the concept of the Buddha. As everything he has experienced will be forever in his memory, although he may not recall it due to his defiled mind, this Buddha concept acts as a seed which will eventually germinate and grow into Buddha-hood when the time is appropriate, although it may be countless lifetimes away. Even if this person may be sinful or evil at present, the very fact that there is a Buddha-seed in his mind, guarantees that he can be saved. In this way, that Buddha whose name he has heard protects and remembers him.

Why by practicing what is taught in the Sutra, aspirants will be reborn in the Western Paradise, has been explained in the previous chapter. Heavenly beings in the Western Paradise will eventually attain enlightenment because this is the way things are in the Western Paradise, as designed by Amitabha Buddha.

A simple, prosaic analogy may help to make this clear. Suppose you are on the ground floor of a large crowded building and wish to go up to the top floor. There is an escalator going from the ground floor to the top floor. If you believe that the escalator exists, want to use it, and follow the proper instruction showing you the way to the escalator, you will undoubtedly find yourself on the escalator — just as if you believe that the Western Paradise exists, want to be reborn in it, and follow the proper instructions to win rebirth there, you will undoubtedly find yourself reborn in the Western Paradise. On the other hand, if you have never heard of the escalator, or do not believe in it though you may have been told, or you have no intention of enjoying a pleasant ride to the top floor, you will forever be lost among the crowd on the ground floor.

But once you are on the escalator, reaching the top floor is a certainty — because its engineer has made it work this way. Similarly once you are in the Western Paradise, attaining enlightenment is a certainty because Amitabha Buddha has created it to work this way.

If the escalator breaks down half way, as it sometimes does, the engineer will repair it and get it going up again; it will never go down because it is not designed to do so. Similarly if some inhabitants in the Western Paradise are too engrossed in savoring the bliss of the paradise that they neglect to cultivate, they will stagnate for some time in their cultivation until teachers or favorable conditions inspire them to cultivate again; but they will never retrogress to a lower spiritual level, because Amitabha Buddha has so created the Western Paradise that retrogression is irrelevant.

Can the passengers on the escalator run down to the ground flow when the escalator breaks down, or even during its process of moving up? They can, if they choose to. Similarly, heavenly beings in the Western Paradise can return to our world, or travel to other worlds (as they frequently do every morning offering mandarava flowers to other Buddhas), or even go to hell, if they choose to. But irrespective of where they go to, their level of spiritual development will not retrogress. Just as the escalator passengers who ran downstairs earlier, can find their way back to the escalator, because they have had understanding and experience of the escalator, inhabitants of the Western Paradise who went elsewhere can find their way back to the Paradise and continue at the level from where they left earlier, because they have had understanding and experience of the Western Paradise.

THE PROCESS OF BEING REBORN

(How You Can Influence Your Own Rebirth)

Thus, a person's state of mind as he dies is very influential in deciding the realm of existence he will be reborn in.

After describing the magnificence of the Western Paradise, explaining how one can win rebirth there, and giving an account of other Buddhas praising the Amitabha Sutra, as explained in the previous four chapters, the Buddha again earnestly advises people to make a vow to be reborn in Amitabha's Pure Land. Then the Buddha reveals that other Buddhas in other worlds also praise him for his difficult task in our Saha world.

The Importance of Making a Vow

Translation

Thus, Sariputra, you all should believe in and accept what I and all other Buddhas have said. Sariputra, if sentient beings have made their vows, or are making their vows, or will make their vows to be reborn in the Buddha-land of Amitabha, they will not retreat from the attainment of Anuttara-Samyak-Sambodhi, and will have been reborn, are being reborn, or will be reborn in this Buddha-land.

Thus, Sariputra, those virtuous men and virtuous women who believe in the teaching of this Sutra, must made a vow to be reborn in the Western Paradise of Eternal Bliss.

Commentary

If someone reads the Amitabha Sutra, understands and believes it, but does nothing much after that, he would have gain some fascinating knowledge, and perhaps some reading pleasure too, but he is unlikely to be reborn in the Western Paradise. If he understands the Sutra, believes it, then cultivates by reciting the name of Amitabha Buddha, he may still not win rebirth in the Western Paradise. Why? Because he has not fulfilled the second of the three conditions, namely:

1. Believe the Western Paradise exists.
2. Make a vow to be reborn there.
3. Cultivate accordingly, like visualization and reciting the name of Amitabha Buddha.

Making a vow is important on at least two counts. One, as illustrative of the democratic spirit in Buddhism, Amitabha Buddha accepts only those who themselves want to be reborn there, and making a vow is a positive indication of this wish. Two, making a vow commits the aspirant seriously to his wish so that he or she will earnestly cultivate to accomplish the objective of the vow.

To show one's earnestness, it is recommended to make the vow in front of an image of Amitabha Buddha or any Buddha or Bodhisattva. If an appropriate image is not available, the aspirant may make his vow towards the sky in the direction of the west. The vow may be made alone, witnessed by other people, or in a group. Burn one or three joss sticks, present some flowers or water, or light a candle as an offering to the Buddha or Bodhisattva.

Then kneel down in front of the Buddha or Bodhisattva image, or in any appropriate places, and place the palms together in front in prayer. Say your vow silently, softly or aloud; the crucial point is that every word of the vow must sink deeply into your heart. You may use your own words in prose or verse to make your vow. The following verse is a translation of a popular vow in Chinese, with some slight modification to facilitate smooth recitation:

I vow to be reborn in the Western Paradise of Eternal Bliss,
Transported to the Pure Land through the lotus calyx with ease.
As the lotus blossoms I see the compassionate Buddha and
samsara ceases,
In the company of Bodhisattvas I cultivate in joy and peace.

After making the vow, prostrate to show your sincerity and gratitude. This is done as follow: from the kneeling position, bend forward, place both palms on the ground (they may be placed downward with the palms in contact with the ground, or upward with the back of the palms in contact with the ground), and gently knock your head on the ground in front once or three times. Some people perform this procedure thrice, i.e. prostrate, stand up; repeat; and repeat.

It may be helpful to remind those who feel uneasy about prostrating, that making a vow for spiritual development is a very honorable thing to do, and therefore should be done with a sense of privilege and fulfillment. Any person who cannot humble himself to divine presence, as demonstrated in the above prostrating in private or in public, is not spiritually mature enough to seek divine help for rebirth in heaven.

If great rulers like Emperor Harsha of India and Empress Wu of China could prostrate before great monks out or respect and not to seek favors, what form of vanity should prevent mere mortals from prostrating before Buddhas and great Bodhisattvas. However, those who feel uncomfortable about prostrating need not do so. Offering of joss sticks or flowers and prostration are a convention followed by many devotees to show respect and gratitude, not a condition imposed by Amitabha Buddha.

Five Defilements in the Saha World

Translation

Sariputra, as I now glorify the incredible merits of all Buddhas, they, too, glorify mine, saying: Sakyamuni Buddha has accomplished such a difficult and rare task; has accomplished in this Saha world of five defilements — the defilements of time, perverse views, passions, sentient beings, and samsara — the attainment of Anuttara-Samyak-Sambodhi, and the teaching which sentient beings find hard to believe. Sariputra, you should understand that in this Saha world of defilements, to accomplish Anuttara-Samyak-Sambodhi, and to teach all beings such an incredible doctrine are indeed very difficult.

Having listened to this sutra, Sariputra and the monks, and all beings, like gods, humans, and spirits, were very happy to accept and practice this teaching of the Buddha. They paid homage to the Buddha, and then departed.

This is the Amitabha Sutra as taught by the Buddha.

Commentary

Our Saha world is inflicted with five defilements, namely the defilements of time, perverse views, passions, sentient beings and samsara. Yet, despite these unfavorable conditions, Siddharta Gautama Sakyamuni has succeeded not only in attaining Anuttara-Samyak-Sambodhi or the supreme perfect wisdom leading to perfect enlightenment, but also in spreading his teaching, especially this teaching about rebirth in the Western Paradise, or Sukhavati, which many people find it hard to believe. This indeed is an incredible achievement, which Buddhas in other world systems praise Sakyamuni Buddha.

Not only is Buddhism probably the religion with the most followers in the world, the Buddha is the only great teacher who was widely accepted by his people during his time. Teachers of other world religions, like Lao Tzu, Confucius, Jesus and Mohammed faced much opposition during their own time. Moreover, among the world's great religions, Buddhism has the longest continuous history, and has never shed a drop of blood in its spread. These are indeed incredible achievements of the Buddha.

The Buddha has taught that his teaching, like any other processes, undergoes four cyclic stages, namely birth, growth, decay and extinction, after which there will be another cycle under the next Buddha, Maitreya Buddha. He predicted that the Amitabha Sutra would be very popular during the decaying period of his teaching when most people, concerned with material comfort, would neglect spiritual development. This is the defilement of time.

Even amongst the few who are spiritually inclined, there are so many diverse views that distract from the supreme true teaching. In Buddhism itself, there are deviations, such as exploiting Buddhist practice to develop one's psychic power for selfish gains or to amass material wealth. This is the defilement of perverse views.

Beings existing in the realm of desire are full of passion, especially for the gratification of the senses. These strong drives to satisfy desire not only take up much of their time, which could otherwise be used for spiritual cultivation, but also perpetuate karma, making it difficult for people to attain nirvana. This is the defilement of passion.

Sentient beings in the lower realms of humans, asuras, animals, ghosts and hell inhabitants are full of greed, hatred and lust; otherwise they will be in the higher realms of devas (heavenly beings) and brahmas (gods). Much time is first needed to eliminate these negative qualities before the aspirant can commence concerted effort in meditation to attain enlightenment. This is the defilement of sentient beings.

Sentient beings are constantly embroiled in samsara, the endless cycle of birth and rebirth. Except brahmas in high spiritual realms who are about to enter nirvana, but who are also usually reborn from the human realm, the only realm in our Saha world favorable for attaining enlightenment is the human realm.

Hell inhabitants are constantly being tortured; ghosts are ignorant, lost and hungry; animals are preoccupied with survival; and asuras are always quarrelling and fighting. The conditions that they are in are unfavorable for spiritual training. The conditions of devas and lower brahmas are not better for spiritual cultivation. This is because they are too embroiled in enjoying themselves. Even humans, who are relatively in the most favorable condition, face many difficulties. This is the defilement of samsara.

Hence, because of these five defilements, spiritual cultivation is hard to accomplish in the Saha world. In comparison, in the Western Paradise of Amitabha Buddha, all these defilements are absent.

It must be emphasized that this teaching of the Buddha regarding the Western Paradise is meant not for humans only, but for all sentient beings. All sentient beings, especially devas, asuras, ghosts and spirits, can win rebirth to the Western Paradise if they practice what the Buddha has taught in this Sutra.

When an ordinary person dies, unless he has won rebirth in the Western Paradise, he will reincarnate in one of the six different types of realms in the Saha world system, namely six realms of devas, and a realm each of humans, asuras, animals, ghosts and hell inhabitants. There are altogether eleven realms, but conventionally they are referred to as the six realms of reincarnation, with all the heavenly realms of devas grouped into one class. These realms will be described in the next chapter; meanwhile let us study what cause rebirth, what determines which realm the being will be reborn into, and how the process of rebirth takes place.

Causes and Determinants of Rebirth

Let us hear from the Buddha's own words as recorded in the *Anguttara Nikaya,* a fundamental Theravada sutra:

Once the venerable Ananda came to see the Blessed One and spoke to him thus:

One speaks of 'Becoming', Lord. How is there a Becoming?
If, Ananda, there were no Kamma ripening in the sphere of sense existence, would there appear any sensual becoming?
Surely not, O Lord.
Therefore, Ananda, Kamma is the field, consciousness is the seed, and craving is the moisture. Of beings hindered by ignorance and fettered by craving, their consciousness takes a hold in a lower sphere. Thus there is, in the future, a re-becoming, a rebirth.

If, Ananda, there were no Kamma ripening in a fine-material sphere, would there appear any fine-material becoming?

Surely not, O Lord.

Therefore, Ananda, Kamma is the field, consciousness is the seed, and carving is the moisture. Of beings hindered by ignorance and fettered by carving, their consciousness takes a hold in an intermediate sphere. Thus there is, in the future, a re-becoming, a rebirth.

If, Ananda, there were no Kamma ripening in an immaterial sphere, would there appear any immaterial becoming?

Surely not, O Lord.

Therefore, Ananda, Kamma is the field, consciousness is the seed, and craving is the moisture. Of beings hindered by ignorance and fettered by carving, their consciousness takes a hold in the lofty sphere. Thus there is, in the future, a re-becoming, a rebirth. Thus, Ananda is there a Becoming.

One should remember that the Buddha's teaching was originally a direct oral transmission; hence important material was often repeated for the listeners' benefit. Sutras are records of the Buddha's exact words. The causes of or factors in rebirth are karma, consciousness and craving, which in this case refer to the rebirth thought. If a person or any being eliminates karma, by overcoming ignorance and craving, he (or she) overcomes the cycle of rebirth and attains nirvana.

The Buddha explains rebirth in the three spheres of existence, namely:

1. the sphere of desire, where beings like humans and devas (heavenly beings) have desire and gross form; mentioned in the above sutra as the lower, sensual sphere.
2. the sphere of form, where beings like brahmas (gods) have overcome desire and have fine form; mentioned above as the intermediate, fine-material sphere.
3. the sphere of non-form, where beings like Arahants and Bodhisattvas have no desire and no form, and exist as pure consciousness; mentioned above as the lofty, immaterial sphere.

These three spheres of existence will be described in some details in the next chapter.

All beings in these three spheres undergo reincarnation, although the life spans of devas and brahmas are so long — in millions of human years — that we may regard them as "everlasting". The life spans of beings in the lofty, formless sphere are reckoned not in millions of years, but in aeons. Bodhisattvas, who exist in this sphere, reincarnate because they choose to; they often manifest themselves in countless forms simultaneously in numerous realms of existence to help other sentient beings.

There is some dispute as whether Arahants are subject to reincarnation, and this dispute was in fact one of the main issues leading to the separate views of Mahayana and Theravada. Because of their great respect for Siddharta Guatama Sakyamuni, Theravadins reserve the term "Buddha" only for him, though they also accept that there were Buddhas in the past, and there will be Buddhas in the future. However, they are not so clear-cut about Buddhas in other galaxies in the present.

Hence, in the Theravada tradition, the highest attainment any being can ever achieve is Arahantship. In other words, when he (or she) attains nirvana, therefore emancipating himself from the process of rebirth, he is still called an Arahant. On the other hand, most Arahants have not reached this supreme level; in fact, many of them are only at the higher brahma realms of the intermediate sphere, others at the lofty, formless sphere, both of which are still subject to rebirth.

Therefore, the issue whether Arahants are subject to rebirth is actually a linguistic problem, which does not occur in the Mahayana and the Vajrayana tradition where any being who has attained nirvana, or enlightenment, is called a Buddha, or the Enlightened One, who is of course not subject to rebirth. This is not only in no way disrespectful to Sakyamuni Buddha, but actually fulfills his great mission, i.e. helping all beings to be Enlightened Ones.

Rebirth in all the three spheres of existence is the ripening of karma (kamma in Pali). The factors that contribute to this ripening are consciousness and craving. Figuratively, karma is the field from which the seed of consciousness, nurtured by the moisture of craving, blossoms.

Karma is the universal law of cause and effect. An effect in turn becomes the cause of other effects. A significant point to note in the operation of karma is that a being is rewarded or punished not *by* some divine force, but *as a result* of his thought, words and deeds. A good cause will produce a good effect; and an evil cause, an evil effect. If a good cause produces an evil effect, or vice versa, as it may sometimes happen, it is due to the intervention of some other causes, which may not be obvious to the beings involved. Moreover, the operation of karma may be immediate, or carried over many lifetimes.

For example, if you plant a good mango seed in fertile soil and water it properly, you will get a good mango plant. If you get a bad mango plant despite your good seed, good field and good moisture, it may be because of intervening factors which you are unaware of, such as the soil being contaminated by chemicals, or insects attacking your plant. If you get an apple plant instead, again it is due to other causes you are ignorant of, such as you mistook an apple seed for a mango seed, or someone had placed a super apple seed earlier at that spot and it grew instead of your mango seed, which may, if conditions are favorable, also grow later.

A person's karma is the base upon which his rebirth will occur. If he has accumulated good karma by having good thoughts, words and deeds in the past, he will have the foundation for a good rebirth. That aspect of him which connects his two lives is his consciousness, and the driving force is his craving or rebirth thought.

Thus, a person's state of mind as he dies is very influential in deciding the realm of existence he will be reborn in. If he is peaceful and happy, focuses on heaven in his rebirth thought, feels confident in and justified for his rebirth in heaven, and has a foundation of good karma, he will be reborn in a heavenly realm.

On the other hand, if he is fearful or remorseful, feels hopeless with no desire to live, and his karma is not good, he will be reborn in one of the lower realms, like as an animal where life is short and he has to fight continually for survival, or as a ghost, lost, hungry and ignorant. If he is full of violence and hatred, feels wicked and vengeful, and his karma is evil, he will be reborn in hell to suffer the creation of his mind.

Can a wicked, vengeful person who has this knowledge about the rebirth process, forces himself to feel peaceful and happy at his dying hour so as to be reborn in a heavenly realm? No, this does not happen. If he can feel peaceful and happy, he is not a wicked and vengeful person in the first place. Just imagine how difficult even for a normal person caught in a traffic jam when he has an appointment to meet, to be calm and patient, although he knows that by being impatient not only does not help him to reach his destination faster, but is also detrimental to his health.

A person's state of mind at his time of death, is a function of his karma. If, as an exception, a normally wicked and vengeful person ever becomes peaceful and happy before he dies, it is because of the effect of his earlier good karma that could have been accumulated in his previous lives.

However, if a wicked, vengeful person repents and starts to cultivate blessings, he may accumulate enough good karma for a good rebirth.

Rebirth Modes and Linkage

According to the Buddha's teaching, all beings are reborn in four modes, namely rebirth by means of moisture, rebirth by means of an egg, rebirth by means of a womb, and rebirth by means of transformation. It needs to be pointed out that this classification of rebirth modes, like many other aspects of the Buddha's teaching, is a provisional means to help us understand the universe, and ourselves better and not meant to be a rigid compartmentalization of phenomena. When a baby is born from a womb, for example, there is also moisture, but it is classified as rebirth by means of a womb.

Examples of rebirth by means of moisture include microorganisms and maggots. It is amazing that many ancient masters, Buddhist as well as non-Buddhist, had knowledge of microorganisms centuries before the discovery of the microscope. One should also note that this moisture mode of rebirth does not say that maggots or other relevant beings are born out of moisture or out of nowhere; it says that these beings (who already existed in their previous lives) are reborn by means of moisture.

Examples of the egg mode of rebirth include birds and reptiles; and from the womb mode, humans and many types of animals. Cosmically speaking, the most widespread mode of rebirth is by means of transformation, in which the being is transported to another realm of existence in the form he was in the previous life. It is the mode for all rebirths to all the heavenly realms. Does a man who has died from an illness and is reborn in heaven, carries his illness with him? No, he is reborn whole and healthy; there is no illness and pain in heaven.

How does the process of rebirth take place? It takes place by way of rebirth linkage, which is of twenty kinds. As these concepts are both unfamiliar and profound, and the description below is compact, those who may not be able to follow the explanation easily should not be discouraged; you will have a clearer idea after you have read about the various realms of existence in the next chapter.

The first ten kinds of rebirth linkage are associated with desire, and therefore lead to rebirth in the sphere of desire. This sphere of desire consists of eleven realms of existence, which are a realm each of hell, ghosts, animals, asuras, and humans, and six realms of heavens. The ten kinds of rebirth linkage, which concern most people, are as follows:

1. Characterized by investigation, accompanied by equanimity, and results from evil deeds.
2. Characterized by investigation, accompanied by equanimity, and results from good deeds.
3. Associated with knowledge, accompanied by pleasure, and is not prompted.
4. Associated with knowledge, accompanied by pleasure, and is prompted.
5. Dissociated from knowledge, accompanied by pleasure, and is not prompted.
6. Dissociated from knowledge, accompanied by pleasure, and is prompted.
7. Associated with knowledge, accompanied by equanimity, and is not prompted.
8. Associated with knowledge, accompanied by equanimity, and is prompted.
9. Dissociated from knowledge, accompanied by equanimity, and is not prompted.
10. Dissociated from knowledge, accompanied by equanimity, and is prompted.

Beings reborn in the lower realms of hells, ghosts, animals and asuras are reborn through the first rebirth linkage. The mind of the being investigates his evil deeds with equanimity, and is reborn in his evil realm according to his karma. If his mind is imprinted with violence, for instance, he is reborn in hell; if imprinted with hopelessness, reborn as a ghost; if imprinted with fear, as an animal; if imprinted with envy, as an asura.

Beings who have merits take the other nine kinds of rebirth linkage and are reborn in the realms of humans or devas. Those who have good karma, possess knowledge of where they want to go, and experience peace of mind will be reborn in a heavenly realm. Their knowledge may be prompted, i.e. told to them just before they died, or after their death but within the forty-nine days when their rebirth has not been finalized; or their knowledge may be unprompted, i.e. they already have the knowledge themselves.

Rebirth to the Brahma Heavens

The next six kinds of rebirth linkage are more concerned with spiritually awakened beings. They lead to rebirth in the sphere of form, which consists of 16 brahma heavens, where the brahma gods have overcome desire and have very fine form. The six kinds of rebirth linkage, which are attained through meditation, are as follows:

1. With concentration, contemplation, gladness, bliss, and unification of consciousness.
2. With contemplation, gladness, bliss and unification of consciousness.
3. With gladness, bliss, and unification of consciousness.
4. With bliss and unification of consciousness.
5. With equanimity and unification of consciousness.
6. With unification of consciousness.

In the above description, concentration and contemplation are two aspects of meditation; gladness refers to mundane pleasure, as contrast to spiritual bliss; consciousness is the vehicle of rebirth.

The depth of advanced Buddhist meditation is classified into eight levels, known as four *dhyanas* and eight *samadhis* (the first four *samadhis* correspond to the four *dhyanas*). The four dhyanas are involved in the above six kinds of rebirth linkage which leads to the realm of form, and the remaining samadhis in the rebirth linkage leading to the formless sphere to be explained later.

An advanced being who has attained the first dhyana, concentrates his thought, contemplates on his rebirth, experiences gladness and bliss intensely, unifies his consciousness and is reborn in one of the first three realms of brahma heavens, depending on whether his rebirth thought is weak, moderate or strong. In the 31 realms of existence (please see the list at the end of the next chapter), these three brahma heavens are realm 12, 13 and 14 when counted from the lowest realm of hells.

An advanced being who has attained the second dhyana, sustains his contemplation of rebirth, experiences gladness and bliss intensely, unifies his consciousness, and, depending on the strength of his rebirth thought, is reborn in one of the next three brahma heavens, which are realms 15, 16 and 17.

The mind of an advanced being who has attained the third dhyana, need not apply initial thought nor sustains contemplation; he perceives clearly what rebirth he will undergo, experiences gladness and bliss, unifies his consciousness, and, depending on the strength of his rebirth thought, is reborn in one of the next three brahma heavens, which are realms 18, 19 and 20.

An advanced being who has attained a weak fourth dhyana, perceives his rebirth with bliss, unifies his consciousness, and is reborn in the 10th brahma heaven, or the 21st realm of existence. One who has attained a moderate fourth dhyana, perceives his rebirth with equanimity, unifies his consciousness, and is reborn in the 11th brahma heaven, or the 22nd realm of existence. One who has attained the full fourth dhyana, perceives his rebirth, unifies his consciousness, and, depending on the nature of his thought, is reborn in one of the five highest heavens, which are the 23rd, 24th, 25th, 26th and 27th realm of existence.

Thus, rebirth to these advanced realms of brahma heavens depends not just on good merits, which are prerequisites, but more importantly on meditation and wisdom. Deeper meditation and greater wisdom are necessary for rebirth to the next and highest sphere of existence, i.e. the sphere of non-form, where very advanced beings exist as pure consciousness.

Rebirth to the Sphere of Non-Form

There are four kinds of rebirth linkage leading to the corresponding four highest realms of existence:

1. Associated with the sphere of the infinity of space.
2. Associated with the sphere of the infinity of consciousness.
3. Associated with the sphere of nothingness.
4. Associated with the sphere of neither perception nor non-perception.

Rebirths to these highest realms are accomplished through very advanced meditation known as the 5th, 6th, 7th and 8th samadhi (the first four samadhis correspond to the four dhyanas for rebirth to the brahma heavens, as explained earlier). In the Theravada tradition, these samadhi levels are collectively called the post-fourth jhana, or the fifth jhana.

The mind of a very advanced being affirms that form is an illusion, fills the infinity of space, fixes at it for a moment, and is reborn in the Sphere of Infinite Space, which is the 28th realm of existence.

In the next realm, the very advanced mind affirms that space is an illusion, experiences the infinity of his consciousness, fixes at it for a moment, and is reborn in the Sphere of Infinite Consciousness, which is the 29th realm.

The very advanced mind affirms that there is nothingness, fixes at it for a moment, and is reborn in the Sphere of Nothingness, which is the 30th realm.

The very advanced mind experiences that there is neither perception nor non-perception, and is reborn in the Sphere of Neither Perception Nor Non-Perception, which is the 31st and highest realm of existence, beyond which the mind attains Buddhahood.

All these twenty types of rebirth linkage help to explain the process of rebirth in the Saha world. Nevertheless, they also suggest some explanation how beings in our Saha world can be reborn in Sukhavati, the Western Paradise of Amitabha Buddha, and help to reassure us that what is taught in the Amitabha Sutra is true and valid.

COSMOLOGY AND METAPHYSICS OF THE SAHA WORLD

(Heavens, Hells and Other Realms of Existence)

The requirements for rebirth in heaven are to avoid all evil, and do good.

The Saha World

Besides Sukhavati, the Western Paradise of Eternal Bliss, there are countless other heavens in other stars and planets. Even in our own Saha world system there are twenty-two heavens. It is useful to have a brief description of them as well as other realms in our Saha world system, so that you may compare the Western Paradise with these realms, and should you decide to go to one of these heavens instead of the Western Paradise, the previous chapter on rebirth process will be very helpful.

Because their knowledge of Buddhism is mainly through Theravada sources which emphasize the Four Noble Truths and the Eightfold Path, many westerners often have the misconception that Buddhism deals only with a moral way of living, and cares little for cosmology and metaphysics. They will certainly be very surprised that, even in Theravada sources, Buddhist cosmology and metaphysics are more detailed and profound than these topics were ever studied anywhere in the world!

This is not an exaggeration; more than twenty five centuries ago the Buddha already taught that there are countless galaxies and countless worlds, and the latest discoveries in modern physics confirm many of the Buddha's teachings, such as the relativity of time and space, the constant interchange of energy and matter, and the holistic inter-penetration of the sub-stratum, implicate order.

According to Buddhist cosmology, at the bottom of our Saha world is the "wheel of void". On top of the "wheel of void" in succession are the "wheel of wind", the "wheel of water", the "wheel of metal", and the "wheel of earth". The "wheel of earth" supports the world's ocean, in the middle of which rises the Sumeru Mountain 84,000 yojanas into the sky, with another 84,000 yojanas sunk into the ocean.

A yojana is an ancient Indian measurement of the average distance in a day's march by a king's military expedition. Different sources have given different interpretations as to how long a yojana is: for example, Indian sources usually refer to a yojana as 30 miles, Chinese sources as 40 miles, and Thai sources as 10 miles. This is because not only the length of a mile varies between cultures, but also between times. If we take the Chinese measurement, the height of Sumeru Mountain is 135,000 times higher than Mount Everest.

Surrounding the Sumeru Mountain is a ring of "fragrant sea", which in turn is surrounded by a ring of "golden mountain range". Surrounding this ring of "golden mountain range" is another ring of "fragrant sea", which again is surrounded by another ring of "golden mountain range". These alternate concentric rings of "fragrant seas" and "golden mountain ranges" go on for seven layers, and are known as internal seas and internal mountain ranges. Outside these seven rings of "fragrant seas" and "golden mountain ranges" is the world ocean.

To the south of the Sumeru Mountain across the ocean is the Jambudvipa, sometimes called the southern continent, which is rectangular in shape and 6,000 by 7,000 yojanas. Many people think this Jambudvipa refers to the Indian subcontinent or central Asia; others think it refers to our whole world.

To the east of the Sumeru Mountain across the ocean is Pubbavideha, the eastern continent, which is triangular in shape, 2,000 yojanas all round. Some people refer to this eastern continent as China or East Asia; others think it refers to another planet.

To the north is Uttarakuru, or the northern continent, which is square in shape, and 2,000 yojanas on each side. It is considered to be the most magnificent of the four continents.

To the west is Aparagoyana, or the western continent, which is circular in shape, with a circumference of 8,000 yojanas. Bulls and cows were used here as the medium of trade.

Besides these four main continents, there are also sub-continents and large islands. Surrounding all these continents, sub-continents, islands, the world's ocean, golden mountain ranges, fragrant seas and Sumeru Mountain is the great, circular Iron Mountain Range, which marks the boundary of our world system.

Buddhism and Science

It is obvious to modern readers that this Buddhist description of the world does not fit the knowledge we get from modern geography and astronomy. Indeed, one day when I was thinking about this problem a picture of our world in the form of a globe suddenly flashed across my mind. In an instant it occurred to me that if we view our world from space, then the Buddhist description becomes strikingly accurate.

The seas and mountains in the Buddhist cosmological description refer not literally to the seas and mountains on earth, but figuratively to space and heavenly bodies. The Buddha refers to our world not from the view seen on the ground, but to our earth in space, surrounded by the solar system, which in turn is surrounded by a sea of space and then a ring of stars successively. The Saha world is not just our earth; some sources interpret it as the solar system, others as our galaxy.

But, what about the wheels of void, wind, water, metal and earth at the "base" of the Saha world? How do they fit into modern astronomy? No definite answers can be given yet, but an important fact is that at a time when most ancient philosophies proposed that the earth was supported by mystical creatures like turtles and elephants, the Buddha taught that the earth and other worlds are suspended in space, as indicated by the "wheel of void".

The "wheel of wind" could be interpreted as what the inhabitants of their respective worlds would regard as the atmosphere; the "wheel of water" as the hydrosphere; the "wheel of metal" the core; and the "wheel of earth" as the mantle of the heavenly body in question. Alternatively, these wheels may represent something in our universe that our astronomers have not discovered.

It should be noted that what our earthly scientists regard as barren rocks or poisonous gas on other planets may be what we call "woods" and "streams" to their inhabitants, invisible to us, who operate under a different set of conditions. We should remember how limited actually is the range of light visible to us, and how infinitesimal is our place in the known universe.

It is also relevant and significant to point out that throughout history our knowledge of science has been constantly revised, and each major revision confirmed what has been taught in Buddhism since ancient times. Some notable examples are our previous conviction that our earth was a few hundred thousand years old, our galaxy was the whole universe, time and space were absolute, living and non-living things were exclusively different, the mind was nothing but a function of the brain, the fundamental stuff of the world was made up of discrete particles, and the external world was objectively real. Many Buddhist concepts that were considered outlandish in the past are now proven by science to be true.

It is understandable that many of us viewing phenomena from the narrow temporal and spatial perspectives of the present moment and from our puny earth, would find it extremely hard to believe that many of what we have accepted as "scientific facts" may not be true after all, just as our predecessors had accepted many assumptions (like "light travels in a straight line", "matter and energy are exclusive") as "scientific facts" but are now found to be mistaken.

Hence, although Buddhism has provided so many examples where it was right and science was wrong, most scientists and many other people today will still not accept some of the Buddhist concepts that are beyond common experience, such as the existence of ghosts and asuras in our world system, or the presence of life in other countless heavenly bodies besides our earth.

Of course, it is never suggested that wherever there is a difference of viewpoint, Buddhism is always right. Buddhist philosophy has always emphasized that one should not accept any teaching on faith alone, but should assess the teaching to the best of his understanding and experience.

Hence, one should not be too condescending to say that since Mount Everest is the highest mountain in the world, the existence of Mount Sumeru, reckoned to be 135,000 times higher than Everest, is pure nonsense. Richard Morris provides some thought-provoking ideas:

> There are some superstring theories that suggest that there might be a kind of matter which interacts with ordinary matter only through the gravitational interaction. Since the production of light and the existence of intermolecular forces are products of electromagnetic interaction, not only would this *shadow matter* be invisible to us, but one could walk right through it, no matter how dense it might be.

Neil McAleer reminded us how limited the physical reality of our senses is:

> The physical reality of our senses — what we see, touch, smell, hear, and taste every day — represents an infinitesimal fraction of the physical reality of the Universe. If the energy spectrum were a yardstick (36 inches; 91 centimeters), then what we see with our eyes in the small visible range would be less than a half inch (about 1.3 centimeters).

Working on the law of probability, it is 70 times to 1 that shadow matter exists. The term "shadow matter" is a misnomer: it is actually physical matter; we normally cannot see it because it falls outside our extremely limited range of visibility. Thus, it is likely, or at least possible, that Mount Sumeru is made up of such shadow matter. Ordinary people may be unable to see Mount Sumeru, but Buddhas, Bodhisattvas and other enlightened beings can see the mountain as well as other sentient beings and phenomena clearly. Let us read what they have discovered for us.

Realms of Existence Invisible to Us

Just as we cannot see shadow matter, there are also many classes of sentient beings normally invisible to our grossly limited human eyes. Even in the Animal Realm, or Tiracchana Yoni, creatures like garudas (gigantic birds) and nagas (dragons) are invisible to us because they live in heavens above our Human Realm, or Manussa Loka.

Classes of beings normally not visible to us include hell inhabitants, ghosts and spirits, asuras (titans), devas (heavenly beings) and brahmas (gods).

In Buddhist metaphysics, there is not one but many hells, each with its sub-hells. But we can be comforted that there are many times more heavens than hells. The hells are found in various places, such as below the continents, the mountain ranges and the seas, where the water appears as fire to hell beings. The realm of hells is known as Niraya.

The major hells are Sanjiva, the hell of continually being killed; Kalasutta, the hell of black rope floor; Sanghata, the hell of crushing and smashing; Roruva, the hell of screaming; Tapana, the hell of fiercely burning fire; and Avici, the hell of suffering without respite. Experience in any hell is of course morbid and scary.

Many people would ask why does a compassionate religion like Buddhism create hells to torture sentient beings, even though these beings have sinned. The answer is thus: Hells are not created by Buddhism; they are created by the mind of the evil doers.

Because his mind is evil, when a person is reborn, the impressions of evilness imprinted in his mind when he thought of or committed evil deeds, lead him to a rebirth to an evil realm. One important aim in Buddhism is to help people not to fall into hells, and to save them if they have fallen. The great Bodhisattva Ksitigarbha, who chooses to go to hells to help others, has helped countless hell inhabitants to ascend to heavens.

One may argue: Since hell is a creation of evil minds, if there are no descriptions of hells, there will be no concepts or ideas regarding hells for people's minds to follow. This is not true, because a person's evil impression is principally derived not from descriptions but from his thought, speech and action. In fact, if he is aware of the scary descriptions of hells, he could be deterred from committing evilness. To take a rough analogy, if a camera is directed at sordid scenes, the photographs when developed will be sordid, irrespectively of whether the photographer has read any sordid descriptions.

Nevertheless, with the distinguished exc*eption of the Bodhisattva Ksitigarbha Sutra* which gives a vivid description of hells and how hell inhabitants can be and have been saved, Buddhist teaching seldom touches on hells, as Buddhist teachers believe that leading followers to heavens and to enlightenment is more positive and rewarding.

Ghosts and nature spirits are different from hell inhabitants, and they exist in a different realm called the Realm of Spirits, or Peta Loka. Unlike hell inhabitants who are confined, ghosts and spirits are free to roam about. They are found in various places, such as on mountains and in forests, and they sometimes exist in the same "space" as the human realm but in a different dimension.

Unlike devas and asuras who can materialize food by visualization, and humans and animals who can find their food — hell inhabitants are too busy suffering to think of food — ghosts are incapable of producing food. As they are always hungry, they are often called hungry ghosts. Hence, it is a common practice in Buddhist monasteries that before every meal, each monk takes out seven grains of rice from his serving to feed hungry ghosts.

Asuras (titans) are beings whose position is somewhere between humans and devas, but because their happiness, despite their abundance pleasures, is far less than that of humans', they are usually placed in a position below the human realm. Like devas, asuras have much enjoyment, and female asuras are exceedingly beautiful, but the males are always quarrelling and fighting amongst themselves, thus they are not happy. Asuras are usually found in forests and on mountains, especially at the lower reaches of Mount Sumeru where they live in magnificent palaces. The asura realm is called Asura Nikaya.

The realms of devas, humans, asuras, animals, ghosts and hell inhabitants are the six realms of existence into which a being will normally reincarnate at his rebirth according to his karma. They are therefore called the six realms of reincarnation. An advanced being may be reborn into a brahma realm, which is higher than the realms of devas, or a brahma may retrogress into a lower realm, though this is unlikely. But by convention Buddhists still talk of the six realms of reincarnation (not seven), with the brahma realms and deva realms regarded as the same class of realms.

It is significant that while there is only one realm each for humans, asuras, animals, ghosts and hell inhabitants, there are six realms for devas and sixteen realms for brahmas. In other worlds, there are twenty-two realms of heavens, and only five realms that are non-heavens. Hence, in Buddhism, unless a person has been particularly wicked, his chance of rebirth in a heaven is 22 to 5.

The Heavenly Realms

The lowest heavenly realm is 42,000 yojanas above our human realm, midway up the Sumeru Mountain. This is Catumaharajika, or the Realm of the Four Great Kings. The terms in this chapter are in Pali, in contrast with other chapters where Sanskrit terms are usually used, as the material here is taken from Pali sources, indicating that Theravada Buddhism is also very rich in cosmology and metaphysics, although Theravadin teachers seldom discuss these topics.

The four great kings who preside over this heavenly realm are Dhataratha (king of devas) in the east, Virupakkha (king of garudas and nagas) in the west, Virulhaka (king of yakkhas who are called kumbhandas) in the south, and Vessavana (king of yakkhas and devas) in the north. Devas are heavenly beings who correspond to humans in the human realm; garudas are gigantic birds; nagas are dragons; and yakkhas are fierce spirits who police the hells but who, because of their good karma, spend some of their time in heaven. The lifespan of a deva in this realm is 500 celestial years, which is 9,000,000 human years.

A deva can transform himself into as big or as small as he (or she) likes. He eats celestial food, but has no urine or excrement. He does not become sick at all. Devas play with their spouses and children, and have fun all the time. The normal height of a deva in this Catumaharajika realm is 0.5 yojanas; a deva king is 0,75 yojanas.

Another 42,000 yojanas above Catumaharajika is Tavatimsa, or the Realm of the Thirty Three Deva Kings. This heavenly realm is at the peak of Sumeru mountain, ruled by thirty three deva kings who stay in heavenly palaces made from gems. The Lord of this realm is Indra.

84,000 yojanas above the realm of the Tavatimsa Heaven is the Realm of Yama, which is above the Sumeru Mountain. The devas here have bright and beautiful faces and bodies. The king is Suyamadevaraja. The lifespan of a deva here is 2,000 celestial years, which is 144,000,000 human years.

168,000 yojanas above the Realm of Yama is the famous Tusita Heaven, or the Heaven of Enjoying Bliss. The King is Santusitadevaraja. The lifespan here is 4,000 celestial years, which is 576,000,000 human years. Sri Ariya Metteyya, who will descend to the earth to become the next Buddha, lives here. The height of a deva here is 2 yojanas.

336,000 yojanas above the Tusita Heaven, is the Nimmana-Rati Heaven, or the Realm of Enjoying Own Creation. The devas here, 4 yojanas tall, create whatever they desire, and play with female devas to their heart content. The lifespan here is 8,000 celestial years, or 2,304,000,000 human years.

672,000 yojanas above the Nimmana-Rati Heaven is the Paranimmita-Vasavatti Heaven, or the Realm of Enjoying Others' Creation. If a deva wishes to have something, it will be created by other devas. Each deva is 8 yojanas tall. There are two kings who never visit or have an audience with each other. The lifespan here is 16,000 celestial years, or 9,216,000,000 human years. This Parnimmita-Vasavatti Heaven is at the highest level of Kamaloka, or the realms of desire. Above this is Rupaloka, or the realms of form.

A deva in any of the Kamaloka realms may die in one of four ways: expiration of his lifespan, expiration of his merits, expiration of food, or expiration due to anger. When his lifespan or merits are spent, the deva undergoes reincarnation to a higher or lower level depending on his karma.

Devas have to take celestial food too; this is apparently simple because they only need to visualize whatever they want to materialize it. Yet, surprising it may seem, a deva may be so engrossed in his enjoyment of heavenly bliss, like playing with a female deva, that he forgets to eat his food, and so dies!

If a deva quarrels or fights with another deva, and if both are angry, they both die, because the fire that is generated in their anger consumes them. However, if any one of them is not angry, water is created and quenches the fire of the other deva, saving both of them. It pays to be calm and peaceful — even in heavens.

Such risk from pleasure or anger, however, does not occur in the two higher spheres, Rupaloka or the sphere of form, and Arupaloka or the sphere of non-form, because here all desire has been eliminated.

The heavenly beings in the Rupaloka are known as brahmas. Brahmas have overcome all desire, but they still retain their bodily form which is of very fine matter. There are sixteen heavenly realms in this sphere of form. While winning rebirth to the deva heavens in the sphere of desire is through good karma, winning rebirth to the brahma heavens in this sphere of form is through meditation.

In ascending order, the first three of these brahma realms are the Parisajja Heaven, or the Heaven of Brahma Retinue; the Purohita Heaven, or the Heaven of Brahma Ministers; and the Maha-Brahma Heaven, or the Heaven of Great Brahmas. An adept, who has reached the first jhana of meditation, when he passes away from earthly life, attains these three realms or even here and now when he is still alive in this world.

Four levels of meditation are used to attain the various brahma heavens in the sphere of form. These meditation levels are known as *jhana* in Pali, *dhyana* in Sanskrit, *chan* in Chinese, and *zen* in Japanese. Accomplishing the first jhana, which enables the adept to reach the first three brahma heavens depending on the relative depth of his meditation, is known in the Theravada tradition as attaining *sotapanna*, which is the first fruit in the cultivation towards nibbana.

The next three brahma heavens above the Maha-Brahma Heaven are Parittabha Heaven, or the Heaven of Brahmas with Minor Lustre; the Appamanabha Heaven, or the Heaven of Brahmas with Infinite Lustre; and Abhassara Heaven, or the Heaven of Radiant Brahmas. These three realms are attained when one accomplishes the second jhana in meditation. This attainment is known as *sakadagamin*, the second fruit of spiritual cultivation in the Theravada tradition.

The next three heavens are Paritta Subha Heaven, or the Heaven of Brahmas with Minor Aura; Appamana Subha Heaven, or the Heaven of Brahmas with Infinite Aura; and the Subha Kinha Heaven, or the Heaven of Brahmas with Steady Aura. These brahma realms are attained through the third jhana of meditation, with the accomplishment of *Anagamin*, the third fruit.

The next two brahma realms are the Vehapphala Heaven, or the Heaven of Greatly Rewarded Brahmas; and the Asanna-Satta Heaven, or the Heaven of Sensationless Brahmas. These two realms are reached in very deep third jhana, or weak fourth jhana.

When the aspirant deepens his meditation in the fourth jhana, he attains, according to the depth of his meditation, the following five brahma realms in ascending order: Aviha Heaven, or the Heaven of Immobile Brahmas; Atappa Heaven, or the Heaven of Serene Brahmas; Sudassa Heaven, or the Heaven of Beautiful Brahmas; Sudassi Heaven, or the Heaven of Clear-Sighted Brahmas; and Akanittha Heaven, or the Heaven of Supreme

Brahmas. When an adept attains these levels he is called an *Arahant*, the fourth and highest fruit of spiritual cultivation in the Theravada tradition.

Understandably, ordinary mortals will find it very hard to appreciate the kind of bliss at these levels above the Aviha Heaven. Unlike in the much lower deva heavens, where the enjoyment of devas like in dancing and feasting is easily comprehensible to humans, in the highest brahma heavens, an Arahant remains blissfully motionless in his heaven for aeons!

The Realms of Non-Forms

Nevertheless, these motionless brahma realms are not the highest realms in the Saha world. Above the sphere of form, or Rupaloka, is the sphere of non-form, or Arupaloka, where there are four formless realms. Here, there is not only no movement, there is also no form.

Enlightened beings, who are Sravakas, Prateyaka-buddhas, Arahants and Bodhisattvas, exist as pure consciousness; but of course if they wish to manifest in any of the lower realms they can take any form they like. Because there is no form, these realms are not normally described as heavens; they are above heavens, a "link" or "transition" between the phenomenal dimension and the transcendental, undifferentiated Supreme Reality, the attainment of which is enlightenment or nirvana.

These four formless realms are Akasananca Yatana, or the Sphere of Infinite Space; Vinnananca Yatana, or the Sphere of Infinite Consciousness; Akincanna Yatana, or the Sphere of Nothingness; and Nevasannanasanna Yatana, or the Sphere of Neither Perception Nor Non-Perception. These realms are attained through the post-fourth jhana in the Theravada tradition, and in the fifth, sixth, seventh and eighth *samadhi* (or *ding* in Chinese) in the Mahayana and Vajrayana tradition. These very high spiritual levels are attainable not necessarily in an afterlife, but here and now.

The Thirty-One Realms

The thirty-one realms of existence in the three spheres of desire, form and non-form are as follows:

Sphere of Non-Form:
   31. Nevasannanasanna Yatana.
      Sphere of Neither Perception Nor Non-Perception.
   30. Akincanna Yatana.
      Sphere of Nothingness.

29. Vinnananca Yatana.
> Sphere of Infinite Consciousness.

28. Akasananca Yatana.
> Sphere of Infinite Space.

Sphere of Form:

27. Akanittha Heaven.
> Heaven of Supreme Brahmas.

26. Sudassi Heaven.
> Heaven of Clear-Sighted Brahmas.

25. Sudassa Heaven.
> Heaven of Beautiful Brahmas.

24. Atappa Heaven.
> Heaven of Serene Brahmas.

23. Aviha Heaven.
> Heaven of Immobile Brahmas.

22. Asanna-Satta Heaven.
> Heaven of Sensationless Brahmas.

21. Vehapphala Heaven.
> Heaven of Greatly Rewarded Brahmas.

20. Subha Kinha Heaven.
> Heaven of Brahmas with Steady Aura.

19. Appamana Heaven.
> Heaven of Brahmas with Infinite Aura.

18. Paritta Subha Heaven.
> Heaven of Brahmas with Minor Aura.

17. Abhassara Heaven.
> Heaven of Radiant Brahmas.

16. Appamanabha Heaven.
> Heaven of Brahmas with Infinite Lustre.

15. Parittabha Heaven.
> Heaven of Brahmas with Minor Lustre.

14. Maha-Brahma Heaven
> Heaven of Great Brahmas.

13. Purohita Heaven.
> Heaven of Brahma Ministers.

12. Parisajja Heaven.
> Heaven of Brahma Retinue.

Sphere of Desire:
   11. Paranimmita-Vasavatti Heaven.
         Heaven of Enjoying Others' Creation.
   10. Nimmana-Rati Heaven.
         Heaven of Enjoying Own Creation.
   9. Tusita Heaven.
         Heaven of Enjoying Bliss.
   8. Yama Heaven.
         Heaven of Yama.
   7. Tavatimsa Heaven.
         Heaven of Thirty Three Deva Kings.
   6. Catumaharajika Heaven.
         Heaven of Four Great Kings.
   5. Manussa Loka.
         Realm of Humans.
   4. Asura Nikaya.
         Realm of Titans.
   3. Tiracchana Yoni.
         Realm of Animals.
   2. Peta Loka.
         Realm of Ghosts and Spirits.
   1. Niraya.
         Realms of Hells.

As it can be seen in the list above, the chance of going to heaven is very high. The requirement for rebirth in heaven is to avoid all evil, and do good. Anyone with good blessings, even if he or she is spiritually ignorant, can be reborn in heaven. However, if you wish to be reborn in one of the higher heavens, you need to cultivate wisdom too, i.e. besides avoiding evil and doing good, you must also cultivate your mind through meditation.

Nevertheless, except for the higher brahma heavens, although you will have tremendous joy in heavens, your opportunity for further spiritual development is rather slim as you will most probably be too engrossed in enjoyment. When your blessings are spent, you will have to undergo reincarnation again. Hence, you still have not gone beyond life and death. One effective way to overcome this problem, as taught by the Buddha in the Amitabha Buddha Sutra, is to be reborn in Sukhavati, the Western Paradise of Eternal Bliss, where you can have both eternal joy as well as a sure opportunity for spiritual development.

THE PURE LANDS

(Canons, Sutras, Heavens and Mahayana)

Mahayana Buddhists believe that there are heavens not only in our Saha world system, but also in countless other stars and planets and in other galaxies.

The Chinese and the Sinhalese Canons

Some Theravada masters and western scholars, most of who do not know Chinese nor practice Mahayana Buddhism, believe that the voluminous Chinese Mahayana Canon was mainly a later adulterated addition to the original teaching of the Buddha. It is useful to examine the historical background to assess if this belief is valid.

The Buddha's teaching was originally transmitted orally, first written mainly in Sanskrit and Pali about four hundred years later, and then translated into Chinese and Sinhalese respectively. As Sanskrit and Pali have become obsolete, the bulk of the Buddhist literature is now found in Chinese and Sinhalese, although some other languages, like Tibetan, Japanese and Thai also contain rich Buddhist literature.

The translation of the Pali Canon into Sinhalese underwent two crucial breaks. The first break lasted about four hundred years from the beginning of the Common Era when Pali became obsolete, to about 400 when some old Pali scriptures were discovered in Sri Lanka and translated for the first time into Sinhalese. The second break lasted about three hundred years in the 17th, 18th and 19th centuries when the Sinhalese sangha (or monastic order) died out and monks had to be repeatedly imported from Thailand and Burma.

On the other hand, the translation of the Sanskrit Canon into Chinese was continuous and complete, carried out by such great, dedicated monks like Paramartha and Kumarajiva from India, Xuan Zang and Yi Xing from China, with imperial patronage. By the 6th century, i.e. long before Sanskrit became obsolete in the 13th century, all of the important Sanskrit scriptures had been translated into Chinese. With an understanding of these historical facts, it becomes obvious why many sutras found in Chinese, which contains the tremendous Mahayana Canon, are not found in Sinhalese, which contains the much smaller Theravada Canon.

It is significant to note that the Chinese Mahayana Canon also includes all Theravada scriptures, as Mahayanists regard the Theravada as the basic teaching of the Buddha. On the other hand, Theravadins generally do not accept the Mahayana teaching, considering it a spurious addition. For some time, as the original Amitabha Sutra in Sanskrit was unknown, many critics regarded the Chinese version as not taught by the Buddha, but written by some zealous Chinese using the Buddha's name. A good answer to this accusation came about 1880 when the great western scholar Max Muller found the original Sanskrit text in Japan.

Max Muller's translation of the Sanskrit text, which he calls *The Smaller Sukhavati-Vyuha*, is exactly the same in meaning as the Chinese version, with only the following one exception:

Beings are not born in that Buddha country of the Tathagata Amitayus as a reward and result of good works performed in this present life.

The same passage translated by the great Kumarajiva in 402 from Sanskrit into Chinese is as follows (please see Chapter 7, page 2, Passage 8):

Sariputra, in order to be born there, one must not lack good spiritual roots and blessings from good karma.

Max Muller himself pointed out this difference, which he suggested was to highlight a theme of the sutra:

Instead of the old doctrine, As a man soweth, so he shall reap, a new and easier way of salvation is here preached, viz. As a man prayeth, so he shall be saved. It is what we know as salvation by faith rather than by works.

The profound and extensive Buddhist literature in Chinese is still virtually untapped by western scholars. This is indeed a great pity because this very rich literature, which deals not only with philosophy and metaphysics, but also sciences like physics, astronomy and psychology, has much to offer to modern societies. The western Buddhist scholar,

Professor Conze, estimates that "numerically speaking, perhaps 5 per cent of the Mahayana Sutras have so far been reliably edited, and perhaps 2 per cent intelligently translated." In my opinion, Conze's estimate is conservative.

Throughout the long history of Buddhism in China, Chinese masters have extensively and intensively explained and commented upon the sutras, thereby adding an invaluable section to the already voluminous Buddhist literature, which with its more than 7000 volumes of basic Buddhist scriptures alone, even without considering the equally tremendous amount of commentaries and original Chinese works, can easily be the most extensive collection of religious works in the world.

The sutras, which are difficult to comprehend by themselves, are explained in depth and detail. Various systems have been developed in their commentaries, and the one by Zhi Yi, the great 6th century master of the Tien Tai School, is the most popular and is still being used today.

The Five Principles of Commentary

Zhi Yi divides a commentary on any sutra into five major sections, namely:

1. Explaining the Title.
2. Elaborating the Substance.
3. Illuminating the Philosophy.
4. Discussing the Use.
5. Discerning the Teaching.

We may have some idea of the depth and scope of Zhi Yi's commentary from the fact that the master took more than thirty sermons to explain just the word "miao", meaning "wonderful", in *Miao Fa Lian Hua Jing*, or the *Sutra of the Wonderful Law of the Lotus*.

Traditionally, masters classify sutras according to their titles into seven groups using the three features of Personality, Methodology and Symbolism. For example, the *Amitabha Sutra as Taught by the Buddha* is classified as a sutra of the Personality group, because both the Buddha and Amitabha are personalities. The four *Agama Sutras* are classified as sutras of the methodology group, because they describe the basic teachings of the Buddha. The *Brahma-Net Sutra* is classified as a sutra of the Symbolism group, because Brahma's net is a symbol.

Fundamental Vows of Ksitigharbha Bodhisattva Sutra is a sutra of the Personality-Methodology group, because Ksitigharbha Bodhisattva is a personality and Fundamental Vows are concerned with methodology. *Sutra of Manjusri Asking About Bodhi* is of the Personality-Symbolism group, because Manjusri is a personality and Bodhi is a symbol. *Sutra of the Wonderful Law of the Lotus* is of the Methodology-Symbolism group, because Wonderful Law is concerned with methodology, and the Lotus is a symbol. *Great Popular Expedient-Means Buddha Flower-Adornment Sutra*, having all the three features, is of the Personality-Methodology-Symbolism group, because Buddha is a personality, Great Popular Expedient-Means is methodology, and Flower-Adornment is symbolism.

The second section of Zhi Yi's system of commentary, i.e. elaborating the substance, is to give a thorough explanation of the content of the sutra. Regarding the Amitabha Sutra, this has been done in Chapters 6 to 9. In a nutshell, the Amitabha Sutra is about the Buddha describing the Western Paradise and Amitabha Buddha, explaining how sentient beings can win rebirth in the Pure Land, and citing Buddhas of other galaxies who also praise Amitabha Buddha.

The third section, illuminating the philosophy, describes the theme of the sutra. While all sutras are the direct teaching of Sakyamuni Buddha, each sutra has its theme and special features. For example, the *Flower-Adornment Sutra (Avatamsaka Sutra)* is noted for its magnificence and grandeur, with describing Sakyamuni"s direct experience of cosmic reality as the theme. The *Surangama Sutra* is noted for its discussion of metaphysics, with its theme of describing various methods of spiritual cultivation, including those of the non-Buddhists. The *Diamond Sutra* is noted for is teaching on emptiness, and its theme is to show Bodhisattvas how to attain the supreme perfect wisdom.

The outstanding features of the Amitabha Sutra, which constitute its philosophy, are the principles of faith, vow and practice; and the theme of the sutra is to teach sentient beings how to be reborn in Sukhavati, the Western Paradise of Eternal Bliss. The gist of the Amitabha Sutra is the Buddha's exhortation to followers to have faith in the Western Paradise, to vow to be reborn in the Western Paradise, and to practice the prescribed methods for rebirth in the Western paradise. Throughout history, masters of the Pure Land School have assured that if a follower satisfies these three requirements, he or she will be guaranteed to be reborn in Amitabha's

Pure Land

The fourth section of the commentary discusses the use of the sutra. For example, why does the Buddha teach the Amitabha Sutra? How do followers use the teaching to accomplish their aims and objectives? The Buddha taught the Amitabha Sutra during the third phase between the 11th and the 18th of his 45 years of life-long teaching.

This phase, which represents the transition from the Hinayana to the Mahayana tradition, is known as the Vaipulya or developmental period. Realizing that many people would face much difficulty in seeking nirvana through the "self-effort approach" of meditation, the Buddha taught this easier "others' help approach" of reciting Amitabha Buddha's name. Details of this practice will be described in a later chapter.

The fifth section of the commentary is discerning the teaching, which gives an overall study of the sutra from different angles. For example, topics like why this Buddha-recitation method is the most suitable for certain people, how it can eliminate defilement, and how it involves all the three Buddhist cultivations of moral purity, meditation and wisdom, are discussed. It is also significant to note that Pure Land masters always remind their followers that going to a Pure Land or heaven is an expedient means, and not the final goal of Buddhism. The final goal, as in all other schools of Buddhism, is attaining nirvana or perfect enlightenment. Hence, the frequent criticism that the Pure Land practice is non-Buddhist because it aims at heaven and not at nirvana, is due to an inadequate understanding of the Pure Land philosophy.

The Concept of Pure Land

Pure Land is a figurative term referring to a heavenly realm where there is no defilement as we know it on earth. It is sometimes called Buddha-land. There are countless Pure Lands, including those of the non-Budddhist, and the Western Paradise of Amitabha is only one of them.

The celebrated modern master, Venerable Yin Sun, classifies Pure Lands into three convenient groups:

(a) Common Pure Lands,
(b) Buddhist Pure Lands,
(c) Mahayana Pure Lands.

Common Pure Lands refer to heavenly realms that may apply to everyone, and are taught by non-Buddhist religions but are accepted by Buddhists, particularly Mahayana Buddhists. A well-known example is Shangrila, the Happy Abode, taught in Indian Tantricism.

Another famous example, which is comparatively unknown to westerners but familiar to the Chinese, is Fenglai, the heavenly island of saints, taught in Taoism. All the heavens taught in other religions also belong to this group of Pure Lands. This is another testimony to the very liberal and healthy attitude of Buddhists, who agree that working for rebirth in any of these non-Buddhist heavens or Pure Lands is a worthy spiritual task, and rejoice with non-Buddhists in their attainment.

Buddhist Pure Lands refer to all the Pure Lands taught in Buddhism, and which may not be accepted by followers of other religions. All the heavenly realms of our Saha world systems, like Catumaharajika Heaven, Tavatimsa Heaven and Tusita Heaven, belong to this group of Pure Lands as they are accepted by all schools of Buddhism, although the Theravada school pays little attention to them.

Tusita Heaven is particularly popular: it is where our historical Buddha (manifested in his reward body) came from, before his appearance on earth as Siddhartha Gautama Sakyamuni; it is also where Bodhisattva Maitreya is now staying, before he will appear as the next Buddha in the human realm on our earth. Tusita Heaven, therefore, is sometimes referred to as the Pure Land of Maitreya Buddha; however, others believe that Maitreya's Pure Land is our own human world in the next aeon when the coming Buddha will transform it from a world of suffering to a world of laughter.

Mahayana Pure Lands refer to those Pure Lands taught in Mahayana Buddhism (including Vajrayana Buddhism), but which are generally not accepted by the Theravada school. These Pure Lands are found outside our Saha world system, in other galaxies presided by other Buddhas. Besides Sukhavati or the Western Paradise of Amitabha Buddha, other well-known examples of Mahayana Pure Lands are the Eastern Paradise of Askhobhya Buddha, and the Crystal Paradise of Bhaisajyaguru Buddha.

But in our human world, the term Pure Land may sometimes be loosely used to mean nirvana, or the direct experience of transcendental cosmic reality. Hence, Zen Buddhists, whose aspiration is to attain nirvana here and now, frequently exclaim that the Pure Land is not millions of galaxies away, but right here in our world, attainable the very moment we become enlightened.

Strictly speaking, a Pure Land is different from nirvana. A Pure Land, like any other realm of existence, is in the phenomenal dimension, where there is separateness and differentiation. In other words, each being or object in a Pure Land is separated and different from any other being or object; and the knower is separated and different from the known. On the other hand, nirvana or enlightenment is in the transcendental dimension, where all separation and differentation cease; and the knower is also the known.

Then, why do Zen Buddhists sometimes use the term Pure Land for nirvana? This is because, firstly, in Buddhism, language is often used provisionally — not because Buddhism is not exact, but because words are not exact. For example, in quantum physics when we mention an electron, we may refer to a particle that is limited in space, or to a wave of electrical charges not limited by any definite boundary. Even in ordinary language, depending on our intention, both the statements 'man is an animal" and 'man is not an animal' are correct.

Secondly, in deep levels of meditation in Zen Buddhism, the attainment of a Pure Land state is often similar to the attainment of Zen, which is nirvana. Many Zen practitioners use the recitation of the Buddha's name as a means to enter meditation. On the other hand, many Pure Land practitioners maintain that when their mind has become one-pointed in the Buddha-recitation, they are in a deep level of Zen.

Mahayana and Theravada Perspectives

For those who lack the higher wisdom of Buddhism, it may be understandable why they reject these Mahayana Pure Lands. Let us look at an analogy. It must be stressed that this analogy is never meant to belittle non-Mahayanist beliefs, although it may be so misconstrued, but a sincere attempt to explain the Mahayana view. Of course, those who disagree can regard this analogy as invalid.

Suppose, during the middle age, an informed person wandered into a jungle and met a primitive tribe with a culture not very different from that of the Stone Age. This informed person, wanting to help the primitives, told them about farming settlements outside their jungle. It would be difficult for the primitives, who had been used to hunting wild animals and living inside caves for their whole lives since their ancestors' time, to believe in the existence of such farming settlements where they could easily obtain their food from their crops and domesticated animals, and stayed in dwellings well protected from natural elements and wild beasts. Such an agricultural life would be heaven for the cave-dwelling hunters.

Next came another outsider, who told them even more fantastic things, like buying food from a market instead of growing crops or rearing animals themselves, thus giving them much leisure to enjoy the comfort of town life that the cave-dwellers could not even dare to dream about.

Then came a Marco Polo who described the incredible wonders and luxuries of Cathay and other magnificent civilizations that lie many lands away beyond the seas. The cave dwellers offended by such blatant fantasies, might cook the Marco Polo over a cave-fire for food.

Looking back over many centuries with hindsight, we in the modern age may laugh at the primitive cave dwellers for being so naive. Yet, many centuries later when our successors will have succeeded in reaching not only happier realms of existence on our very earth but also more advanced and blissful worlds many galaxies away beyond the seas of space, will they similarly chide us for being so primitive as to consider our puny earth as the only habitable world in the whole universe?

Hence, it is surprising that Theravada masters, while believing in heavens in our Saha world system and in the existence of advanced life forms in countless stars and planets of other galaxies, do not accept the Pure Land concept. Theravada masters explicitly state that the teaching regarding the Pure Land is non-Buddhist, implying that sutras concerning Pure Lands, like the Amitabha Sutra and the Bhaisajyaguru Sutra, are fictitious additions by later writers impersonating the Buddha.

The issue is not just the use of the term "Pure Land", but also the implication that other than the heavens found in our Saha world system, there are no heavens in other stars and planets in other galaxies, or if there are, they are not taught or mentioned by the Buddha.

The crucial point is not whether Theravadins place any importance on these other heavens in their cultivation, but whether they belief these other heavens exist. Theravadins, one must be fair to note, generally place little importance on attaining after-life in a heaven, because they aim at nirvana, even if it may need countless reincarnations on earth to attain it. But to rationalize that it is unimportant whether these other heavens exist or not, is invalid in Mahayana philosophy because their existence is crucial to the Mahayanist cultivation of Buddha-recitation.

The Mahayana view is different from the Theravada's. Mahayana Buddhists belief that there are heavens not only in our Saha world system, but also in countless other stars and planets and in other galaxies, many of which are superior to our Saha heavens in certain ways. For example, people lacking in blessings from meritorious deeds have no chance to enter any Saha heavens, but through the grace of Amitabha Buddha, they may, despite their bad karma, be reborn in the Western Paradise of Eternal Bliss where they will continue their spiritual training without any regression.

Secondly, Mahayana Buddhists belief that as the Buddha possesses annuttara-samyak-sambodhi, or the supreme perfect wisdom (a concept also shared by Theravadins), he has a thorough understanding of these other heavens. As the Buddha has great compassion (another concept common to both Mahayanists and Theravadins), Mahayanists belief that he definitely imparts this knowledge to his followers, especially those who may progress very little spiritually had they employed the usual method of meditation.

Therefore, if sutras containing teaching of these heavens are found in the Mahayana Canon but not in the Theravada Canon, it is more likely that for some reasons these sutras were unwittingly missed out in Theravada, rather than they were wittingly added in Mahayana. To suggest that heavens are found only in our comparatively minute Saha system and absent in all other systems when we know how infinitely extensive the other systems are, is logically untenable. To imagine the Buddha to be ignorant of these heavens, or to withhold such wisdom from his followers, is extremely unjust and disrespectful to our all-knowing, all-compassionate Teacher.

THE IMPORTANCE OF FAITH

(Various Kinds of Faith in Amitabha Cultivation)

Our world as we know it, exists because it is created by our mind, not just in the present lifetimes, but also throughout millennia and imprinted in our alaya or collective consciousness.

Four Kinds of Faith

If we wish to win rebirth in Sukhavati, the Pure Land of Eternal Bliss, faith is exceedingly important. The modern Pure Land master, Yuan Yin, explained that there are four kinds of faith, namely:

1. Faith in the Buddha.
2. Faith in Existence of the Western Paradise.
3. Faith in countless other Buddhas.
4. Faith in the belief that the Saha world is defiled.

The first kind is to have faith in the Buddha, who in his great compassion and wisdom, strongly recommends people living in the decadent period of a spiritual cycle to practice the Amitabha teaching, because many of these people would find other modes of spiritual cultivation difficult if not impossible. Followers of the Pure Land School have faith that the Buddha cannot be wrong in his exhortation.

The second kind of faith is to belief without the slightest doubt that Sukhavati, the Western Paradise, exists and that its existence is created and sustained by Amitabha Buddha, who out of great compassion and using his incredible powers, transports sentient beings, including humans, who have fulfilled the three requirements, to Sukhavati. The Western Paradise is not a matter of imagination; it is as real as the respective worlds the beings are now living in.

Thirdly the follower should have faith in all the Buddhas who bear witness to the glories and tremendous merits of Amitabha Buddha. These are Buddhas of other stars and other galaxies, like Akshobhya Buddha,

Merudhavaju Buddha, and Meruprabhasa Buddha of the East; Yasahprabha Buddha, Maharchiskandha Buddha and Anantavirya Buddha of the South; Amitaskandha Buddha, Mahaprabha Buddha and Suddharasmiprahba of the West; Dushpradharsha Buddha, Adityasambhava Buddha and Jalenipradha Buddha of the North; Simha Buddha, Yasas Buddha and Dharmadhara Buddha of the Nadir; Brahmaghosha Buddha, Salendraraja Buddha and Ratnapalasri Buddha of the Zenith.

The fourth kind of faith is to believe that the Saha world we are now staying in is polluted with five defilements, namely the defilements of time, perverse views, passions, sentient beings, and samsara. (Please see Passage 16 in Chapter 9). Because of these defilements, it is very difficult to succeed in spiritual cultivation. An ordinary being may have to go through countless lifetimes before he can overcome these defilements and appreciate what enlightenment is. In Sukhavati these five defilements are absent; hence it is much easier to attain enlightenment in this Pure Land of Amitabha Buddha.

Personal Self and Universal Self

Besides the four kinds of faith described by the Venerable Yuan Yin, another famous description of faith is found in a Pure Land classic, *Important Explanation on Amitabha*, written by the Venerable Ou Yi. This master mentions six kinds of faith:

1. Faith in Self.
2. Faith in Buddha.
3. Faith in Cause.
4. Faith in Effect.
5. Faith in Phenomena.
6. Faith in Principle.

These six kinds of faith are in pairs: self and Buddha; cause and effect; phenomena and principle.

Some readers may wonder why is there "faith in self" when Buddhism is popularly known for its teaching on non-self. The doctrine of non-self (or *anatta* in Pali) is emphasized only in the Theravada tradition. In the Mahayana tradition this doctrine of non-self, like other doctrines, is regarded as an expedient means to help people overcome their attachment to self, and certainly not as a rigid dogma insisting that the self does not exist. In the same way, the doctrine of suffering (*dukkha*) and the doctrine of impermanence (*anicca*) are expedient means to help people overcome suffering and the illusion of an objective world; these doctrines do not mean that there is no joy in living or that reality is impermanent!

Indeed the very concept "attachment to self" indicates that the self exists. If the self does not exist, there is no need to free oneself from the attachment to self. Without the self (soul, spirit, mind, consciousness or call it whatever you may) the whole teaching of the Amitabha Sutra becomes meaningless. If the being that is going to be reborn in the Western Paradise is not yourself, it makes no sense to you or anybody to cultivate for such rebirth, or for any form of spiritual attainment. If the self or soul does not exist, or is always suffering (who is suffering?), or never permanent (who is impermanent?), then it would be meaningless to cultivate for nirvana (who or what enter nirvana?).

If the self or soul exists, then how does this non-soul doctrine help sentient beings free themselves from their attachment to their selves or souls? The answer represents an example of higher wisdom which according to Mahayanists and Vajrayanists, Theravadins may not have.

The self or soul or whatever term we may use for this concept, exists only at the phenomenal level. At the transcendental level, or the level of ultimate reality, the self or soul does not exist. In other words, the self or soul is an illusion: what we believe to be our personal self at the phenomenal level, is actually the universal self at the transcendental level. It is due to our ignorance that we imagine our illusory soul to be imprisoned inside our illusory body; when we are enlightened, we realize that we are actually the Supreme Reality. It is to help us understand and experience this great cosmic truth that the Buddha teaches the doctrine of non-self or non-soul.

If the self is illusory, then does it exist? The answer, depending on various factors, can be yes or no, yes and no, neither yes nor no, neither yes and neither no. Interestingly, modern scientists are using a similar language. The world renowned scientist Robert Oppenheimer says:

> If we ask, for instance, whether the position of the electron remains the same, we must say 'no'; if we ask whether the electron's position changes with time, we must say 'no'; if we ask whether the electron is at rest, we must say 'no'; if we ask whether it is in motion, we must say 'no'.

We must remember that saying the personal self is illusory does not necessarily mean that it does not exist but we imagine it to exist. In Buddhist teaching, at the transcendental dimension, your wife or husband is illusory, the house you are living in and the mountain you are looking at are illusory, the sun and the moon are illusory, and the whole external, "objective" world is illusory! But at our ordinary phenomenal dimension, your self or soul is as "real" as your wife or husband, the house and the mountain, the sun and the moon, and the whole external world.

As in quantum physics like Oppenheimer's quotation above, this description of your wife (or husband) being illusory in transcendental reality but "real" in the phenomenal world, is not some sort of a joke or a play of words, but is serious matter at the very center of Buddhism.

Suppose you look at your wife through a gigantic, powerful electron microscope yet to be built by scientists. Your wife will not be there. Where has she gone? She has not gone anywhere, because she was an illusion in the first place. Now, with the help of the gigantic, powerful instrument, you only see patterns of subatomic particles. If the microscope is more powerful, you will not even see particles; there remains only an undifferentiated spread of cosmic energy — the realization of the united field theory. Buddhist masters do not normally use electron microscopes; they use their wisdom-eye developed through their spiritual cultivation.

As ordinary people do not have wisdom-eyes, they mistakenly regard phenomena, which actually is derived from a Greek word meaning appearances, as ultimate reality, and consider that aspect of the Universal Self limited in their phenomenal bodies as their personal selves. However, when the Venerable Ou Yi mentions "faith in self" as one of the six kinds of faith in the cultivation of Amitabha recitation, the master refers not to the personal self, but to the Universal Self.

To have faith in the Universal Self means to have the higher wisdom concerning the phenomenal and the transcendental aspects of ultimate reality, realizing that transcendentally the personal self is actually the Universal Self, and that phenomenally the external world (like the Western Paradise) is a creation of the mind. This explains that if an aspirant's mind has become one-pointed in reciting the name of Amitabha Buddha and his faith in the Buddha's promise is so strong, the Western Paradise will be manifested for him.

To take a very gross analogy, if you tape-record the same beautiful scene and nothing else into countless video-cassettes, every time you play a video-cassette you will see only the beautiful scene. It should be noted that the Western Paradise does not exist in the aspirant's imagination; it is as real to him as his own fingers.

Buddha and Karma

Faith in Buddha is in three parts, namely faith in Sakyamuni Buddha, in Amitabha Buddha, and in countless other Buddhas. Sakyamuni Buddha, considering that cultivation by reciting Amitabha's name is an excellent method, especially during the decadent period of a spiritual cycle, spontaneously teaches the Amitabha Sutra to the Saha world — unlike in many other sutras which are direct answers to disciples' questions. Aspirants have faith that Sakyamuni's judgment and teaching are right.

The Western Paradise is created and sustained by Amitabha Buddha as a result of his vows. He declared that if he could not fulfill his vows, he would refuse to enter Buddhahood. Amitabha has become a Buddha for ten aeons, thus demonstrating that his vows have been fulfilled. Aspirants therefore have faith that by following Amitabha's instruction, they will be reborn in his Pure Land.

Countless Buddhas of various galaxies have testified to the validity of Sakyamuni's teaching and Amitabha's promise. Buddhas never tell untruths, and this characteristic results in their having long, wide tongues. If aspirants practice the Amitabha teaching correctly and devotedly, yet cannot be reborn in the Western Paradise, it means either that Sakyamuni, Amitabha or these countless Buddhas have lied, or that this Amitabha Sutra is a false scripture.

It may not be easy for ordinary people to verify whether these Buddhas have lied and are therefore not true Buddhas, but he can have tremendous circumstantial verification from the fact that the Amitabha Sutra (which testifies to the truthfulness of the Buddhas) has been accepted as true throughout many centuries by great masters whose wisdom and character are impeccable, and who would not gain any benefit from lying.

Moreover, though it may be difficult for the uninitiated to believe, countless people in moments of spiritual inspiration in both ancient and modern times have actually seen Sukhavati, the Western Paradise! A method for the pious to seek this incredible experience will be explained in a later chapter.

Faith in cause refers to the belief in the cause of karma. A Buddhist tenet teaches that even a mere but meaningful mention of the term "Buddha" or of any Buddha's name by a person will generate the relevant energy in his mind, acting like a seed that will eventually germinate into Buddhahood.

The Venerable Ou Yi asks rhetorically, "Even a random mention of a Buddha's name acts like a Buddha-seed that will one day germinate into Buddhahood, what more will be a devoted recitation of Amitabha Buddha's name by a one-pointed mind! Won't such one-pointed recitation result in a rebirth in the Pure Land?" Aspirants have faith that it certainly will.

Returning to our gross analogy, even if you have randomly tape-recorded a beautiful scene only once, if you play the cassette this beautiful scene will eventually appear. Won't this beautiful scene appear if you have purposely and constantly tape-recorded this scene?

Faith in effect, which is complementary to faith in cause, postulates that if you follow certain procedures, you will get the expected result. For example, as explained in your car manual and described here in a simplified manner, if you ignite your car engine, put on the first gear and step on the accelerator, you will get the expected result of moving your car forward.

Similarly, aspirants who have faith in effect, will have no doubt that if they believe in the Western Paradise, have made a vow to be reborn there, and have recited the name of Amitabha Buddha whole-heartedly for at least ten times, they will be reborn in Amitabha's Pure Land.

Doctrine of Four Realms

The next two kinds of faith, faith in phenomena and faith in principle, are complementary and are quite profound. A brief explanation of the doctrine of four realms taught by the Hua Yen (Avatamsaka or Flower Adornment) School is helpful.

The Hua Yen School, the Mahayana school that emphasizes on the Buddha's teaching of cosmic reality, teaches that the universe may be interpreted in four ways, as follows:

1. the realm of phenomena,
2. the realm of principles,
3. the realm of the inter-penetration of phenomena and phenomena,
4. the realm of the inter-penetration of phenomena and principles.

The world we normally perceive is the realm of phenomena, where objects and processes such as tress and people, eating a meal and earthquakes exist as separated and differentiated. In the language of science, this is the world of classical physics, where every event in the universe can be determined if we have sufficient information.

The realm of principles is the world of the new physics, where reality or different levels of reality, are perceived in terms of mathematical equations. This dimension of our world is normally unknown to ordinary people, although they exist in it. Because of their spiritual cultivation, Buddhist masters can experience this dimension directly, such as perceiving their physical bodies as empty, or witnessing heavenly beings in heavenly realms.

The realm of the inter-penetration of phenomena and phenomena refers to that dimension of the world where objects and processes, while separated and differentiated, are actually inter-connected. At shallow levels, the inter-connection can be perceived by ordinary people, although they may have to observe and ponder, such as every time a tree sways or we eat our meal, the environment is affected in some subtle ways.

At deeper levels, some ordinary people who lack the knowledge, may regard such inter-connection as ridiculous, such as if you harbor wicked thoughts against others you are actually ruining your own future, or if you pray sincerely for a sick friend (even without his knowing) you can help him to recover.

The realm of the inter-penetration of phenomena and principles may be used to explain psychical happenings or events that many would consider miraculous or fraudulent. Using this inter-penetration of phenomena and principles, the great Indian master Bodhidharma, for example, crossed the Yangtze River on a reed, and Bodhisattvas can manifest into numerous forms at different places at the same time to help people.

Phenomena and Principles

In Ou Yi's six kinds of faith, faith in phenomena refers to the realization that the phenomenal realm of the Western Paradise is a creation of the mind. Thus, if an aspirant beliefs that the Western Paradise exists, and if his mind has become one-pointed through his devoted recitation of Amitabha Buddha, the Western Paradise will appear before him. It must be stressed again that this does not mean the Western Paradise exists only in his imagination.

Our world as we know it, exists because it is created by our mind, not just in the present lifetimes, but also throughout millennia and imprinted in our alaya or collective consciousness. The same world will be very different for other sentient beings, like bacteria and crocodiles, because their alaya consciousness is different. For most ordinary people, many realms of existence in this world such as the realms of ghosts and asuras, are non-existent because, among many reasons, they do not belief in them.

Why, then, familiar objects like tables and chairs continue to exist even though we try to believe they are non-existent? This is because they have been imprinted so deeply in our alaya consciousness that even if we try in our normal consciousness to believe they do not exist, our unconsciousness accepts their existence. But those with powerful minds can influence matter. Yogis, for example, may make themselves invisible by their will. Even for ordinary people, their thoughts often modify reality. For example, whether your neighbor is your friend or your enemy often depends on how you think of him.

Faith in principles is perceiving the issue from the other perspective. While faith in phenomena expounds that what we experience is the result of our mind, faith in principles postulates that our mind can decide on what we experience.

Hence, if an aspirant intensely wants to be reborn in the Western Paradise, he can be reborn there. This explains why besides having faith, it is very important to make a vow. For those who are "this-worldly", this doctrine also suggests that in the final analysis whether their life in this world is happy or miserable, depends not so much on where they live, and the wealth and company they have, but on the state of their mind.

UNDERSTANDING AND EXPERIENCE

(How You May Verify the Buddha's Teaching)

Buddhism never says faith is unimportant; but it advocates that acceptance should not be based on blind faith. Otherwise it may become superstition. Secondly, Buddhism always emphasizes understanding and verification.

Faith and Understanding

Faith is a crucial factor in the cultivation for rebirth in the Western Paradise of Eternal Bliss. As explained in the previous chapter, the master Yuan Yin mentioned four kinds of faith, namely faith in the Buddha, in the existence of the Western Paradise, in
countless other Buddhas, and in the belief that the Saha world is defiled. Another master, Ou Yi, mentioned six kinds of faith, namely faith in self, in Buddha, in cause, in effect, in phenomena, and in principles.

Yuan Yin's four kinds of faith are easy to understand, and are therefore more suitable for most people aspiring to Sukhavati, the Western Paradise. Ou Yi's six kinds of faith are profound, and will be of interest and benefit to the more philosophical minded. Most masters of the Pure Land School believe that in the cultivation methods of their school, having strong faith is more important than having deep understanding.

Probably because of this special feature, some critics claim, possibly because of inadequate understanding of the Pure Land philosophy that the Pure Land School is for the "dull mind". Pure Land School masters have provided some convincing answers to this criticism, and they will be discussed in a later chapter.

Some people may wonder why faith is such an important factor in this Pure Land School of Buddhism, when the Buddha has stressed that followers should not accept his teaching on faith alone, but to assess his teaching to the best of their understanding and experience. One should note that, firstly, Buddhism never says faith is unimportant; but it advocates that acceptance should not be based on blind faith. Otherwise it may become superstition. Secondly, Buddhism always emphasizes understanding and verification.

Faith, obviously, is an essential aspect of all religions, so much so that a person's religion is often referred to as his faith. Buddhism is probably the only world's religion where her greatest teacher and other masters have taken the trouble to remind their followers not to accept the religion on faith alone. At the beginning stage, when the beginner does not have sufficient understanding and experience, faith is comparatively more important, but as he progresses in his spiritual development, the importance of faith becomes less until at the advanced stage Buddhism is mainly direct experience.

Yet, even at the beginning stage, understanding and experience are necessary. A beginner may not have the understanding or experience of advance concepts like other realms of existence and seeking a Bodhisattva's help through his mantra. He would, therefore, have to accept such teachings on the faith that advanced practitioners have experienced and explained these truths, or he could refuse to accept these teachings.

He can test many of these teachings through his own experience, such as following closely the procedure in seeking a Bodhisattva's help, and confirming or rebuking this teaching. He should also realize that sometimes failure to have his prayers answered may not necessarily mean that this Buddhist teaching concerning Bodhisattvas' help is false, because the failure can be due to other factors beyond his ordinary comprehension. It must be stressed that this is not some form of trick or rationalization. Buddhists are sincere in wanting to verify their beliefs, as well as open-minded enough to accept that some factors may operate beyond their present state of understanding and experience, but they would not allow such acceptance to degenerate into dogma or superstition.

For example, sometimes it is better for a person that his selfish prayers are not answered, or his karma is such that granting him some selfish wishes is just delaying his karmic burden which could be better relieved earlier even if it would cause him some pain, or granting him some petty favors would deprive him of some lessons for development. A simple, prosaic analogy is a child asking his parents to do his homework.

The Significance of Direct Experience

It is indeed a remarkable distinction for Buddhism that every doctrine, no matter how incredible it may appear to the uninitiated, can be explained intellectually and appreciated experientially, if the person in question has attained the appropriate developmental level for the understanding and experience. This is so, because every teaching of the Buddha is the result not of speculation, but of direct experience that has been verified by countless masters. For example, when a master teaches that the external world is an illusion, this teaching is not a result of some theorizing supported by mathematical proofs, but the result of his direct, personal perception of reality during deep meditation.

A beginner, of course, could not have such spiritual experience; he is not even expected to understand the intellectual explanation of such attainment. For such advanced teaching, he has a choice: accepting it on faith with the frequent reminder that he should understand what he beliefs, and then seek personal verification as he progress; or reject it for the time being until he is ready to understand or experience the teaching. But he can, and should, verify whatever Buddhist teaching at his level.

For example, instead of accepting on blind faith the Buddha's basic teaching that life in our Saha world is suffering, and that Buddhism reduces and eventually eliminates this suffering, the beginner in Buddhism should verify for himself the truth or otherwise of this teaching. If he is not able to review his own birth during meditation, and not ready to let a hypnotist regress him to his birth, to verify whether he had suffered while being born, he can, for instance, study whether the births of babies, besides the obvious joy they bring to the world, cause any suffering to themselves as well as to their parents. This simple experience can serve to verify the truth or otherwise of the Buddha's teaching that birth is suffering.

Similarly, the Buddha's teaching that aging, sickness, death, meeting of hated ones, parting of loved ones, failure to get what one desires, and the five aggregates (matter, perception, thought, activity and consciousness) that make up a human being, are causes of suffering, can be verified by means of appropriate studies and experiences.

One way to assess the five aggregates is to review whether the matter that makes up your physical body, or the perception that makes up your psyche, has ever caused you any suffering. One should remember that this doctrine of suffering does not necessarily mean that there is no joy in life, or that your physical body and psyche have not brought you any joy. When a person has the relevant understanding and experience, he can rightly say he accepts the Buddha's teaching on the First Noble Truth.

He should then assess how true is the claim that Buddhism overcomes suffering. If, for example, after learning fundamental teachings from Buddhist teachers (or good books), and practicing Buddhism for a reasonable length of time, he still does not feel happier or more peaceful than before, then he should leave Buddhism (at least for the time being), and pursue other religious teachings or other wholesome activities.

Verifying the Truth on Suffering

The first Noble Truth of Buddhism states that life is suffering. Without adequate or proper understanding, it is easy to conclude that Buddhism is pessimistic. Actually, Buddhism is a religion of joy, explaining as well as providing practical ways how people and other sentient beings can overcome suffering and attain eternal bliss in nirvana. To say life is suffering, therefore, must not be interpreted, as there is no joy in life. In our human realm, the amount of joy and suffering is about equal; but the main objective of teaching this Noble Truth is to make us aware that despite its joy, life in samsara, i.e. the continuous cycle of birth and rebirth, is still suffering, because if we cling to samsara we would deny ourselves the opportunity to attain nirvana, which is the supreme aim of Buddhism.

Some of us may think that it is mere platitude to say that our human realm has about equal amount of joy and suffering. Indeed the human realm is unique in the Saha world in this respect.

In the realm of hells, there is only suffering and no joy; in the realms of ghosts and of animals there is much suffering and little joy; in the realm of asuras, there is more suffering than joy; and in the heavenly realms of devas and brahma gods, and the formless realms of Sravadas, Prateyakabuddhas, Arahants and Bodhisattvas, there is only joy and no suffering.

Yet, even in the heavenly realms, there are two other types of suffering, known as "destructive-suffering" due to the impermanence of form, and "samsaric-suffering" due to being subject to reincarnation. These two kinds of suffering are also present in the desire realms of hells, ghosts, animals, asuras and humans. In the formless realms, which are above the heavenly realms, there are no suffering due to desire, and no destructive-suffering due to impermanence, but samsaric-suffering is still present.

The following is a simple method you may use to verify the truth of this Buddhist teaching on suffering. Take a clean sheet of paper and draw a line down the middle. On one side of the line, list all the instances of suffering you have experienced today; and on the other side list all the instances of joy. Repeat for yesterday and the day before, or as many days as you wish. Compare whether your instances of suffering are more than those of joy.

You may make this method more sophisticated. Grade each instance of joy from 1 to 10 : 1 for slight joy and 10 for extreme joy. Similarly, grade each instance of suffering from -1 to -10. Total up your grades to see whether your score is plus or minus. If you often have a plus score, as I do, count yourself as being one of the very lucky few. Otherwise, the Buddha's teaching will help you to improve your score.

Similarly we can investigate to verify, at our respective developmental levels, other teachings of the Buddha. We can, for example, verify the Second Noble Truth, whether suffering is caused by craving, as taught by the Buddha. If someone you know passes away, you would probably feel sad. Why must you suffer when someone else dies? It is because of your craving, such as craving for his company, or for the attachment of emotion, thus verifying the Second Noble Truth. If you have no craving, such as you do not crave for his company or you have risen above emotional attachment, you might not suffer any sadness at his passing away. This therefore verifies the Third Noble Truth, i.e. to overcome suffering you have to overcome craving.

One way to overcome craving is to practice the Noble Eightfold Path. Let us investigate the first of the eight tenets, namely right view. If you have perverse views, such as thinking that was the end of your friend, or his death was a punishment from a god, you would continue to suffer the consequence of your wrong views. But if you have right view, and understand that his physical death is the result of the expiration of his karmic forces which hold his mental and bodily aggregates together, and that he would be reborn in another place, perhaps in the Western Paradise, you would have overcome your craving for his continued existence on this earth (to serve your interest), and would have eliminated your suffering.

But how would one verify the teaching on Sukhavati? How would he be certain that if he has faith, makes a vow and recites the Buddha's name devotedly, he would be reborn in Amitabha's Pure Land?

It is not as easy to verify the existence of Sukhavati as one would verify the four Noble Truths. Hence, this is why faith is of utmost importance in this cultivation method of Amitabha-recitation to win rebirth in the Western Paradise. There is, nevertheless, much indirect evidence from personal witness of many people, both past and present, that Sukhavati exists. It is recorded in sutras that through his miraculous powers the Buddha enabled thousands of people, including Ananda, King Bimbisara and Queen Vaidehi, to see the Western Paradise. Maudgalyayana used his own miraculous powers to view this Pure Land. The modern Chinese master, Yin Sun, reported his view of Sukhavati, as well as of Amitabha Buddha, Bodhisattva Guan Yin, Bodhisattva Da Shi Zi and other saints appearing before him.

In the above examples, faith is involved: one needs to have faith that all these reports are true. Is there any method, without having to leave this world, to experience Sukhavati, so as to verify the Buddha's teaching?

Vow to See Amitabha and Sukhavati

The Venerable Shan Dao, considered by many as a manifestation of Amitabha Buddha himself in our world to help humanity, taught the following method whereby we may perceive Amitabha Buddha and Sukhavati.

Those who cultivate with the Pure Land method and wish to see Sukhavati in their meditation should, before they go to bed, with a one-pointed mind clasp their palms together in prayer, facing the West, either sitting or standing or kneeling down, recite ten times Amitabha Buddha, Bodhisattva Guan Yin, Bodhisattva Da Shi Zi and other saints of the pure, tranquil sea of Sukhavati, and then make a vow as follows: I, disciple so and so, now a mortal in samsara, deep and heavy in defilement, entangled in the cycle of rebirth in the six realms, am enduring unspeakable suffering. Now I have the opportunity to meet the virtuous and wise, from who I learn about Amitabha Buddha and his great vows and merits. I recite the name of Amitabha Buddha whole-heartedly, and vow to be reborn in Sukhavati. May the Buddha be kind and compassionate without reserve, and have mercy on me. I, disciple so and so, have no knowledge of the magnificent and radiant body of the Buddha; may the Buddha manifest so that I may have a chance to see the Buddha, and also to see Bodhisattva Guan Yin, Bodhisattva Da Shi Zi and other Bodhisattvas, as well as to see the grandeur of Sukhavati, pure, tranquil and magnificent, radiant and wondrous. After making the vow, you must go into meditation with right thought, or go to sleep with right thought. You must not say any irrelevant words, or harbor any irrelevant thoughts. You may perceive Sukhavati, Amitabha Buddha and the Bodhisattvas immediately in your meditation, or see them in your dream. If you follow the procedure with focused determination, you will certainly realize your vow.

Anyone wishing to attempt the above method should bear in mind the following three points. One, it is unreasonable to expect success after one or two tries. The above method demands much meditation skill as well as deep spirituality. Focused determination is necessary.

Two, if an aspirant fails to see Amitabha Buddha or Sukhavati despite many tries, it does not necessarily mean that Amitabha Buddha or Sukhavati does not exist. Many people, for example, fail to reach the South Pole or win the football world cup final despite numerous attempts, but, of course, that does not mean the South Pole or the world cup final does not exist.

Three, if an aspirant is sincere in seeking for verification that Sukhavati exists, and if he eventually succeeds in perceiving Sukhavati, he will make a mockery of his original purpose if, instead of accepting his own experience as the most simple, most direct and most logical verification for the Buddha's teaching, he rationalizes that his experience of Sukhavati is his own fantasy or hallucination, or he tries to think up any excuse to justify his disbelief.

Indeed it is amazing what length some people may go to so as to refute evidence that is most direct, simple and logical. For instance, when Dr Jules Cloquet reported to his medical academy that he had successfully removed a breast tumor from a woman in 1829 after mesmerizing her, or when dentist Oudet extracted a tooth after mesmerizing the patient in 1837, instead of having their cases accepted as simple, direct and logical evidence showing the validity of mesmerism, they were told that their patients pretended to feel no pain!

In this connection it is pertinent to note that throughout its history, scientific progress has always been guided by the faith that the best explanation for phenomena is to adopt the simplest hypothesis which coordinates all known observations.

COMPASSION AND CARE IN BUDDHISM

(Structure and Content of a Liturgical Chanting)

When one studies the meanings of these supportive songs and verses, as well as of the main sutra itself, one cannot help to be touched by the typical Mahayanist philosophy of selflessness and caring for others.

Songs and Praises

Anyone who has followed a liturgical chanting of a Buddhist sutra in any temple or religious gathering, or has examined a typical Buddhist scripture, would be impressed with the feeling of devotion and compassion in the Buddhist liturgy. A sutra is seldom chanted by itself, though this can be done, as there are no hard and fast rules in sutra chanting. Usually the chanting of a sutra is preceded and followed by various songs of phrases and relevant mantras or dharanis, and virtually always concluded with the transference of merits to others.

When one studies the meanings of these supportive songs and verses, as well as of the main sutra itself, one cannot help to be touched by the typical Mahayanist philosophy of selflessness and caring for others. Almost all the prayers are devoted to the benefit of others, including strangers and non-human beings; there is very little asking for one's benefit. When a devotee ever refers to himself or herself in the liturgy, it is usually repentance of wrong doings in the past (including past lives), and seldom seeking for rewards in future, beautifully stated in the Chinese expression "zhi qiu chan hui, bu qiu fu bao".

It may not be easy for many people to appreciate the deep wisdom and spirituality in this attitude; some may regard it as weak or negative. In a nutshell, the onus of a typical Buddhist liturgy is not "Buddha, please help me to be successful in my endeavor" but "May whatever merits obtained by me in this service be transferred to all sentient beings so that they can be free from suffering."

The following is an example of a fairly complete sutra chanting session. Most sessions, however, are shorter. The procedure is a convention; none of the items are obligatory.

A chanting session begins with three dignified soundings of a drum or "wooden fish" (which is a Buddhist liturgical music instrument made of wood, shaped like a fish, roughly oval and hollow inside, giving a mallow sound when struck), followed by a gentle but rich sounding of a small copper bell. The soundings of the drum and bell may be more in some chanting sessions. Then devotees chant the "Praise of Fragrance" calling for the Buddha (or Buddhas) and Bodhisattvas to preside over their gathering. The devotees usually kneel in front of a statute of the Buddha or a Bodhisattva while chanting, but other positions like standing or sitting cross-legged, are also permissible.

When the sutra to be recited in the session has special significance to a particular Bodhisattva, then a special opening song or gatha (verse) pertaining to that Bodhisattva, rather than the above Praise of Fragrance, may be chanted. For example, in the chanting of the "Chapter on Guan Shi Yin Bodhisattva's Gate for the Masses in the Lotus Sutra", which is a very popular sutra, the opening song is usually "Praise to the Water of Purification", which has special reference to Guan Shi Yin Bodhisattva.

Mantras and Paying Homage

Next is the chanting of various mantras, such as for cleansing the mouth, cleansing the body, and bringing peace to local deities. As a sign of respect, it is commendable for devotees to wash their mouth, have a shower, change into clean clothing and tidy up their hair before engaging in sutra chanting. Then they chant the relevant mantras to spiritually cleanse themselves. If, for some reasons, it is not feasible for them to cleanse themselves physically first, these cleansing mantras may be a poor substitute. When we chant a sutra, many other beings like ghosts, nature spirits and gods may gather around to listen. It is meritorious to chant a mantra for their blessings.

Mantras are in Sanskrit, and transliterated into Chinese according to sound, not according to meaning. Most devotees do not know their meanings; it is in fact not necessary to know the meanings because their operation depends on sound patterns. Mantras are like the esoteric signals Buddhas and Bodhisattvas have given to their followers, and have promised that when these signals are sounded they will come to the followers' help.

Because the sound system of the Chinese language, like any languages, has changed throughout the ages, when mantras that were written many centuries ago are read now, the words may be pronounced differently from what they were before. For example, what is pronounced as "an" was originally "om"; "Ju Lai" (meaning the Tathagata or the Buddha), in classical Chinese is now pronounced as "Ru Lai".

If the sound system has changed, will the Buddhas and the Bodhisattvas recognize their mantras when they are now recited according to modern phonetics? Of course they can; if a linguist can recognize the changes, what more can these great beings do. Let us look at a simple analogy. Suppose you tell your very young children that whenever they need help, just call "Daddy". If your children cannot pronounce it clearly, and say "da da" instead, you would not have much difficulty knowing they need help. Buddhas and Bodhisattvas look after us with more care and loving-kindness than most parents do with their children.

Next, a vow is chanted. It is usual for a gathering to chant in unison a vow that is commonly used, but anybody may chant his own vow silently if he wishes. The nature of the vow is usually related to the sutra that will be recited, and frequently includes an affirmation to repay those who have benefited us, and to help the unfortunate to be relieved of their suffering.

For example, in the chanting of the Guan Yin Sutra mentioned above, which is particularly noted for bestowing compassion to others, some masters whose ability to go to heaven, if not nirvana itself, is beyond doubt, categorically indicate in their vow their desire to be reborn in the world or even a lower realm so as to help others.

It is worthy to note that at their level, there is no question of making an empty vow: they fully know that their thoughts will generate the appropriate karmic force that will inevitably work out in their future reincarnations the ways their minds at present think. This is an example of practicing the Bodhisattva ideal.

After making or reconfirming their vow, the devotees pay homage to Sakyamuni Buddha, the Great Teacher of our aeon, by chanting his name three times: "Homage to our Teacher Sakyamuni Buddha", or "Namo Ben Shi Shi Jia Mou Ni Fo" in Chinese.

Simultaneous with chanting the name, devotees make three prostrations as follows. From the clasped hands in prayer position, kneel down on your right knee (if you start from the standing position), and place your right hand palm downward on the ground about a foot or two in front. Then kneel down on your left knee and place your left hand palm downward on the ground about a foot or two in front. Now with both knees and both palms on the ground, bow your head forward to touch the ground with your forehead, with your palms quite parallel a short distance in front.

While the head is still touching the ground, turn both hands so that the palms face upward, in a poise of receiving the feet of the Buddha or a Bodhisattva. Remain in this prostration for a few seconds. Then turn the hands so that the palms face downward again. Raise your left knee, lift your left palm, raise your right knee, lift your right palm, stand upright and bring both palms together in front in prayer position. This completes the first prostration. Repeat twice, making three prostrations altogether, while simultaneously chanting the Buddha's name thrice.

It is worthy of note that the prostration is our way of showing our highest respect and gratitude to the Buddha and Bodhisattva. The action comes willingly from our part. No one needs to prostrate, even while others are prostrating, if he does not sincerely want to do so.

Rare Opportunity Indeed

Next, the devotees chant the "The Gatha to Start the Sutra", whereby they verbalize the great truth, though it is little realized by most people, that it is indeed very rare to have access to the supreme true teaching of the Buddha. The devotees affirm their determination to understand the true meaning of this very precious teaching. If we are aware that a being has to spend countless lives before he can have a chance to be a human, and has gone through countless human reincarnations before he can have a chance to come across a sutra, then to be sufficiently matured spiritually before he can seriously consider studying the meaning of a sutra; further, the sutra is not by any ordinary instructor, scientist, or philosopher on some mundane topic like how to make money or whether the circle is the perfect form, but by the Buddha himself, considered by many as the greatest of all teachers, on how we can transcend the phenomenal world to attain eternal bliss — then we can appreciate how precious is the opportunity to study the sutra.

Following this opening gatha is the chanting of the sutra proper, which will take up most of the time of the chanting session. First the devotees pay homage to the Buddha or the Bodhisattva who is the central figure in the sutra, by chanting his name and simultaneously prostrating thrice.

Often the appropriate appellatives are affixed to the name of the Buddha or Bodhisattva. For example, for the Guan Yin Sutra, devotees will chant "Namo Great Compassion Guan Shi Yin Bodhisattva"; and for the Khsitigarbha Bodhisattva Sutra, which is an important sutra frequently recited to help lost souls, the chant is "Namo Great Sacrifice Khsitigarbha Bodhisattva", because this Bodhisattva, who could enjoy eternal bliss in nirvana, has made great sacrifices to go to hells to help suffering souls there.

The name of the sutra is always included in the chanting. The name of the translator is always written at the start of the sutra, thus giving a sense of authority and responsibility, but it is often not chanted.

After the chanting of the sutra proper, a long gatha or verse recapitulating the main points of the sutra is sometimes sung. In the Guan Yin Sutra, this long gatha is incorporated into the sutra itself. This is usually followed by recitation of mantras or dharanis related to the sutra. For example, after chanting the Diamond Sutra, which is a very important sutra that explains the meaning of emptiness or cosmic reality, mantras like "Boundless Store of Wisdom Mantra", "Heart of Diamond Mantra" and "Repentance Mantra" are frequently recited.

The chanting session usually ends with singing praises to the Buddha or the Bodhisattva principally connected with the sutra, and paying homage to all Buddhas and Bodhisattvas, with three prostrations each. The conclusion of the chanting proper, however, is not the end of the gathering yet. This sutra chanting results in blessings, often loosely referred to as merits, being acquired by the participants. Usually before completing the whole liturgical procedure, the devotees recite or chant a prayer to transfer these merits to other beings.

The various items for the full chanting procedure are listed below for easy reference. Most chanting sessions, however, do not include all the items; some people, especially if they are chanting alone, chant only a sutra, a part of a sutra, a dharani, a mantra, or just the name of a Buddha or Bodhisattva.

1. Praise of Fragrance, or other Praises.
2. Mantras for cleansing, for bringing peace to local deities, and for reducing karmic effect of past sins.
3. Vow.
4. Homage to Sakyamuni Buddha, with prostration.
5. Gatha to Start the Sutra.
6. Homage to the Buddha or Bodhisattva central to the sutra, with prostration.
7. Sutra proper.
8. Gatha to recapitulate.
9. Mantras or dharanis related to the sutra.
10. Praises to Buddhas and Bodhisattvas.
11. Homage to the central Buddha or Bodhisattva, with prostration.
12. Transfer of Merits.

The following are some examples of the various items in a chanting session. The examples chosen are those frequently used in the chanting of the Amitabha Sutra.

Praise of Fragrance
(Sing, chant or recite three times)

Fragrance from the incense
Permeates the whole dharma realm.
The sea of Buddhas know and hear this calling,
Thus everywhere into propitious clouds forming,
To our sincerity and with expedient means responding,
The Buddhas reveal themselves with compassion and love.
Homage to the Bodhisattvas and Mahasattvas of the fragrant clouds above.

(Note: It is a convention, but not a essential condition, to burn incensed joss sticks as a token of homage just before the chanting. Dharma realm, here, means cosmos. This Praise is sung not only to Sakyamuni Buddha, but to all Buddhas. The Buddhas may reveal themselves as Bodhisattvas. Mahasattvas means Great Beings.)

Mantra for Cleansing the Mouth

Xiu li xiu li
Mo he xiu li
Xiu xiu li
Sa po he.

(Note: "He" in Romanized Chinese is pronounced like the English "her", not "hee", and corresponds to the Sanskrit "ha".)

Mantra to Cleanse the Body

An.
Xiu duo li, xiu duo li
Xiu mo li, xiu mo li
Sa po he.

(Note: "An" is the modern pronunciation of the ancient "om", which is the primordial sound of the cosmos.)

Mantra to Bring Peace to Local Deities

Nan mo san man duo
Mo tuo nan
An
Du lu du lu
Di wei suo po he.

(Note: "Nan mo" was pronounced as "nam mo" in the past, and corresponds to the Sanskrit "Namo", meaning "pay homage to". "Mo tuo nan" was pronounced as "mou tuo nam". Many modern devotees chant the mantra following the ancient sound.)

Mantra to Reduce Karmic Effect of Past Sins
Known as "Seven Buddhas Eliminate Sins"
(To be chanted or recited thrice)

Li po li po di. Qiu he qiu he di.
Tuo luo ni di. Ni he la di.
Pi li ni di. Mo he qie di.
Zhen ling qian di. Suo po he.

(Note: Before reciting this mantra, it is recommendable to say a prayer of repentance, such as, "I so and so sincerely repent for all the sins I have committed consciously and unconsciously in the past, including all my past lives, and vow that to the best of my ability I will not commit any sins again. May the compassionate Buddhas and Bodhisattvas have mercy on me." Some readers may wonder how is it possible to eliminate karmic effects of sins already committed. It is possible because karmic effects operate as impressions in the mind, and this mantra of repentance helps to eliminate these impressions.)

Vow

Prostrating before the Most-Honored One of the three cosmic planes,
Paying homage to Buddhas of ten directions,
I now make a great vow
To devote myself to this sutra
So as to repay my debts to the four kinds of gratitude I owe above,
And to eliminate the suffering of the three realms below.

May everyone who sees or hears of this sutra
Understand it and awaken the bodhi heart;
Using fully this reward body which is the result of our past merits,
Together let us be reborn in the Land of Eternal Bliss.

(Note: Three cosmic planes refer to the planes of desire, of form, and of non-form. Ten directions mean everywhere. The four kinds of gratitude refer to that towards the Buddha, our parents, the land where we live, and all the sentient beings whose efforts have made it possible for us to be alive. The three lower realms are those of animals, ghosts and hells. The bodhi heart is the heart or mind seeking spiritual wisdom. The vow must be made in sincerity and with a one-pointed mind.)

Gatha to Start the Sutra

The marvelous dharma, unsurpassed and profound,
Millions of aeons may not occur a meeting.
With this sutra, rare indeed the chance is found,
I vow to understand the Tathagata's teaching.

(Note: Tathagata means "Suchness" or the Supreme Reality. Here, the Tathagata is personified in Sakyamuni Buddha. After this opening-verse, homage to the Buddhas and Bodhisattvas of the Western Paradise is to be chanted thrice, if the sutra to be recited is the Amitabha Sutra.)

Homage to Buddhas and Bodhisattvas
(Three times)

Homage to the Sea of Buddhas and Bodhisattvas of the Lotus Pond.

(Note: All beings are reborn in the Western Paradise at the Lotus Pond. After paying homage to Buddhas and Bodhisattvas, the sutra proper is chanted, often followed by a gatha to recapitulate the main points of the sutra. The complete Amitabha Sutra is given in the next chapter, and an example of the recapitulating gatha is given below.)

Gatha of Praise

Amitabha Buddha, lord of forty-eight great vows
Of compassion and mercy is his boundless grace

From his third eye white light radiates
Illuminating beings to his happy place
Eight meritorious waters and lotus of classes nine
Seven rows of marvelous trees of superb sublime
We must have faith, and make a vow
Praising the Tathagata may all be blessed
The name of Amitabha Buddha we constantly recite
All will be reborn in the Paradise of the West

(Note: A special feature of Sukhavati is that people may be reborn in this Western Paradise by means of a lotus, carrying their karma with them. These heavenly inhabitants are divided into nine classes according to their karma.)

Dharani for Eliminating All Previous Karmic Hindrances For Rebirth in the Pure Land

Namo a mi duo po ya, Duo tuo jia duo ya
Duo di ya tuo, A mi li dou po pi
A mi li duo, Shi dan po pi
A mi li duo, Pi jia lan di
A mi li duo, Pi jia lan duo
Jia mi li, Jia jia na
Shi duo jia li, Sa po he

(Note: The title of this dharani is very long; it is often shortened to "Rebirth Dharani". It is one of the better-known dharanis, and is often recited for someone who has just passed away to help him acquire a better rebirth.)

Praise to Amitabha Buddha

The body of Amitabha shines in gold
Radiant is his appearance without compare
Like Mount Semuru his white turf unfolds
Over the four seas his eyes glow with care
Countless Buddhas from his radiance made
Countless Bodhisattvas from his Pure Land won
With forty-eight vows sentient beings are saved
Ferrying souls in nine classes to the shore beyond

(Note: Amitabha is the Buddha of Infinite Light presiding in the Western Paradise billions of light years from our earth. When manifested in his reward body (so that sentient beings can see him), the turf of white hair at his forehead is like five Mount Sumerus. Through his great compassion he ferries sentient beings from our world of suffering to his Pure Land where the heavenly inhabitants are classified into nine classes according to their spiritual development, and the highest become Bodhisattvas (Beings of Great Wisdom) and Buddhas (Enlightened Beings). The above song of praise to Amitabha Buddha was composed by the Venerable Ze Yin in the Song Dynasty.)

Homage to Amitabha Buddha

Homage to the Great Compassionate,
the Great Merciful Amitabha Buddha of the
Western Paradise of Eternal Bliss.
Namo Amitabha Buddha.

(Note: The first phrase is to be recited three times, simultaneous with three prostrations. The other phrase "Namo Amitabha Buddha" is to be recited many times, which may range from three to thousands. Following this is paying homage to the Bodhisattvas of the Western Paradise.)

Homage to Bodhisattvas of Sukhavati

Namo Guan Shi Yin Bodhisattva, Mahasattva.
Namo Da Shi Zhi Bodhisattva, Mahasattva.
Namo sea of Bodhisattvas, Mahasattvas of the Pure Land.

(Note: Each phrase of homage is to be recited three times, simultaneous with three prostrations, making nine prostrations altogether. Should anyone think that prostrating three times for Amitabha Buddha and nine times for these Bodhisattvas in a row is too much of trouble, please remember that they help us to overcome the greatest problem facing humankind, i.e. the problem of life and death. While it is true that devotion and gratitude need not be demonstrated by outward form, it is also true that if someone is not humble enough to prostrate, it is because his devotion and gratitude is not sufficiently deep. In their pilgrimage to famous temples of Bodhisattvas on sacred mountains, some well-known monks practiced "three steps one prostration". They made one prostration towards the direction of the

Bodhisattva for every three steps from the bottom of the mountain to the temple. However, no one needs to prostrate if he is not ready. In Buddhism, devotion and gratitude are shown willingly from those below, never demanded from above.)

Transfer of Merits

May the rebirth be in the Pure Land of the West
Born out of the lotus, fatherless and motherless
Seeing the Buddha, and transcending life and death
Together with Bodhisattvas in the spiritual quest

(Note: The merits derived from chanting the sutra can be transferred to other beings, or transferred back to yourself. In line with the Mahayana philosophy of helping others, the merits are usually transferred to other beings, human or non-human. If you wish to direct the merits to a particular person or persons, who may be alive or have passed away, so that he or they be reborn in the Western Paradise, you may start as follows: "May the rebirth of so and so be in ..." If chanting this sutra is part of your cultivation to be reborn in the Western Paradise, you should start with "May I be reborn in ..." Irrespective of whom (including yourself) you wish to direct the merits to, you must recite the Transfer of Merit in sincerity and with a one-pointed mind.)

RECITING THE AMITABHA SUTRA

(The Benefits and Procedure in Reciting a Sutra)

The Buddha's teaching, among other things, explains the Supreme Reality, and where we came from and where we shall go to.

Benefits of Sutra Chanting

What are the benefits one can get by reciting a sutra? Throughout the book the terms reciting and chanting are interchangeable, although reciting suggests an inclination towards reading whereas chanting towards singing.

A sutra is the teaching spoken by the Buddha himself. The Buddha is the Enlightened One, possessed of the highest supreme wisdom. Even if any person may or may not agree with what an enlightened being has taught, it is certainly worth his while to study the teaching, then assess the teaching to the best of his understanding and experience.

What the Buddha teaches is not about some mundane topics, but about the most important question any person would face, i.e. the question of transcending life and death. The Buddha's teaching, among other things, explains the Supreme Reality, and where we came from and where we shall go to. The whole range of the Buddha's teaching is collected in a few thousand sutras. While all the sutras contribute towards the central theme, i.e. how we can attain eternal bliss in nirvana, each sutra focuses on one principal aspect of the overall teaching. For example, the various Agama sutras focus on cultivating moral purity, and the colossal volumes of Wisdom sutras focus on cosmic reality. This Amitabha Sutra, which belongs to a group of sutras called Vaipulya sutras, explains how any being may cultivate to go to Sukhavati, the Western Paradise of Eternal Bliss.

Because the concepts in the sutras are very deep, and written or translated concisely in a classical style, it is generally difficult to understand without the help of explanation or commentary. Thus, many devotees recite the sutras without actually understanding in detail what they mean, though most of them would have a rough idea of their general purposes. The Amitabha Sutra is particular relevant in this respect. Literally thousands of followers of the Pure Land School of Buddhism chant the

Amitabha Sutra every day in many parts of the world, but most of them may not know its profound meaning, although virtually all of them would know that their devoted chanting will help them to go to Sukhavati, the Western Paradise of Eternal Bliss.

Does this devotion without understanding contradict the fundamental Buddhist principle that one must not accept the teaching on faith alone? Apparently it does, but a deeper investigation will show that this teaching is *not* based on faith *alone*, but on understanding and experience, as various chapters in this book have demonstrated. While most followers may not have attained the developmental level to have an intellectual understanding or direct spiritual experience of Amitabha's Pure Land, many masters have.

In fact the Pure Land School, in contrast with the Zen School, is appropriate for those who may not possess a sharp mind. This, of course, does not mean that followers of this school are necessarily "dull minded"; indeed some of the followers of the Pure Land School were, and are, exceedingly intelligent.

Even if we leave aside the meaning of the Amitabha Sutra, or any sutra, and work only on the mechanics or the sound of one's chanting, there are still many great benefits. Anyone who devotes himself to chanting sutras or scriptures of any religion, even mechanically, would "have entered the stream", i.e. on the path of spiritual development. How long he needs to cultivate before he will eventually attain the highest goal of his chosen religion will depend on a few other factors, but it is certain that he will not retrogress spiritually. Compared to those who are spiritually lost, irrespective of whether they are thieves or emperors, illiterates or philosophers, this entering the stream is a great achievement.

One who has entered the stream of spiritual development experiences inner peace, and is free from neurotic or psychotic problems, which are fairly prevalent in our modern societies. He may not be materialistically rich, but he is usually free from worldly worries as well as generally healthy. According to the Buddhist teaching, those who recite the sutras conscientiously are always protected by gods, and are therefore generally free from calamities. It is not easy to prove this claim scientifically, and some people may regard this belief as superstition, but if we look around objectively or care to take the trouble to investigate how many people involved in accidents are spiritual, it is not difficult to see its validity. Personally, I have not met someone who chants sutras conscientiously becomes an inmate of an asylum or dies in an accident.

In line with the Mahayana teaching of saving others beside ourselves, when we chant a sutra we also help other beings, although most of us would be unaware of this very meritorious deed, and some may find it "crazy". Our sutra chanting will not only benefit other people who may learn from the sutras, as well as gain from the soothing vibrations created by the chanting, but also benefit other non-human beings like ghosts, nature spirits and even gods who may gather around to hear the Buddha's teaching recited by us. Ghosts who are lost, for example, are very pitiful, and we can help them greatly with guidance provided by the sutra.

You need not worry about any language barrier, as these non-human beings can pick out the meaning from your thought vibrations if you chant or recite with a one-pointed mind.

Reciting the Sutra

In a liturgical chanting, a sutra is usually, but not necessarily, preceded and followed by various praises and mantras, as explained in the previous chapter. In a less formal occasion, a sutra can be recited by itself, although it is better to start and end a sutra with paying homage to the respective Buddha or Bodhisattva, and concluding the whole recitation session with a transfer of merits.

The following is an example of a helpful procedure. The complete Amitabha Sutra is presented, preceded and followed by paying homage to Amitabha Buddha, and are presented continuously so that it is easy for readers to refer to them. A sutra is recited or chanted from memory, but may be read from a text.

The name of the sutra is always recited. The name of the translator is always given, vouching for its warranty, but is usually not recited. It is respectful, but not essential, to light a lamp, burn a joss stick, or offer some flowers or water to Amitabha Buddha at the start of the recitation, and prostrate when reciting his name. If a statute or picture of Amitabha Buddha is not available, the devotee may face the west instead. The recitation of the sutra proper may be carried out while kneeling down, sitting cross-legged, standing or in any suitable position.

佛説阿彌陀經

　　如是我聞：一時，佛在舍衛國、祇樹給孤獨園，與大比丘僧千二百五十人俱，皆是大阿羅漢，眾所知識—長老舍利弗、摩訶目犍連、摩訶迦葉、摩訶迦旃延、摩訶俱絺羅、離婆多、周利槃陀伽、難陀、阿難陀、羅睺羅、憍梵波提、賓頭盧頗羅墮、迦留陀夷、摩訶劫賓那、薄拘羅、阿㝹樓馱，如是等諸大弟子；並諸菩薩摩訶薩—文殊師利法王子、阿逸多菩薩、乾陀訶提菩薩、常精進菩薩，如是等諸大菩薩，及釋提桓因等；無量諸天大眾俱。

　　爾時，佛告長老舍利弗：「從是西方過十萬億佛土，有世界名曰『極樂』。其土有佛，號『阿彌陀』，今現在説法。」

　　「舍利弗！彼土何故名爲極樂？其國眾生無有眾苦，但受諸樂，故名極樂。」

　　「又舍利弗，極樂國土七重欄楯、七重羅網、七重行樹，皆是四寶，周帀圍繞，是故彼國名爲極樂。」

　　「又舍利弗，極樂國土有七寶池，八功德水充滿其中。池底純以金沙布地，四邊階道，金、銀、瑠璃、玻瓈合成。上有樓閣，亦以金、銀、瑠璃、玻瓈、硨磲、赤珠、瑪瑙而嚴飾之。池中蓮花大如車輪，青色青光，黃色黃光，赤色赤光，白色白光，微妙香潔。」

　　「舍利弗！極樂國土成就如是功德莊嚴！」

　　「又舍利弗，彼佛國土，常作天樂，黃金爲地，晝夜六時，雨天曼陀羅華。」

　　「其土眾生，常以清旦，各以衣祴，盛眾妙華，供養他方十萬億佛，即以食時還到本國，飯食經行。」

　　「舍利弗！極樂國土成就如是功德莊嚴！」

　　「復次舍利弗，彼國常有種種奇妙雜色之鳥：白鶴、孔雀、鸚鵡、舍利、迦陵頻伽、共命之鳥。是諸眾鳥，晝夜六時，出和雅音，其音演暢：五根、五力、七菩提分、八聖道分，如是等法。其土眾生，聞是音已，皆悉念佛、念法、念僧。」

　　「舍利弗！汝勿謂此鳥實是罪報所生，所以者何？彼佛國土，無三惡道，舍利弗！其佛國土，尚無惡道之名，何況有實？是諸眾鳥，皆是阿彌陀佛欲令法音宣流，變化所作。」

「舍利弗！彼佛國土，微風吹動，諸寶行樹，及寶羅網，出微妙音，譬如百千種樂，同時俱作。聞是音者，自然皆生念佛、念法、念僧之心。」

「舍利弗！其佛國土成就如是功德莊嚴。」

「舍利弗！於汝意云何，彼佛何故號『阿彌陀』？舍利佛！彼佛光明無量，照十方國，無所障礙，是故號為『阿彌陀』。」

「又舍利弗，彼佛壽命及其人民，無量無邊阿僧祇劫，故名『阿彌陀』。」

「舍利弗！阿彌陀佛成佛以來，於今十劫。又舍利弗，彼佛有無量無邊聲聞弟子，皆阿羅漢，非是算數之所能知，諸菩薩眾亦復如是。」

「舍利弗！彼佛國土成就如是功德莊嚴！」

「又舍利弗，極樂國土眾生生者，皆是阿鞞跋致。其中多有一生補處，其數甚多，非是算數所能知之，但可以無量無邊阿僧祇說。」

「舍利弗！眾生聞者，應當發願，願生彼國。所以者何？得與如是諸上善人，俱會一處。舍利弗！不可以少善根、福德因緣，得生彼國。」

「舍利弗！若有善男子、善女人，聞說『阿彌陀佛』，執持名號，若一日、若二日、若三日、若四日、若五日、若六日、若七日，一心不亂，其人臨命終時，阿彌陀佛，與諸聖眾，現在其前。是人終時，心不顛倒，即得往生阿彌陀佛極樂國土。」

「舍利弗！我見是利，故說此言：若有眾生，聞是說者，應當發願，生彼國土。」

「舍利弗！如我今者，讚歎阿彌陀佛不可思議功德之利，東方亦有：阿閦鞞佛、須彌相佛、大須彌佛、須彌光佛、妙音佛，如是等恒河沙數諸佛，各於其國出廣長舌相，偏覆三千大千世界，說誠實言：汝等眾生，當信是稱讚不可思議功德，一切諸佛所護念經。」

「舍利弗！南方世界有：日月燈佛、名聞光佛、大燄肩佛、須彌燈佛、無量精進佛，如是等恒河沙數諸佛，各於其國，出廣長舌相，偏覆三千大千世界，說誠實言：汝等眾生，當信是稱讚不可思議功德，一切諸佛所護念經。」

「舍利弗！西方世界有：無量壽佛、無量相佛、無量幢佛、大光佛、大明佛、寶相佛、淨光佛，如是等恒河沙數諸佛，各於其國出廣長舌相，徧覆三千大千世界，說誠實言：汝等眾生，當信是稱讚不可思議功德，一切諸佛所護念經。」

「舍利弗！北方世界有：燄肩佛、最勝音佛、難沮佛、日生佛、網明佛，如是等恒河沙數諸佛，各於其國，出廣長舌相，徧覆三千大千世界，說誠實言：汝等眾生，當信是稱讚不可思議功德，一切諸佛所護念經。」

「舍利弗！下方世界有：師子佛、名聞佛、名光佛、達摩佛、法幢佛、持法佛，如是等恒河沙數諸佛，各於其國，出廣長舌相，徧覆三千大千世界，說誠實言：汝等眾生，當信是稱讚不可思議功德，一切諸佛所護念經。」

「舍利弗！上方世界有：梵音佛、宿王佛、香上佛、香光佛、大燄肩佛、雜色寶華嚴身佛、娑羅樹王佛、寶華德佛、見一切義佛、如須彌山佛，如是等恒河沙數諸佛，各於其國，出廣長舌相，徧覆三千大千世界，說誠實言：汝等眾生，當信是稱讚不可思議功德，一切諸佛所護念經。」

「舍利弗！於汝意云何，何故名爲一切諸佛所護念經？舍利弗！若有善男子、善女人，聞是經受持者；及聞諸佛名者，是諸善男子、善女人，皆爲一切諸佛之所護念，皆得不退轉於阿耨多羅三藐三菩提。是故；舍利弗！汝等皆當信受我語，及諸佛所說。」

「舍利弗！若有人已發願、今發願、當發願，欲生阿彌陀佛國者；是諸人等，皆得不退轉於阿耨多羅三藐三菩提，於彼國土，若已生、若今生、若當生。是故；舍利弗！諸善男子、善女人，若有信者，應當發願，生彼國土。」

「舍利弗！如我今者稱讚諸佛不可思議功德。彼諸佛等，亦稱讚我不可思議功德，而作是言：釋迦牟尼佛能爲甚難希有之事，能於娑婆國土、五濁惡世─劫濁、見濁、煩惱濁、眾生濁、命濁中，得阿耨多羅三藐三菩提，爲諸眾生說是一切世間難信之法。舍利弗！當知我於五濁惡世，行此難事，得阿耨多羅三藐三菩提，爲一切世間說此難信之法，是爲甚難。」

佛說此經已；舍利弗及諸比丘、一切世間天、人、阿修羅等，聞佛所說，歡喜信受，作禮而去。

The Amitabha Sutra as Taught by the Buddha

Homage to Amitabha Buddha,
    Receiver and Guide of the Western Paradise.
Homage to Amitabha Buddha,
    Receiver and Guide of the Western Paradise.
Homage to Amitabha Buddha,
    Receiver and Guide of the Western Paradise.

The Amitabha Sutra as Taught by the Buddha.

[Translated from Sanskrit to Chinese by Tripitaka Master Kumarajiva of the Yao Qin Dynasty in 5th century CE. Translated from Chinese to English by Wong Kiew Kit of Malaysia in 20th century CE.]

Thus have I heard. Once, the Buddha was at Anathapindika Park of Jeta Grove in the country of Sravasti, with a great following of 1,250 monks, who were all great Arahants, known and recognized by the public. Among them were the Venerable Sariputra, Maudgalyayana, Mahakasyapa, Mahakatyayana, Mahakaustila, Revata, Suddhipanthaka, Nanda, Ananda, Rahula, Gavampati, Pindola-Bharahaga, Kalodayi, Mahakapphina, Vakkula, Aniruddha, and other great disciples; and great Bodhisattvas and Mahasattvas, such as Manjusri, the Prince of the Dharma, Bodhisattva Ajita, Bodhisattva Gandhahasti, Bodhisattva Nityodyukta, and other great Bodhisattvas; and also Sakradeva Indra and countless heavenly beings.

At that time the Buddha told the Venerable Sariputra: passing over ten thousand billions of Buddha-lands to our west is a world known as Sukhavati, where a Buddha called Amitabha teaches the Dharma.

Sariputra, why is this world called Sukhavati or Eternal Bliss? It is because the inhabitants of this world not only have no suffering, but also have boundless bliss. Thus, it is named Sukhavati or Eternal Bliss.

Then, Sariputra, this Paradise of Eternal Bliss is surrounded by seven tiers of ornamental railings, seven curtains of netted tapestries, and seven rows of tress. All these are made of four treasures. Thus, this world is called Eternal Bliss.

Sariputra, in this Paradise of Eternal Bliss there are ponds of seven treasures, filled with waters of eight merits. The bottoms of the ponds are purely covered with gold sand. On all sides the walks are made of gold, silver, lapis-lazuli and crystal. Above are built towers and pavilions, adorned with gold, silver, lapis-lazuli, crystal, beryl, red pearls and carnelian. In the ponds are lotus flowers as large as carriage wheels — green-colored with green radiance, yellow-colored with yellow radiance, red-colored with red radiance, white-colored with white radiance, subtle, wonderful, fragrant and pure. Oh Sariputra, thus is the Paradise of Eternal Bliss, brought to such a glorious state of magnificence through the merits of Amitabha Buddha.

Sariputra, celestial music is always heard in the air. Day and night for six times heavenly mandarava flowers with exquisite fragrance rain from the sky onto the ground of gold. Often at dawn the heavenly beings of this Pure Land receive with their robes these marvelous, beautiful mandarava flowers, and present them in reverence to ten million billion Buddhas of other worlds. At meal times, these heavenly beings return to the Western Paradise for their meals. Sariputra, such is this world, brought to so glorious a state of excellence through the merits of Amitabha Buddha.

Next, Sariputra, in the Western Paradise there are marvelous, multi-colored birds, like white cranes, peacocks, parrots, swans, jiva-jivas and the kalavindas. These birds sing six times days and night in melodious voices to proclaim doctrines like Five Roots, Five Powers, Seven Branches of Bodhi, and Eightfold Path. When the heavenly beings hear these voices, they will spontaneously think of the Buddha, the Dharma and the Sangha.

Sariputra, do not be mistaken that these birds are reborn here in the animal realm as the result of their sinful karma in their previous lives. Why is this so? There are no three evil realms of existence in this Pure Land. Sariputra, even the names of the evil realms are unknown here; how can there be products of the evil realms. These various birds are the creation of Amitabha Buddha as a means to dissipate the sounds of the Dharma so that the heavenly beings will cultivate towards enlightenment.

Sariputra, when breeze blows through the Western Paradise, the rows of precious trees and curtains of tapestries send out subtle, wondrous music, as if hundreds and thousands of heavenly orchestras are playing. When the beings hear the heavenly music, they spontaneously think of the Buddha, the Dharma and the Sangha. Sariputra, such is this Buddha-land, brought to so glorious a state of excellence through the merits of Amitabha Buddha.

Sariputra, what is your opinion? Why is this Buddha called Amitabha? Sariputra, the radiant light of this Buddha is boundless, illuminating all the lands of ten directions without any obstruction. Thus he is called Amitabha. Also, Sariputra, the lifespan of this Buddha as well as of the inhabitants of his Buddha-land is boundless, lasting for assamkhyeyas kalpas. So he is called Amitabha.

Sariputra, Amitabha Buddha has become a Buddha for ten kalpas. Besides, Sariputra, this Buddha has countless, limitless Sravaka-disciples, who are all Arahants, and their number is beyond computation. In the same way, there are countless, limitless Bodhisattvas. Thus, Sariputra, is this Buddha-land, brought to so glorious a state of excellence through the merits of Amitabha Buddha.

Next, Sariputra, all the sentient beings in this Western Paradise of Eternal Bliss are Avarvartyas, among them are numerous Ekajati-Pratibuddhas. There are so many of them that their number is beyond computation, but may be described as immeasurable, limitless assamkhyeyas kalpas.

Sariputra, sentient beings who have heard about this teaching, should make a vow, vow to be reborn in this Western Paradise. Wherefore? To be in the company of advanced, virtuous beings. Sariputra, in order to be born there, one must not lack good spiritual roots and blessings from good karma.

Sariputra, if a virtuous man or a virtuous woman, hearing this teaching about Amitabha Buddha, recites the Buddha's name for one day, or two days, or three days, or four days, or five days, or six days, or seven days, recites whole-heartedly without any other thoughts, when this person is about to pass away in his or her physical life, Amitabha Buddha and other holy beings will appear before him or her. At the time of death, if his or her mind is free from mundane distraction, this person will be reborn in Amitabha's Paradise of Eternal Bliss.

Sariputra, as I see the great benefit of this teaching, I therefore preach it. If sentient beings hear of this teaching, they should make a vow to be reborn in this Western Paradise.

Sariputra, as I now praise and appreciate the incredible merits of Amitabha Buddha, and the benefits of winning rebirth in his Pure Land, in the East there are Askhobhya Buddha, Merudhavaju Buddha, Mahameru Buddha, Meruprabhasa Buddha, Manjudhvaja Buddha, and other Buddhas as immeasurable as the sands of the River Ganges, each in their respective Buddha-land, revealing the characteristics of their long, wide tongue, spreading the teaching over the countless worlds in the myriad galaxies, proclaiming truthfully thus: May all sentient beings have faith in this Sutra which glorifies the incredible merits of Amitabha Buddha, and which is guarded and meditated by all Buddhas.

Sariputra, in world systems in the South there are Chandra-Suryapradipa Buddha, Yasahprabha Buddha, Maharchiskandha Buddha, Merupradipa Buddha, Anantavirya Buddha, and other Buddhas as immeasurable as the sands of the River Ganges, each in their respective Buddha-land, revealing the characteristics of their long, wide tongue, spreading the teaching over countless worlds in the myriad galaxies, proclaiming truthfully thus: May all sentient beings have faith in this Sutra which glorifies the incredible merits of Amitabha Buddha, and which is guarded and meditated by all Buddhas.

In world systems in the West, there are Amitabha Buddha, Amitaskandha Buddha, Amitadhvaja Buddha, Mahaprabha Buddha, Mahnyata Buddha, Maharatnaketu Buddha, Suddharasmiprahba Buddha, and other Buddhas as immeasurable as the sands of the River Ganges, each in their respective Buddha-land, revealing the characteristics of their long, wide tongue, spreading the teaching over countless worlds in the myriad galaxies, proclaiming truthfully thus: May all sentient beings have faith in this Sutra which glorifies the incredible merits of Amitabha Buddha, and which is guarded and meditated by all Buddhas.

In world systems in the North, there are Archiskandha Buddha, Vaisvanaranirghosa Buddha, Dushpradharsha Buddha, Adityasambhava Buddha, Jalenipradha Buddha, and other Buddhas as immeasurable as the sands of the River Ganges, each in their respective Buddha-land, revealing the characteristics of their long, wide tongue, spreading the teaching over countless worlds in the myriad galaxies, proclaiming truthfully thus: May all sentient beings have faith in this Sutra which glorifies the incredible merits of Amitabha Buddha, and which is guarded and meditated by all Buddhas.

Sariputra, in the Nadir there are Simha Buddha, Yasas Buddha, Yasasprabhava Buddha, Dharma Buddha, Dharmadhvaja Buddha, Dharmadhara Buddha, and other Buddhas as immeasurable as the sands of the River Ganges, each in their respective Buddha-land, revealing the characteristics of their long, wide tongue, spreading the teaching over countless worlds in the myriad galaxies, proclaiming truthfully thus: May all sentient beings have faith in this Sutra which glorifies the incredible merits of Amitabha Buddha, and which is guarded and meditated by all Buddhas.

Sariputra, in the Zenith there are Brahmaghosha Buddha, Nakshatraraja Buddha, Gandhatama Buddha, Grandhaprabhasa Buddha, Maharchiskandha Buddha, Ratnakusumasampushpitagtra Buddha, Salendraraja Buddha, Ratnapalasri Buddha, Saruarthadarsa Buddha, Semerukalpa Buddha, and other Buddhas as immeasurable as the sands of the River Ganges, each in their respective Buddha-land, revealing the characteristics of their long, wide tongue, spreading the teaching over countless worlds in the myriad galaxies, proclaiming truthfully thus: May all sentient beings have faith in this Sutra which glorifies the incredible merits of Amitabha Buddha, and which is guarded and meditated by all Buddhas.

Sariputra, why do you think this Sutra is named "The Sutra that is Protected and Meditated by All Buddhas"?

Sariputra, it is because if there are virtuous men and virtuous women who hear this Sutra, accept its teaching and practice it, and hear the names of the Buddhas just mentioned, they will be protected and remembered by the Buddhas, and will never retreat from attaining Anuttara-Samyak-Sambodhi, or the supreme perfect wisdom.

Thus, Sariputra, you all should belief in and accept what I and all other Buddhas have said.

Sariputra, if sentient beings have made their vows, or are making their vows, or will make their vows to be reborn in the Buddha-land of Amitabha, they will not retreat from the attainment of Anuttara-Samyak-Sambodhi, and will have been reborn, are being reborn, or will be reborn in this Buddha-land.

Thus, Sariputra, those virtuous men and virtuous women who believe in the teaching of this Sutra, must made a vow to be reborn in the Western Paradise of Eternal Bliss.

Sariputra, as I now glorify the incredible merits of all Buddhas, they, too, glorify mine, saying: Sakyamuni Buddha has accomplished such a difficult and rare task; has accomplished in this Saha world of five defilements — the defilements of time, perverse views, passions, sentient beings, and samsara — the attainment of Anuttara-Samyak-Sambodhi, and the teaching which sentient beings find hard to belief. Sariputra, you should understand that in this Saha world of defilements, to accomplish Anuttara-Samyak-Sambodhi, and to teach all beings such an incredible doctrine are indeed very difficult.

Having listened to this sutra, Sariputra and the monks, and all beings, like gods, humans, and spirits, were very happy to accept and practice this teaching of the Buddha. They paid homage to the Buddha, and then departed.

This is the Amitabha Sutra as taught by the Buddha

Homage to Amitabha Buddha,
    Receiver and Guide of the Western Paradise.
Homage to Amitabha Buddha,
    Receiver and Guide of the Western Paradise.
Homage to Amitabha Buddha,
    Receiver and Guide of the Western Paradise.

May the merits accredited from the recitation of this sutra
    Be transferred to all sentient beings
So that all who have vowed to go to the Western Paradise
    Will be reborn in Amitabha's Pure Land.

CULTIVATION FOR SUKHAVATI

(Vow, Amitabha Recitation and Transfer of Merits)

Paying homage to the compassionate Buddha
I vow to cultivate for spiritual growth
Transferring merits to all sentient beings
To repay four kinds of gratitude I owe
And fulfill the transference in three folds
May all sentient beings in the dharma realm
Attain perfect wisdom as vowed in this psalm

Requirements for Going to Sukhavati

Amitabha Buddha has promised that any being can be reborn in Sukhavati, the Western Paradise of Eternal Bliss created by him, if the being fulfills the following three conditions:

1. Have faith that Sukhavati exists,
2. Make a vow to be reborn there,
3. Sincerely and with a one-pointed mind recite his name at least ten times, or practice any other appropriate cultivation.

The various cultivation methods to go to Sukhavati may be conveniently classified into three kinds:

1. Reciting Amitabha's name.
2. Reciting the Amitabha Sutra, the Amitayus Sutra or the Meditation on Amitayus Sutra.
3. Visualization through meditation.

The easiest, and therefore the most popular, is reciting Amitabha's name. Various ways to do so are described in this chapter.

It is recommendable to start the recitation of Amitabha's name with reaffirming the vow, and conclude with a transfer of merits to others or a focus of merits for oneself contributing to his cultivation to go to Sukhavati.

However, especially during informal recitation, it is permissible just to recite the Buddha's name.

Vows to be Reborn in Sukhavati

You can formulate your own words in making your vow. Some examples of such vows composed by past masters and popularly used by many devotees are also given below. It is very important that your vow must be made in sincerity and with a one-pointed mind.

Mahayana Buddhism teaches that we work not only for our own enlightenment but also the enlightenment of others. If we want rebirth in the Western Paradise, we will also help others with similar intention to be reborn there too. Thus, at the conclusion of each cultivation practice, we transfer our merits to others to help them in this direction, or in other ways that will bring peace and happiness to them. Like your vow, you can formulate your own transfer of merits, but some examples formulated by masters and popularly used by many devotees are also given in this chapter.

The following vows, in verse as well as in prose, were taught by the great Pure Land master Venerable Lian Chi, quoted in Venerable Yin Guang's book, *Explanation of Amitabha Sutra.*

Homage to the Great Teacher, Receiver and Guide
   To the Western Paradise of the blissful.
With this great vow to be reborn in the Buddhaland
   May I be accepted by the Great Merciful.

I, so and so, am indebted to four kinds of gratitude and wander in the three planes of existence. Because sentient beings of the dharma realm seek from various Buddhas, the one and unsurpassed way of wisdom, I devotedly and with a one-pointed mind specially recite the infinite virtuous name of Amitabha Buddha, aiming to be reborn in the Pure Land.

Also, because of my heavy karmic burden but little merits, deep hindrances but shallow wisdom, I can be easily deluded by miscellaneous thoughts; it may be difficult for me to attain the virtue of purity. Now before the Buddha, prostrating on all five points of my body, from the depth of my heart, I sincerely repent for all the sins I have done in the past. All sentient beings and I from countless aeons till now have been deluded from our original pure heart. From greed, anger and doubt, we build up our three kinds of karma, and for infinite time and limitless space have created all sorts of karma for which I now vow to eliminate.

From today onwards I vow deeply and greatly to avoid all evil; vow not to create any more bad karma; vow to cultivate the way of the sage; vow never to retrogress; vow to attain enlightenment; vow to save all sentient beings.

(Note: Four kinds of gratitude refer to gratitude towards the Buddha, towards parents, towards the place of inhabitance, and towards all sentient beings whose efforts sustains his life. Three planes of existence are the planes of desire, of form and of non-form. Dharma realm and "original pure heart" means the Supreme Reality or the Ultimate Truth. Three kinds of karma are that of thought, words and deeds. It is significant to note that for the aspirant making this vow, going to Amitabha's Pure Land is not the end itself; it is a means for further cultivation to attain the one and unsurpassed way, i.e. enlightenment or Buddhahood.)

May the compassionate power of Amitabha Buddha's vows cause me to be awakened; when I am weak, arouse me; when strengthened, motivate me. I vow that in my meditation, or in my sleep, I will see Amitabha Buddha in his golden light, that I will experience the precious, majestic land of Amitabha Buddha. May Amitabha Buddha bless me on my head with his fragrant dew, shine on me with his radiant light, touch me on my head and protect me with his dress, so that my hindrances will be eliminated, my spiritual roots developed, my delusion dispersed. Instantly ignorance is destroyed, the perfect, marvelous heart of wisdom is awakened, and the light of ultimate reality is revealed in front of me.

When the time comes for completing this physical life, I will know beforehand. There will be no illness and no suffering at all; no trace of greed or delusion; all roots are liberated; the right thought is clear; leaving peacefully, like entering meditation. Amitabha Buddha, Guan Yin, Shi Zhi and other holy sages radiate their light to welcome me. I raise my hands to accept. Buildings and banners, marvelous fragrance and heavenly music, holy scenes of the Western Paradise appear before me, so that all sentient beings, seeing and hearing all these, are happy and full of praises, and awaken their heart towards bodhi.

At that time I will be taken by the diamond seat, following the Buddha, in the time of flipping a finger, and be reborn in the Land of Eternal Bliss, in the pond of seven precious gems, amidst glorious lotus flowers. When the lotus flower blossoms, I see the Buddha, see numerous Bodhisattvas, hear the marvelous sound of dharma, and realize that all dharmas are originally without birth and without death. I will personally receive the Buddha's teaching. After receiving the teaching, my three bodies, four wisdoms, five levels of seeing, six classes of miraculous abilities, boundless methods of dharnanis, and all forms of merits are understood and attained.

Then I will not remain in this Land of Peace and Cultivation, but return to the Saha world, manifest into countless bodies, spread over all directions, using incredible, spontaneous, marvelous powers and various expedient means to save and liberate sentient beings to free themselves from miscellaneous pollution, to return to the pure heart, and altogether be reborn in the Western Paradise and enter the stage of never retrogress in spiritual cultivation.

Thus is my great vow. The world is boundless, sentient beings are endless, karmic effect and delusion are limitless, so my vow is infinite.

(Note: Like in the previous vow, going to the Western Paradise is a means, not an end. But unlike in the previous vow where the aspirant aims at Buddhahood, the aspirant here goes to Western Paradise for training, to be equipped with incredible miraculous powers so that he can come back as a Bodhisattva to our world of suffering to help others. He knows that as sentient beings are endless, his great vow to help others is therefore infinite. Notice that when seeking confirmation of Amitabha's authenticity, he is not contented with just a general presence of Amitabha, but is specific, like asking to be flooded by Amitabha's golden radiance and touched on the head by Amitabha's hand. To be transported to the Western Paradise in a diamond seat is to be reborn at the highest level, the level of Bodhisattvas. The three bodies are spiritual body, reward body and transformational body. Four wisdoms and five levels of seeing refer to different developmental stages. Land of Peace and Cultivation is another name for Sukhavati.)

Paying homage to the compassionate Buddha
I vow to cultivate for spiritual growth
Transferring merits to all sentient beings
To repay four kinds of gratitude I owe
And fulfill the transference in three folds
May all sentient beings in the dharma realm
Attain perfect wisdom as vowed in this psalm

(Note: The Mahayana philosophy of universal salvation is clearly seen in this vow. The aspirant is concerned not with his personal enlightenment, but with the enlightenment of all sentient beings. He prays that the merits that he has acquired will be transferred to all sentient beings as a form of gratitude to repay his four kinds of debt to the Buddha, his parents, his country and all sentient beings whose effort has in any way made it possible for him to be alive. There are three forms of merit transfer: from self to others, from cause to effect, and events to principles.)

Recitation Methods

The recitation or chanting of Amitabha Buddha's name may be carried out in Sanskrit, or in any languages. In Sanskrit, the recitation is:

Namo Amitabha Buddha.

In English, it is:

Homage to Amitabha Buddha.

In Chinese:

Nan Mo A Mi Tuo Fo.

In Japanese:

Namu Amida Butsu.

In Vietnanese:

Nammo A-Di-Da Phat.

Whatever is the language used, the recitation must be carried out in sincerity and with a one-pointed mind. There must be no other thoughts. The recitation may range from a few times to a few thousand times or more. Amitabha Buddha's name is often chanted rhythmically, and sometimes with music. There are many methods of recitation with variations to suit individual needs; the following are just some examples. Generally, better results are obtained if you stick to one chosen method, instead of changing methods now and then. You may, within reasons, modify any procedure to suit your needs, or devise your own method.

1. Recitation with Visual or Mental Focus.
Kneel, stand or sit cross-legged before an image of Amitabha Buddha and focus your eyes on the image. Or you may close your eyes and visualize Amitabha Buddha clearly in your mind. Whenever you visualization blurs away, open your eyes to focus on the image again. Simultaneously recite "Homage to Amitabha Buddha" (or its equivalent in any language) clearly aloud, softly or silently, and listen to each syllable attentively with your ears or mind.

2. Recitation with Visualization of Sukhavati.
Assume any suitable position. You may kneel before an image of Amitabha Buddha, or lie comfortably on your bed. Close your eyes and gently focus on your breathing for a short while. Then visualize the conditions in or environment of Sukhavati, like what is described in the Amitabha Sutra. Recite Amitabha Buddha's name while gently holding the vision in your mind.

3. Recitation with Rosary.
Decide on the number of times of recitation. Say a few hundred or thousand times. Make a mark on your rosary. Kneel, stand or sit cross-legged in front of an image of Amitabha Buddha. If an image is not available, face the west. Move a bead for each recitation of the Buddha's name. When your legs are tired, circumambulate in a clockwise direction while reciting and moving the beads. Complete when you reach the mark in the rosary.

4. Continuous Recitation.
Recite, or chant musically, "Homage to Amitabha Buddha" continuously while you are engaged in some other activities, such as traveling in a train, waiting for a friend, or working in your garden. You may recite aloud, softly or silently, but you must recite clearly and without any hurry.

4. Four Steps One Recitation.
This is a simple method that you can use when you go for a walk, or combine the recitation with walking meditation. Recite "Namo Amitabha Buddha" (or its equivalent in any language) once every four steps. You can of course choose another number of steps to suit your situation, but it is best to keep to the same number of steps to become habitual so that without having to worry about the mechanics of recitation, you can recite with a one-pointed mind.

5. One Breath, One Recitation.

Recite "Namo Amitabha Buddha" once for each time you breath. You may recite while breathing in, or while breathing out; or part of the phrase while breathing in and the remaining part while breathing out. Keep to the same procedure, once you have found which one suits you best. You may use this method informally while doing something else, or formally in front of the Buddha's image. You may also use it in conjunction with meditation.

6. Ten-Recitation Method.

If there is an image of Amitabha Buddha, make three prostrations to the Buddha. If an image is not available, make one prostration, or even just a deep bow, towards the direction of the west. Then in one breath, recite "Namo Amitabha Buddha" (in any language) continuously. For those whose breathing is deep and long, they may recite ten, twenty or more times; those whose breath is short, may recite only a few times. Altogether recite in ten breaths. Next, direct the blessings to yourself or transfer them to others. Complete with three prostrations to the Buddha image, or one prostration or a deep bow to the west.

7. Recitation in Meditation.

Sit in a double-lotus or single-lotus position. Close or half-close your eyes gently. Clear your mind of all thoughts. Recite Amitabha Buddha's name, immersing your total consciousness into the recitation. Soon you will be in deep meditation. This approach, known as Zen-Amitabha approach, is often used by Zen practitioners besides Pure Land devotees, and may lead not only to Sukhavati but to nirvana itself.

8. Recitation with Investigation

Sit in a double-lotus or single-lotus position. Chant "Namo Amitabha Buddha" as a means to go into meditation. When your mind is one-pointed or concentrated, contemplate on the meaning of "Namo", "Amitabha" and "Buddha" separately, then together as one phrase. Investigate, for example, why are you paying homage to Amitabha; who or what is the "you" that is paying homage; is Amitabha real, and how do you know he is real; if not, why are you paying homage to him; how or what is the Buddha, and how do you become one.

9. Enlightenment through Sound.

Go into deep meditation. Then chant "Namo Amitabha Buddha", or praising the Buddha in any language, aloud or in your heart. Listen intensely to the every sound. Let every sound resonates inside you. At the advanced stage, you will find that your physical body has disappeared; you have become the sound vibration. Although most people depend on sight, sound is also a very important medium for attaining enlightenment. The great compassionate Avalokitesvara Bodhisattva attained his enlightenment through sound.

Transfer of Merits

After acquiring blessings from a meritorious deed, like reciting a sutra, helping another person or donating money to a charitable organization, you may like to direct the merits to someone (including yourself) or to a particular cause. The merits will not be wasted even if you have not directed it, but the effect will be enhanced if you give the merits some focus. As reciting or chanting Amitabha Buddha's name is a very meritorious deed, you may like to focus the blessing towards your effort to be reborn in Sukhavati, or transfer the merits to others.

There is no need for any elaborate ritual; you can direct your blessings by saying a simple phrase or by focusing your mind. After you have done a good deed, for example, you can focus your blessings by saying to yourself, "May the merit from this kind deed add to my blessings so that I will always be safe and peaceful." Or you may transfer the merit to someone, irrespective of whether he is living or has passed away, by saying or thinking to yourself, "May this merit contribute to John's recovery from his illness", or "May Mary's soul find peace and happiness in another world".

Here the term "merits" and "blessings" are used loosely, and are generally interchangeable. In some situations, especially in Zen Buddhism, a distinction is made between "merits" and "blessings". Merits refer to progress towards nirvana, whereas blessings refer to progress towards rebirth in heaven. Merits are acquired through wisdom, such as in meditation, whereas blessings are acquired through good thoughts, words and deeds, such as helping others. The classical example is when Emperor Liang Wu Di, who had done numerous kind deeds in the spread of Buddhism, asked whether he had any merits. The great master Bodhidharma answered "No!" If you yourself gain spiritual wisdom while reciting a sutra, you gain merits; when others benefit from your sutra recitation, you gain blessings.

The following are examples of verse and prose often used by aspirants in their focusing or transfer of merits or blessings. You may find many expressions in the Transfer of Merits similar to those in the Vow. This is because these two aspects are closely related.

May the merits from this recitation
Glorify the magnificence of the Buddha's Pure Land
Repaying four kinds of gratitude above
Helping three realms of suffering below
May whoever sees or hears of this teaching
Understand and awaken his bodhi heart
Making the best use of our reward bodies
May all be reborn in the Land of Eternal Bliss
Buddhas of ten directions and three times
The foremost is Amitabha Buddha
Saving sentient beings in nine classes
His glories and virtues are boundless
Now I give my life to this noble cause
I deeply repent for all sins I have done
To all blessed and virtuous beings
I sincerely transfer my merits
May all who recite the Buddha's name
Experience the manifestation of their cultivation
Be reborn in the Western Land
Attain wisdom in front of their eyes
Those who see and hear this effort
Together be reborn in the Land of Eternal Bliss
Seeing the Buddha and overcoming life and death
As what the Buddha has vowed to save
Limitless delusion will be destroyed
Boundless spiritual means I cultivate
I vow to save all sentient beings
Ultimately attain the Buddha way

We disciples are now ordinary people undergoing endless cycles of life and death. Heavy with karmic burden, we wander endlessly in the six realms of existence, enduring inexplicable suffering. Now we have the rare opportunity to meet knowledgeable friends, and learn about reciting Amitabha Buddha's name. We wish that all our merits be channeled to the recitation with a one-pointed mind, so that we will be reborn in Amitabha Buddha's Pure Land. May the Buddha in his great compassion have mercy on us and accept us. We disciples have no knowledge of the radiant, beautiful characteristics of the Buddha's body. May the Buddha manifest to let us see, and also see Guan Yin, Shi Zhi and other Bodhisattvas in the Paradise, pure, magnificent and dignified, radiant with wonderful characteristics. May we see Amitabha Buddha.

With all my heart, I give my life to this noble cultivation. May Amitabha Buddha of the Paradise of Eternal Bliss flood me with the radiance of his purity, and save me with his great compassion. Now I have right understanding, recite the Tathagata's name, practice the Bodhi way, seeking rebirth in the Pure Land.

In the past the Buddha made this fundamental vow: If there are sentient beings wishing to be reborn in my Land, make a vow, have faith and recite my name ten times, if they are not thus reborn, I will not accept Buddhahood. Thus is the cause and effect of reciting the Buddha's name, enabling us to enter the sea of the Tathagata's great vow, with the help of the Buddha's compassionate power, miscellaneous sinful effect will be eliminated, good spiritual roots will develop, when the time comes for leaving this world, I will know, without illness and suffering, without greedy attachment, with a determined will, like entering deep meditation, the Buddha and his sacred group, holding golden lotus seats in their hands, come to receive me.

In just one thought, I will be reborn in the Land of Eternal Bliss. When the lotus flower opens, I will see the Buddha, listen to his teaching, awaken the Buddha wisdom, save all sentient beings, fulfilling the Bodhisattva vow. Homage to all Buddhas of the ten directions and the three time dimensions. Homage to all Bodhisattvas and Mahasattvas. Homage to the great wisdom that ferries us to the shore of enlightenment.

SETTLING DOUBTS

(Some Common Questions and their Answers)

Sharing with others the wonderful benefits of the teaching presented in this book is one way of manifesting the compassionate heart.

Can One Really Go to Heaven?

Despite all that has been written in this book, some people may still be doubtful and ask, "Is it really true that by reciting the name of Amitabha Buddha one can go to heaven?" Indeed the method suggested in this book is so comparatively simple, although readers who have read this far will most probably agree that the philosophy behind is profound, that many people may find it too good to be true.

Doubt is one of the main hurdles that hamper spiritual progress. The Buddha refers to doubt as one of the "three poisons" causing delusion, the other two being greed and anger.

Of course, it is never implied that one should accept any teaching blindly; it is a basic Buddhist tenet that one should accept the Buddhist teaching only after he has assessed it to the best of his understanding and experience. It is also important to remember that the teaching described in this book is not my idea or invention; the wisdom in the teaching is far, far beyond what I could even dare to dream of. This is certainly not modesty. It is simply the truth. I merely report what the Buddha, considered by many as the greatest teachers amongst men and gods, has taught; and I attempt to make the profound teaching easier for modern readers by explaining with illustrations what great masters throughout the ages have provided, and expressing in an imagery and vocabulary that western readers can readily understand.

That anyone who follows the teaching described in this book can go to Sukhavati, the Western Paradise, is taught by the Buddha out of his boundless compassion to help suffering beings in samsara, and this teaching has been attested and found valid by some of the greatest minds in human history. Venerable Yin Guang, one of the most respected contemporary Mahayana masters who is now in Sukhavati, told Venerable Kuan Jing, who chose to come back to our Saha world to help others:

When you have returned to the human realm, convey to all fellow cultivators that if they regard discipline as teacher, conscientiously practice moral purity, recite Amitabha Buddha's name whole heartedly, have faith, vow and practice, there is no doubt whatsoever that they shall certainly be reborn in Sukhavati.

Venerable Yuan Yin explained that if Suddhipanthaka, who was considered to be stupid, could attain enlightenment by following his breathing, it would be easier for anyone with some common sense to attain rebirth in Sukhavati by reciting Amitabha Buddha's name, because not only is rebirth in heaven easier than enlightenment, but Amitabha Buddha's name is so much more holy and powerful in spiritual cultivation than mere breathing. Suddhipanthaka was so slow in learning that he could not remember even a line from the sutra. Sakyamuni Buddha, who always used the appropriate expedient means according to the nature and needs of different followers, told Suddhipanthaka to focus his mind on the word "sweep" each time he swept the floor. Soon his mind was clear of all thoughts. Then the Buddha asked him to count his breathing in sets of tens, focusing only on his breathing in. In this way Suddhipanthaka attained nirvana.

The method to go to heaven by reciting Amitabha Buddha's name is also taught by Sakyamuni Buddha. Finding that many people due to their developmental stage could not attain nirvana in their present life because of the "five defilements in the Saha world" (please see Passage 16, Chapter 10), the Buddha in his great compassion to save these people has taught this comparatively easier method so that while enjoying heavenly bliss they can continue their spiritual cultivation in Sukhavati where the five defilements are absent, and eventually attain nirvana.

Is Reciting Amitabha's Name Spiritual Cultivation?

Because they have not freed themselves from stereotyped thinking, some people have a fixed, narrow concept of what constitutes spiritual cultivation, often insisting that their method is the only way. Some common cultivation means, independently claimed by their followers as the only way, include submitting totally to the grace of the Supreme Divine Being, performing sacred rituals, devotional prayers, recitation of scriptures, and meditation.

Mahayana Buddhists belief that while the spiritual goal is one, the ways to the goal are countless, and these ways are called expedient means, or *upayas* in Sanskrit, and *fang bian* in Chinese. Figuratively Mahayanists say that there are 84,000 expedient means to suit the different needs and nature of spiritual aspirants.

All the means of spiritual cultivation practiced by various religions as mentioned in the above paragraph are accepted by Mahayanists. In fact, all these means are practiced in the Pure Land School of Buddhism: the unfaltering faith in the grace of Amitabha Buddha, prostration to Buddhas and Bodhisattvas as a form of ritual, chanting of mantras and gathas as devotional prayers, recitation of the Amitabha and other sutras, and one-pointed mindfulness as meditation.

However, some Buddhists, especially those from the Theravada tradition, do not consider the practices of the Pure Land School as Buddhist spiritual cultivation, because they belief that the orthodox way of Buddhism towards nirvana is through discipline, meditation and wisdom as described in the Noble Eightfold Path.

For a typical Theravadin, spiritual cultivation generally means having the wisdom to realize that living in samsara is suffering, cultivating discipline to overcome greed, anger and lust, and practicing meditation to experience nirvana directly. Moreover, cultivating to go to heaven, instead of striving for nirvana, is "unBuddhist" according to Theravada philosophy, which adamantly declares that the soul does not exist, and therefore going to heaven is irrelevant (although, interestingly, authoritative Theravada scriptures which many ordinary followers may be unaware, describe various gods and heavens.)

Mahayanists believe that the Theravada approach is excellent, but they also stress that it is only one of numerous expedient means, and that it is applicable to only a small minority who have reached a high spiritual level where the necessary meditation practice can be undertaken.

Even among Theravada followers, the great majority of them can only content themselves with cultivating discipline, hoping that, despite their disbelief in the soul or self, in their future reincarnations they may become monks to further their spiritual training.

According to Mahayana philosophy, this hope of the great majority is very slim, because while they are being tossed about in this sea of samsara, wandering in the endless cycles of six realms, they are constantly distracted by various defilements. Mahayanists therefore employ many expedient means to overcome this setback, and one effective way is by reciting Amitabha Buddha's name.

Some critics say that reciting the Buddha's name is not spiritual cultivation; at its best, it is just a form of devotion, which may act as a reminder for followers to be religious minded. Such thinking shows a superficial understanding, or a lack of a deeper appreciation of the Amitabha philosophy and practice.

The three aspects of spiritual cultivation involve what are known in Buddhism as "body, mouth, and mind", which are better understood in English as "deeds, words and thoughts". These three aspects generate karma, thus perpetuating samsara.

In other words, what a person thinks, says and does will create an endless matrix of cause and effect with unlimited repercussion, which directly affects the present and future lives of this person. For example, if he is constantly filled with fear for survival, always complains of what a donkey life he has, and does nothing more than struggling in the mad rat race, he will have a good chance of being reborn as an animal in his next life.

As long as a person has thoughts, words and deeds — for good or for bad — he generates karma, and he will forever remain in the cycle of birth and rebirth. If his thoughts, words and deeds are noble, he will be reborn in noble conditions; if they are evil, his resultant station will be evil. This is a great karmic law. The whole purpose of the Eightfold Path — right understanding, right thought, right speech, right conduct, right livelihood, right effort, right mindfulness and right concentration — is concerned with cultivating right thoughts, words and deeds, so as to improve the followers' karma and then ultimately to transcend their karma to attain nirvana.

When a devotee practices Amitabha recitation, he does the same thing in a simpler but not necessarily less effective way; he involves himself in the cultivation of right thoughts, words and deeds. When the devotee, with unwavering faith and after making a great vow to be reborn in Sukhavati, recites the name of Amitabha Buddha with a one-pointed mind, every sound comes from his heart, is enunciated from his mouth and perceived by his ears. His total involvement is such that every syllable and all syllables permeate his whole being, with every recitation his mind recites as his mouth recites, his mind hears as his ears hear, each recitation follows each other recitation without hindrance and without discontinuity, so that his thoughts, words and deeds are all dissolved into one unity.

Hence he attains a very deep level of meditation whereby "although the Buddha is in his mind, there is no mind outside the Buddha." This is cultivation of thought. Indeed when an aspirant has reached this level of cultivation, he can attain not only rebirth in heaven but nirvana itself.

Before a serious devotee practices his Amitabha recitation, he cleanses his mouth not only physically but also spiritually by chanting some appropriate mantras. He venerates Amitabha Buddha's name deeply, making sure that it would not be desecrated by a polluted mouth that has spoken anything squalid or defiled. Some masters have advised their followers that whenever they feel like talking ill of any people or saying anything improper, they should remind themselves that as reciters of Amitabha Buddha's name, they should never allow their mouths to be soiled. A Chinese saying advises, "Spend less time gossiping, more time reciting the Buddha's name." Thus, devotees of the Amitabha recitation method practice cultivation of speech conscientiously.

Similarly, devotees who habitually recite Amitabha Buddha's name, are very conscientious of their morality. As all deeds as well as words of a person are derived from thought, when his thought has been purified by the recitation of Amitabha Buddha's name, all his deeds as well as words are also sanctified.

A devotee whose thought is constantly thinking of cultivating to go to paradise, imbued with loving-kindness manifested by the Buddha, has no time or space in his mind for evil words or deeds. Teachers of the Pure Land School have a simple but effective way of teaching their followers to cultivate right conduct and right livelihood: they advise the followers that whenever there is even an inkling of doing anything evil, remind themselves that they are spiritual cultivators on the sure path to the Western Paradise, and therefore will not be so stupid as to undo years of cultivation just because of some moments of evil doing.

Teachers also emphasize that besides the devotional chanting of Amitabha Buddha's name, which is regarded as "principal cultivation" and which corresponds to "purifying the mind", cultivators must also practice "supportive cultivation", which involves "avoiding evil and doing good". Even if they cannot do good, they must at the very least avoid evil, the minimum requirement of which is to practice the well known five precepts of not killing, not stealing, not telling lies, not involving in sexual misconduct, and not drinking intoxicants.

Hence, the seemingly simple means of reciting Amitabha Buddha's name is an excellent cultivation method that can be practiced by anybody — old and young, male and female — anywhere — without the need of any elaborated preparation or procedure. This method not only assures the cultivator of going to heaven, but by purifying his thoughts, words and deeds, may also lead him directly to nirvana.

Can a Cultivator Know his Death in Advance?

Not only many advanced spiritual cultivators know when their physical bodies will die, some masters can even control their physical death! In the seventh month the great Zen master, Hui Neng (638-713), gathered his disciples and said, "In the eighth month I wish to leave this world. If you have any doubts please let me know so that I can remove them." Hearing this all his disciples except Shen Hui wept. The master continued,

> Young monk Shen Hui has attained detachment from the dualism of good and evil, and is neither affected by blame nor praise. Neither sorrow nor joy can trouble him. All the others have not reached this achievement. What have you been cultivating all these years in the monastery? For whom are you now weeping so sorrowfully? Are you worried that I do not know where I am going? I certainly know where I am going. If I do not know, then I would be unable to inform you of my going. You weep sorrowfully because you do not know where I am going; if you know where I am going, you will not weep. The Supreme Reality is ultimately without birth or death, without coming here or going away.

While explaining *Anapanasati*, or meditation by means of mindful breathing, the modern Thai Theravada teacher, Buddhadasa Bhikkhu, says, "through becoming well-versed in our practice of Anapanasati we become experts regarding the breath. We will know instantly whether we are going to die during this present breath or not. Then we can predict the final breath of our life."

A Mahayana monk, the Venerable Jing Kong, says that he has personally come across about twenty cases of cultivators who knew the time of their death. He provided the following two examples.

One day the Venerable Xiu Wu asked his fellow monks of the Pure Land School to provide him with some firewood and chant the Amitabha sutra to send him off. On appointed day, Xiu Wu sat in meditation in the courtyard of their monastery. The monks requested, "Venerable Xiu Wu, as you are leaving us, can you please leave behind a gatha for our guidance?" Xiu Wu replied, "I came from a poor laboring family, and I am not well versed in letters, but I will leave the following words from my own experience for remembrance: That which can be described but cannot be practiced, is not real wisdom." Soon Xiu Wu left his physical body for Sukhavati. The body remained intact, without any smell and without any gathering of flies. People were very surprised.

The second case occurred in 1935. Zheng Xi Bin of Jingdao in West China was a pious lay follower of the Pure Land School. One day he told his fellow cultivators to find him a room because he was going to leave. The house-owner who was also a lay follower of the Pure Land School, asked him, "Why do you want a room when you are leaving?"

The following are some of the reasons.

It is easy to recite the phrase, "Namo Amitabha Buddha" or its equivalent in any language. Even those who are illiterate or of low intelligence, do not have much difficulty remembering and reciting the name. There is no need to perform ceremonies or rituals, to enter retreats and meditation, to study scriptures or commentaries, to understand theories or philosophy. All the devotee has to do is to belief in Sukhavati, make a vow to be reborn there, and recite Amitabha's name wholeheartedly.

Why is Buddha-Recitation the Most Convenient?

This Buddha-recitation method of cultivation can be practiced anytime and anywhere. There is no need to enter a monastery, to seek a teacher, to renounce home life or change one's way of living. There is no age or sex limitation, no economic or social barrier. It can be practiced by the young or old, male or female, rich or poor, king or pauper.

Once an aspirant has set his heart to cultivate, there is no danger of retrogression in the Buddha-recitation method, because his progress is assured by the grace of Amitabha Buddha. According to the belief of the Pure Land School, when a devotee makes a vow to go to Sukhavati, a new lotus springs up in the Western Paradise; he will be reborn there through this lotus.

Spiritual progress in other schools is long and often hazardous, stretched over countless lifetimes with inexhaustible temptations and pitfalls. For example, Cao Tang Qing was a well-known Zen cultivator of the Song Dynasty. At his old age, in a moment of weakness, he was tempted by the pomp of the Prime Minister retiring to his home village, thus implanting in him a karmic force that resulted in his being reborn as a glamorous prime minister in his next life. Hence, his many lifetimes of cultivation was exchanged for a lifetime of honor and fame.

Another great convenience or advantage of the Buddha-recitation method is the feature of "carrying karma for rebirth in heaven." It means that even if a person has bad karma, which would normally result in a low-level rebirth, if he for some reasons is fortunate enough to learn of this Buddha-recitation method and practice it, he still can go to the Western Paradise to enjoy heavenly bliss. In prosaic terms, through the grace of Amitabha Buddha, he is given a reprieve, for which he has to cultivate harder and for a longer period to cleanse off his bad karma.

Is the Buddha-Recitation Method Mahayanist?

Because the principal aim of the Buddha-recitation method is to gain rebirth in the Western Paradise, some critics argue that it is Hinayanist rather than Mahayanist in spirit, because it is concerned with self-salvation rather than with saving others. This argument is invalid as it misses the deeper philosophy of this method. Masters of the Pure Land School have often emphasized that going to the Western Paradise is an expedient means, and is not the final aim which is attaining Buddhahood. In fact, this method was taught by Sakyamuni Buddha particularly to help those people who might not have any chance of salvation if not for the grace of Amitabha Buddha. Thus the very source of this method, in its function to help others achieve salvation, is indisputably Mahayanist in spirit.

Followers of the Buddha-recitation method, besides earnestly reciting the name of Amitabha for their own salvation, consider it their duty to help others to attain salvation too. Their typical vow is "May others hear and learn of this method, and may all be reborn in the Paradise of Eternal Bliss." Reciting Amitabha's name is "primary cultivation", helping others is "supportive cultivation".

Their sincere wish to share the wonderful benefits of their cultivation is reflected in their habitual expression: whenever they want to express greetings, gratitude, concern or other feelings, instead of saying "Good morning", "Thank you", "How are you?" or "Not at all", they say "Ami Tuo Fo" or "Amitabha Buddha", which means "May the blessings of Amitabha Buddha be with you".

A celebrated master, the Venerable Yuan Yin, advises that those who wish to fulfill the Bodhisattva Vow, which is the hallmark of Mahayana Buddhism, should practice the Buddha-recitation method, because it assures that they will be reborn in the Western Paradise where they can become Bodhisattvas. Then, when they are adequately prepared, they can choose to come back to our mundane world, or to any worlds or realms of existence including hells, where they can exercise their Bodhisattva powers to save other beings.

The path of the Bodhisattva calls for great dedication and sacrifice. It is easy to make the Bodhisattva Vow but extremely difficult to fulfill it. The following story about Sariputra, probably made up by Mahayanists to tease Hinayanists, suggests an indication of the difficulty.

The ideal of the Mahayanists is the Bodhisattva; whereas the ideal of the Hinayanists, who are today usually called Theravadins, is the Arahant. Bodhisattvas are concerned with saving others, whereas Arahants are concerned with seeking their own enlightenment. One day, Sariputra, reputed to be the wisest of the Arahants, wished to manifest the "Bodhisattva's heart". A deva or god wanted to test Sariputra, so he came down from heaven and pretended to wail profusely. When Sariputra saw the wailing man, the Arahant was filled with pity.

"What's the matter with you?" Sariputra asked the man.

"My aged mother is sick, and I could not obtain the medicine the doctor prescribed. My mother will surely die, Oh my dear mother!"

"What's the medicine the doctor prescribed?"

"The eye of a spiritual cultivator. But which cultivator is willing to give me his eye? Only a Bodhisattva could do that, as a Bodhisattva has vowed to answer all entreats."

Sariputra thought to himself, "I have wanted to be a Bodhisattva; I'll give him my eye to save his aged mother." Gallantly he plucked out his right eye and offered it to the wailing man.

"You fool! I want a left eye; why did you pluck out your right eye?"

Sariputra was slightly annoyed. "He could have told me that before I plucked out my right eye," he thought to himself. But Sariputra easily overcame his initial annoyance. "A Bodhisattva is an embodiment of compassion," he said to himself, "since I have decided to help him, I would not stop half way." His compassion prevailed over the pain of losing his eyes. He plucked out the other eye and gave it to the filial son to cure his aged mother.

The man put the eye to his nose. "What a smelly eye," he said, "of what use can such a smelly eye be!" He tossed the eye away.

Sariputra shook his head. "It is indeed difficult to be a Bodhisattva," he sighed, "I'd better remain an Arahant!"

Of course you need not pluck out your eyes if you wish to be a bodhisattva. Sharing with others the wonderful benefits of the teaching presented in this book is one way of manifesting the compassionate heart.

SELECTED COMMENTARIES FROM THE CLASSICS

(What Past Masters Have Said About the Amitabha Sutra)

Through reciting and reciting Buddha's name, we attain perfect enlightenment; eventually we realize that the phenomenal world is actually a creation of the mind.

Commentaries Through the Centuries

Although many people who practice the recitation of Buddha's name may not be aware of it, much has been written concerning the philosophy and practice of the Buddha-recitation method since its establishment in the 5th century until now. Fortunately it is not difficult to examine these influential writings because 179 of the most important, ranging from the Tang Dynasty right until the present time, have been selected and edited by Mao Shi Yuan in his "Principles and Practice of the Buddha-Recitation School".

The following quotations are all taken from this invaluable book, and are translated from classical Chinese into English. To illustrate the profound philosophy of this Buddha-recitation method through the years, a text from each dynastic period is presented.

The Buddha-recitation method is the most popular means of spiritual cultivation in Buddhism. Basically it involves reciting the name of a Buddha, to the exclusion of all other thoughts, hundreds or even thousands of times per session. Sometimes the relevant sutra is first recited, followed by chanting the name of the Buddha, and sometimes of a Bodhisattva, usually in a rhythmic and often musical manner. The name of the Buddha most popularly chanted is Amitabha. This Buddha-recitation method is the most important means of cultivation in the Pure Land School, but it is also widely used in all other Mahayana schools.

Classical Chinese is a very concise language, and background information which the initiated are expected to know (but which modern readers may not be familiar with) is often left out in the classical writings.

Such information is included in brackets in the quotations below for readers' convenience. The quotations are only selected parts, not whole pieces of the classical writings. If readers find some of the translated expression "funny", please remember that while both are great languages, Chinese and English are vastly different in style and vocabulary; in the translation, especially in translating the titles of the various selected pieces below, I often keep to the original style and vocabulary so as to capture the flavor of the Chinese masters.

One-Pointed Recitation

Treatise on One-Pointed or Assorted Cultivation for the Pure Land by the great Venerable Shan Dao (meaning Kind Guidance") of the Tang Dynasty. The Venerable Shan Dao is regarded by many as an incarnation of Amitabha Buddha himself.

Why is the cultivation method not meditation, but a direct, specific recitation of Amitabha's name? The reasons are that sentient beings have heavy obstacles impeding their cultivation, their ability to visualize is weak and gross, their consciousness scattered and mental concentration dispersed. Hence it is difficult for them to succeed if they use meditation.

The great sage (i.e. Amitabha) is compassionate; he exhorts a direct recitation of his name. As the name recitation is easy, continuous recitation will result in rebirth (in the Western Paradise). If one can recites Amitabha Buddha's name continuously, with one's lifetime as the period (for cultivation), when he recites ten times, he enhances (the possibility of such a) rebirth ten times; when he recites a hundred times, he enhances a hundred times.

Why is this so? Without external, irrelevant conditions, the aspirant (when he recites Amitabha's name) will attain the right thought, (thus generating a mental frequency) that responds correctly to the vow of the Buddha. This is not going against his teaching, but following the Buddha's instruction.

If some people use other cultivation methods instead of this one-pointed recitation, it is difficult to find one or two successes out of a hundred attempts, three or four out of a thousand. Why is this so? It is because as varied conditions prevail, right thought (in focusing on rebirth in the Pure Land) is lost. Such is not in correspondence with the Buddha's vow; it is against his teaching, and not according to the Buddha's instruction. As the thought (of rebirth in the Western Paradise) is not continuously kept in mind, as the heart is not constantly thinking of repaying the Buddha's kindness, as karma which will perpetuate the quest for worldly fame and mundane benefits is generated, as people are glad to involve themselves with mundane conditions, obstacles arise that block themselves and others in the practice to gain rebirth (in the Western Paradise).

May all people and all other beings be virtuous in their thoughts and daily activities. May they be able to control their hearts and subdue their selves, and not waste their days or nights (for not cultivating). (If we can maintain the practice that) as soon as a thought (of Amitabha) is spent, another thought (of Amitabha) arises, we will forever enjoy supramundane bliss, till we attain Buddhahood. Be quick to make up your mind to cultivate.

Faith, Practice and Vow

Three Times Important Business in Reciting Buddha's Name by the Venerable Pu Zhao (meaning "Omniscient Radiance") of the Song Dynasty.

The teaching of the Pure Land School is derived from the power of the great merciful, great compassionate forty eight vows of Amitabha Buddha, who will transport and receive all sentient beings of the ten directions possessing strong faith, to be reborn (in his Western Paradise). The faithful believe in the existence of the Western Pure Land, and believe in the truth of Amitabha Buddha receiving sentient beings. We the sentient beings believe in the opportunity to be reborn (in the Western Paradise).

Although Amitabha receives sentient beings to be reborn (in his Western Paradise, on the other hand), it is necessary for us to have faith that this manifestation (of the Western Paradise) is in line with (the creation of) our mind, so that there is interaction of mutual correspondence (between Amitabha's grace and our own mind). Ultimately (the Western Paradise is) not obtained from the outside. Such belief is regarded as right faith.

Faith without practice is not right faith. Practice, according to the Lankavatara Sutra, involves all the six roots (of eye, ear, nose, tongue, body and consciousness); purity (of mind) and recitation (of Amitabha's name) are mutually related. The Amitabha Sutra says, "hearing this teaching about Amitabha Buddha, recites Buddha's name for one day, or two days, or three days, or four days, or five days, or six days, or seven days, recites wholeheartedly without any other thoughts." Such is practice, which is named right practice.

Practice without (making a) vow does not constitute the right practice. The aspirant making this vow must be in mutual correspondence with the forty eight great vows of Amitabha Buddha, so that his vow is a great vow. Faith, practice and vow are like the three legs of a gigantic three-legged cauldron, and it is not possible to lack any one factor. The aspirant should know that each recitation of Amitabha's name is originally perfect and constant (in line with the Supreme Reality). Faith, practice and vow are originally our virtuous self-nature (or Supreme Reality); now self-nature manifests and radiates in full glory.

When deluded mind and irrelevant thoughts arise, if the aspirant can hold on to the one thought of the great Compassionate Lord, and accordingly recite the six-word sounding name, with each word leaving the mouth and entering the ear, the irrelevant thoughts will naturally disappear with the recitation of Amitabha Buddha's name. He proceeds from one recitation to ten recitations, to continuous recitations without interruption; this is what is mentioned as the interaction of purity and recitation in the Pure Land School.

Followers of the Buddha-recitation method must have unquivering faith concerning the natural operation of right cause, seriously realize the misery of the cycle of life and death in samsara, and deeply abhor the pain of the defiled world. If they constantly recite the name of the Buddha, without harboring any perverse views, till the mind is one-pointed, they can attain the extinction of dualism. The attainment (of this recitation method) need not be described again here. Wherefore is there any futile effort and regret in following this path. Thus the miraculous art of the practice and verification (of the Buddha-recitation method) is the right path that surpasses other expedient means.

Pure Land of the Mind

Precious Mirror of the Lotus School by the Venerable You Tan (meaning "Beautiful Clouds") of the Yuan Dynasty.

In the cultivation of Buddha-recitation to subdue the mind, if you are desirous to attain samadhi (or deep meditative state) quickly, counting the breath as a means to overcome drowsiness is most important. Whenever you intend to meditate, first think of your body in a ball of light, then silently observe your breathing through your nose. Think of breathing out and in, and recite Amitabha Buddha once with each breath.

Regulate your breathing expediently, ensuring that it is neither slow nor quick. Your mind and your breathing are merged together as one unity. And you follow your breath out and in while you are walking, standing, sitting, or lying down. Practice in this manner, and do not allow the practice to be interrupted. Practice regularly and constantly until you have attained a deep level of meditation, whereby your breathing and recitation are both forgotten. Thus your body and mind and the open space are gradually united, your mind's eye is open, and samadhi occurs. This is called Pure Land of the Mind.

The Treatise of Precious King says, "Those employing the cultivation of one characteristic Buddha-recitation samadhi, should unremittingly recite (the name of the Buddha) while they are walking, standing, sitting or lying down, so that even from a drowsy, sleepy state, a practitioner can be awakened to proceed with his practice. Do not discontinue the practice due to work; do not let greed, anger, etc interrupt your cultivation. As soon as you make a mistake, repent immediately. Do not let your thought (of Amitabha Buddha) be interrupted; do not let your thought be deviated (from thinking of the Pure Land); do not (let your cultivation) be interrupted by days; do not (let your cultivation) be interrupted by time (i.e. do not disrupt your cultivation on any day and at any time). Every recitation (made by you) is never unrelated with the Buddha; every recitation leads to tranquility and purity, perfection and enlightenment. This is the attainment of one-characteristic samadhi.

Bodhisattvas (here, "bodhisattvas" means devoted cultivators working for their own as well as other's salvation) who practice at home, worship the Buddha, and follow the (Buddhist) precepts. Those people who, because of daily work and family commitments, are unable to cultivate wholeheartedly (like monks), should wake up early, pray to the Triple Gem (as represented by the Buddha, the Teaching, and the Monastic Order), and recite Buddha's name in accordance with their own aspiration. Similarly, in the evening they should worship the Buddha and recite his name. This constitutes the regular service. If you miss any service because of commitment elsewhere, seek repentance from the Buddha the next day.

This school of cultivation places no restriction on your occupation. The intelligentsia may carry on with their studies, those who live by the earth may continue with their farming; workers may continue with their jobs; those involved in trade may carry on their buying and selling. Besides the morning and evening services, one should also in the twelve time-periods (of the day), amidst their work, take some time off to recite Buddha's name hundreds of times, thousands of times. If you cultivate sincerely, attainment will (surely) come; at the end of your life-period, you will be reborn in the Pure Land.

Mind and Cosmic Reality

Collection of Spiritual Teachings in the Clouds by the Venerable Lian Chi (meaning "Lotus Pond") of the Ming Dynasty.

The Mind (i.e. the Supreme Reality) is actually without thought. When thought arises, there occurs the vehicle (that transforms transcendental reality into the phenomenal world). From the beginningless beginning sentient beings have had the habit of deluded thought, and this habit has not changed. At present the teaching of Buddha-recitation is (employing the principle of) using poison against poison, using soldiers to stop soldiers. There are many ways in this method of Buddha-recitation. Now this special way of using Buddha's name is the middle of the ways, the way of the ways, because the Buddha possesses infinite merits. This four-word name (i.e. A-Mi-Tuo-Fo, meaning Amitabha Buddha) is sufficient to be the nucleus, as Amitabha (Buddha) is the whole Heart (i.e. the Universal Mind). The Heart includes all merits, which are permanent, blissful, universal and tranquil (i.e. the four cardinal aspects of cosmic reality). Self-enlightenment and original enlightenment, ultimate reality and Buddha nature, bodhi and nirvana, hundreds of thousands terms are all in one name (of Amitabha Buddha), where nothing is not included in it. When sentient beings following the True Teaching, there are infinite methods to practice. Now this one method of reciting the Buddha's name is sufficient to be the nucleus (that includes all methods). This method of reciting Buddha's name is (the method) to the one (and only one) Mind. The Mind is the nucleus of myriad methods, the Four Noble Truths and the Six Paramitas, and eighty four thousand cultivation methods, as numerous as the sand grains of the Ganges River and as fine as minute dust particles. What this (method of reciting Buddha's name) includes is boundless.

There are numerous ways to recite Buddha's name, such as open cultivation, i.e. reciting aloud; silent cultivation, i.e. reciting silently; and half-open-half-silent cultivation, i.e. reciting by slightly moving the lips, or what mantra experts refer to as diamond cultivation. Also there is the cultivation where the number of recitations is accounted for, and where it is not accounted for. The aspirant may use whatever way is suitable.

Moreover, these recitation methods may be classified as "event-based" and "understanding-based". If though-recitation is continuous without any interruption by any event, it is called event-based cultivation. If there is thorough experience without interruption, it is called understanding-based cultivation.

By thought-recitation is meant that the aspirant always thinks of the recitation of Buddha's name, with the mind as the source, with every word clearly enunciated, each word following the earlier one without break. Whether walking, standing, sitting or lying down (the aspirant) is filled with this one thought (of Amitabha Buddha) and without a second thought. He is never at all distracted by greed, anger, or miscellaneous deluded thoughts, and he achieves what the Enlightened Meditation Sutra refers to as: "Space becomes tranquil as one mind; even in the midst of miscellaneous defilements there is one mind, until goodness and evil lose their meaning in one mind."

In terms of events, this kind of cultivation is successful, but in terms of understanding, it is not yet thorough. Thus, although there is faith, as the aspirant has not seen the Tao (or cosmic reality in its transcendental dimension), this method is called event-based cultivation to attain the One Mind.

In the understanding-based cultivation where the aspirant has thorough experience, the aspirant not only thinks of, recites and hears the Buddha's name, but he also meditates (on Amitabha Buddha) as he recites. He thoroughly experiences and investigates, seeks the roots and source (of the experience). The deep experience comes from his mind; suddenly his mind and cosmic reality are united in his body as two in one.

Originally cosmic reality and wisdom are not two. When meditating outside the mind, there is no Buddha outside the mind to meditate on: this is the concept of no reality outside wisdom. Outside the Buddha, there is no mind to meditate on the Buddha: this is the concept of no mind outside reality. There is non-reality and non-wisdom; thus it is the one Mind. The two (reality and wisdom) are directly manifested, and are difficult to be conceptualized. If we say they exist, then the mind that can conceptualize is actually empty; the Buddha that is conceptualized is therefore not attainable. If we say they do not exist, then the mind that can conceptualize is clearly perceptible; the Buddha that is conceptualize is discernibly differentiated. If we say they are either existent or non-existent, then both thought and non-thought become both extinguished. If we say they are neither existent nor non-existent, then both thought and non-thought are both retained. Non-existent means constantly tranquil; non non-existent means constantly manifested. Neither existent nor non-existent means non-tranquil and non-manifested, and tranquil and manifested. This is the end of verbalization and conceptualization; there is no way to name it; thus it is one Mind. This is the extinction of the senses, existence and non-existence become infinite, the original body (of the cosmos) becomes pure and tranquil. Therefore are there methods that can (enable the aspirant to) perceive the truth from such difficulty and confusion, (except) this cultivation of one Mind (through understanding and direct experience)?

For those who are expert in events, if they approach from the perspective of understanding, they will attain understanding but will meet obstacles of events, (and vice versa). It is necessary to proceed from both perspectives, and not to be biased on one side. When focusing on events, the aspirant recites (Buddha's name); then it is possible to have mutual correspondence (between events and understanding), and without futility enter the effort of attainment. On the other hand, if he merely focuses on understanding, but does not realize the significance (of practice), he may have the calamity of being futile.

Words, Deeds and Thoughts

Forty Eight Important Points in the Buddha-Recitation Method by the Venerable Miao Kong (meaning "Wonderful Emptiness") of the Jing Dynasty.

Recite the name of the Buddha with a one-pointed mind. Do not have any miscellaneous thoughts of kindness or evil. Except for daily chores which are absolutely necessary to be done, do not do anything else. Once you have completed your chores (or whatever necessary work) leave it behind; do not let it linger and hamper your (concentration of) Buddha-recitation. As you use your mouth to recite Buddha's name, you must not use your mouth to mention anything to do with killing, robbing, sexual misconduct, delusion (and other unwholesome words). If there are any inklings (on these unwholesome activities), you must immediately remind yourself that cultivators of the Buddha-recitation method should not be thus. Vigorously recite the name of the Buddha a few times as a reminder and a neutralizer (of these unwholesome thoughts).

As you use your body to recite Buddha's name (i.e. this Buddha-recitation method is carried out in your physical body), your movement, standing, sitting and lying down (i.e. whatever you do) must be upright. When the body is upright (i.e. when all our actions are righteous), the heart will be tranquil and pure.

As you recite once, push up one bead with your fingers. Just recite four words (i.e. A-Mi-Tuo-Fo, meaning Amitabha Buddha); do not confuse yourself with six words (i.e. Na-Mo-A-Mi-Tuo-Fo, meaning Homage to Amitabha Buddha). Use the four words as a phrase. You may push up one bead at the word "A", or at the word "Fo". Decide on the system to use; do not be mistaken or confused (such as not remembering whether the bead should be counted at "A" or "Fo"). This is the technique of using the bead to tame the heart (i.e. by focusing the recitation with the aid of the beads, you attain a one-pointed mind).

If you mind is drowsy, or when delude thoughts arise, brace yourself up and recite loudly Buddha's name a few hundred times. This will naturally change your perception (i.e. your mental condition). As the root of the ear (i.e. ear-consciousness) is most sensitive, external influences can easily enter (into your mind). Whenever you hear any sound, your mind will move, and miscellaneous thoughts become familiar. Thus, you must recite Buddha's name loudly so as to protect the ear-root (from hearing other distracting sounds), and open the soul of the heart. The heart listens to your own sound (of the Buddha-recitation); every sound is decisive and full. All irrelevant thoughts will naturally be eliminated.

If the mind becomes dispersed and lost, or when you are exceedingly fatigued, there is no need to recite loudly, but keep your consciousness intact and recite softly and gently, until your energy is restored and your mind alert, then you can recite loudly.

If your heart energy is not flowing smoothly (such as the mind or the heart is irritated), or if there are any hindrances (or disturbances) from people or places, then just move your lips and recite using the special diamond method (i.e. pronouncing the words with the lips but without sound or very softly audible only to yourself).

It does not matter how little or much you recite, but every word must pass the heart. When the heart has meditated on the word, it is moved by the tongue; when the tongue has moved the word, it returns to the heart. When the tongue makes any sound, the ear hears your own sound. This is the technique of the heart reciting and the heart hearing. When your heart hears its recitation, the eye does not see delusively, the nose does not smell delusively, the body does not move delusively. The host (i.e. your Buddha-nature or your real self) is invited out by the four words of A-Mi-Tuo-Fo (i.e. your real self has realized the Universal Self or you have attained Buddhahood).

Or you may use the special diamond technique, which is still reminiscent of its trace (i.e which still reminds us of its popular use in the past). In the ancient times, this diamond technique was regarded as a marvelous expedient means. There is no need to move the mouth to emit any sound, but it enables the condition of focusing the heart. When the tongue gently drums on the front teeth, the heart reacts accordingly. The sound is spontaneous, and it does not escape from the mouth. Realizing the nature (of the Supreme Reality) you become internally merged (i.e. the so-called "inside" merges with the so-called "outside", thus overcoming dualism and attaining the realization of transcendental, undifferentiated reality.

The heart reflects the function of the tongue, this function uproots thoughts (and when thoughts no longer arise, karma ceases and the cycle of rebirths is overcome). Thus, from hearing you enter the stream (i.e. you employ the ear-consciousness as an expedient means to enter the stream of spiritual cultivation), and realize your self nature (which actually is transcendental cosmic reality). This is the merging of the three (which means the mind, phenomena and ultimate reality are actually the same — we perceive them as separate and differentiated because of our ignorance). Through reciting and reciting Buddha's name, we attain perfect enlightenment; eventually we realize that the phenomenal world is actually a creation of the mind.

(Note: what the Venerable Wonderful Emptiness teaches is not just rebirth in the Western Paradise, but perfect enlightenment through reciting the name of Amitabha Buddha.)

Zen and Amitabha Buddha

Collection of Teachings by the Venerable Xu Yun (meaning "Empty Clouds") of the modern times. Xu Yun is a celebrated Zen master.

Practicing Zen and reciting the name of the Buddha appear like two separate methods to those who have just started to cultivate. For those who have cultivated for a long time, they are the same method. In practicing Zen, the aspirant meditates on a *hua-tou* (*mondo* or Zen question, such as what was your face like before you were born?), which overcomes the continuous flow of life and death. The aspirant starts with unwavering faith: if he falters in persisting with his *hua-tou*, he would not be successful in his Zen cultivation.

If his faith is strong and steadfast, and he stubbornly embraces his *hua-tou* and perseveres in its meditation until he does not realize it is tea when he drinks tea, nor rice when he eats rice. When his cultivation is ripe, his defilement will be dropped, and enlightenment will appear before him. This is similar to the ripening of Buddha-recitation when the Pure Land appears before him.

When such a stage is reached, principles and phenomena merge perfectly. The mind and the Buddha are not different. (In the transcendental dimension where reality is undifferentiated and unseparated) Buddhas are the same as sentient beings; there is only One, and not two (which means there is only infinite unity and no dualism). Wherefore is the difference (between Zen and Buddha-recitation)?

AMITABHA SUTRA

Thus have I heard. Once, the Buddha was preaching to twelve hundred of his disciples at the Anathapindika Garden of Jeta Grove in the country of Sravasti. The Buddha said:

"Sariputra, passing over ten million Buddha-lands to our west is a world known as the Western Paradise of Eternal Bliss, where a Buddha called Amitabha teaches the Law.

Sariputra, why is this world called the Paradise of Eternal Bliss? It is because the inhabitants of this world not only have no suffering, but also have boundless bliss, unlike the inhabitants of our world who have to endure the suffering of birth, age, sickness and death.

This world is beautiful and majestic, surrounded by lush plants and jeweled trees, with magnificent buildings of gold, silver, lapis-lazuli, crystals and pearls, and there are ponds with lotus flowers of many colors. The air is filled with celestial music, and heavenly showers of mandarava flowers. Such is this world, brought to so glorious a state of excellence through the merits of Amitabha Buddha.

In this Pure Land, there are marvelous birds like cranes, peacocks, parrots, swans, jiva-jivas and kala-vinkas, singing harmoniously. Hearing their sweet singing spontaneously makes the inhabitants think of the Buddha, Dharma and Sangha.

Sariputra, do not think that these birds are born there due to their previous bad karma. In this Pure Land there is no evil, so how can there be a realm of animals suffering from their bad karma? Actually these birds are created by Amitabha Buddha to help spread the teaching of the Buddha. And when gentle breeze blows through the jeweled trees, gentle music is created as if thousands of musical instruments are playing in harmony. When the inhabitants hear such harmonious music, they spontaneously meditate on the Buddha, Dharma and Sangha. Such is this Buddha-land, brought to so glorious a state of excellence through the merits of Amitabha Buddha.

Sariputra, why do you think this Buddha is called Amitabha? It is because the radiant light of this Buddha is boundless, illuminating all lands in all directions without hindrance. Also, the existence of this Buddha and all the inhabitants of this Buddha-land is boundless, of infinite kalpas. Thus he is called Amitabha Buddha. Ten kalpas have passed since Amitabha became a Buddha. Here, there are countless Sravaka-disciples, Arahats and Bodhisattvas. The inhabitants of this land of Eternal Bliss are Avarvartyas, i.e. beings who will never retreat from the Bodhi path. Many are Ekajati-Pratibuddhas, i.e. those who will become Buddhas in just one more lifetime.

Sariputra, all sentient beings who hear this sutra should make a great vow, vow to be born in this Buddha-land so as to be with such virtuous beings. But one must not be lacking in virtues and merits to be born here.

Sariputra, if virtuous men and virtuous women, hearing the name of Amitabha, recite his name for one day, or two days, or three days, or four days, or five days, or six days, or seven days, keeping their mind undisturbed, when these men and women are about to pass away, Amitabha Buddha and various holy beings will appear before them. If these men and women are firm in their aspiration, they will be born in Amitabha's land of Eternal Bliss. As I see such great benefit, so I give this advice: sentient beings who hear this sutra should make a vow to be reborn in this Buddha-land.

Sariputra, as I now praise the incredible merits of Amitabha Buddha, in the East there are Akshobhya Buddha, Merudhvaja Buddha, Mahameru Buddha, Meruprabhasa Buddha, Manjudhvaja Buddha, and countless other Buddhas numerous like the sands of River Ganges, each in his own country, speaks forth sincerely and truthfully with omnipotent tongue, pervading all the worlds in the countless universes, proclaiming thus: May all sentient beings have faith in this sutra which extols the incredible merits of Amitabha Buddha, and which is guarded and recited by all Buddhas.

Sariputra, in the South there Chandra-Suryapradipa Buddha, Yasahprabha Buddha, Maharchiskandha Buddha, Merupradipa Buddha, Anantavirya Buddha, and countless other Buddhas numerous like the sands of River Ganges, each in his own country, speaks forth sincerely and truthfully with omnipotent tongue, pervading all the worlds in the countless universes, proclaiming thus: May all sentient beings have faith in this sutra which extols the incredible merits of Amitabha Buddha, and which is guarded and recited by all Buddhas.

Sariputra, in the West there are Amitayur Buddha, Amitaskandha Buddha, Amitadhvaja Buddha, Mahaprabha Buddha, Mararatnaketu Buddha, Suddharasmiprahba Buddha, and countless other Buddhas numerous like the sands of River Ganges, each in his own country, speaks forth sincerely and truthfully with omnipotent tongue, pervading all the worlds in the countless universes, proclaiming thus: May all sentient beings have faith in this sutra which extols the incredible merits of Amitabha Buddha, and which is guarded and recited by all Buddhas.

Sariputra, in the North there are Archiskandha Buddha, Vaisvanarairghosha Buddha, Dushprabharasha Buddha, Adityasambhava Buddha, Jeleniprabha Buddha, and countless other Buddhas numerous like the sands of River Ganges, each in his own country, speaks forth sincerely and truthfully with omnipotent tongue, pervading all the worlds in the countless universes, proclaiming thus: May all sentient beings have faith in this sutra which extols the incredible merits of Amitabha Buddha, and which is guarded and recited by all Buddhas.

Sariputra, in the Nadir there are Simha Buddha, Yasas Buddha, Yasasprabhava Buddha, Dharma Buddha, Dharmadhvaja Buddha, Dharmadhara Buddha, and countless other Buddhas numerous like the sands of River Ganges, each in his own country, speaks forth sincerely and truth-fully with omni-potent tongue, pervading all the worlds in the countless universes, proclaiming thus: May all sentient beings have faith in this sutra which extols the incredible merits of Amitabha Buddha, and which is guarded and recited by all Buddhas.

Sariputra, in the Zenith there are Brahmaghosha Buddha, Nakshatraraja Buddha, Gandhatama Buddha, Grandhaprabhasa Buddha, Maharchiskandha Buddha, Ratnakusumasampushpitagtra Buddha, Salendraraja Buddha, Ratnapalasri Buddha, Saruarthadarsa Buddha, Semerukalpa Buddha, and countless other Buddhas numerous like the sands of River Ganges, each in his own country, speaks forth sincerely and truthfully with omnipotent tongue, pervading all the worlds in the countless universes, proclaiming thus: May all sentient beings have faith in this sutra which extols the incredible merits of Amitabha Buddha, and which is guarded and recited by all Buddhas.

Sariputra, why do you think this sutra is guarded and recited by all Buddhas? It is because if there are virtuous men and virtuous women who hear this sutra and recite the name of Amitabha, or the names of the Buddhas just mentioned, they will be protected and favored by the Buddhas, and will never retreat from attaining Anuttara-Samyak-Sambodhi, or the supreme wisdom.

Thus, you all should believe in what I and all other Buddhas have said. Sariputra, if sentient beings have made their vows, or are making their vows, or will make their vows to be born in the Buddha-land of Amitabha, they will not retreat from the attainment of Anuttara-Samyak-Sambodhi, and accomplish their vows.

Sariputra, as I now glorify the incredible merits of all Buddhas, they, too, glorify mine, saying: Sakyamuni Buddha has accomplished such a difficult and rare task; has accomplished in this Saha world of five defilements — the defilements of time, perverse views, passions, sentient beings, and samsara — the attainment of Anuttara-Samyak-Sambodhi, and the teaching which sentient beings find hard to believe. Sariputra, you should understand that in this Saha world of defilements, to accomplish Anuttara-Samyak-Sambodhi, and to teach all beings such an incredible doctrine are indeed very difficult."

Having listened to this sutra, Sariputra and the monks, and all beings, like gods, humans, and spirits, were very happy to accept and practice this teaching of the Buddha. They paid homage to the Buddha, and then departed.

Bibliography

Chapter 1

1. Karl Ludvig Reichelt, Truth and Tradition in Chinese Buddhism, Paragon Book, New York, 1928, reprinted 1968, p. 146.
2. August Karl Reischauer, Studies in Japanese Buddhism, Ams Press, New York, 1917, reprinted 1970, p.218.

Chapter 4

1. Robert Oppenheimer, in Lawrence LeShan, Clairvoyant Reality, Turnstone Press, Wellingborough, 1982, p.73
2. Alastair Rae, Quantum Physics: Illusion or Reality?, Cambridge University Press,
   1986, p.50.

Chapter 5

1. The Lotus Sutra, quoted in W.E.Soothill, The Lotus of the Wonderful Law, Claredon Press, Oxford 1930, p. 74-75.
2. The Lotus Sutra, ibid., p.73.
3. Quoted in Grahman Philips, The Missing Universe, Penguin Books Australia, 1994, p.70.
4. Edward Conze, A Short History of Buddhism, Unwin Paperbacks, London, 1986, p.43.
5. Ibid., p.59.
6. Ibid., p.104.
7. Some accounts say the Buddha taught for forty nine years.
8. William James, The Varieties of Religious Experience, Penguin Books, New York, 1902, reprinted 1958, p.321.

Useful Addresses

MALAYSIA

Grandmaster Wong Kiew Kit,
81 Taman Intan B/5,
08000 Sungai Petani, Kedah, Malaysia.
Tel: (60-4) 422-2353
Fax: (60-4) 422-7812
E-mail: shaolin@pd.jaring.my
URL: http://shaolin-wahnam.tripod.com/
index.html
http://www.shaolin-wahnam.org

Master Ng Kowi Beng,
20, Lorong Murni 33,
Taman Desa Murni Sungai Dua,
13800 Butterworth, Pulau Pinang,
Malaysia.
Tel: (60-4) 356-3069
Fax: (60-4) 484-4617
E-mail : kowibeng@tm.net.my

Master Cheong Huat Seng,
22 Taman Mutiara,
08000 Sungai Petani, Kedah, Malaysia.
Tel: (60-4) 421-0634

Master Goh Kok Hin,
86 Jalan Sungai Emas,
08500 Kota Kuala Muda, Kedah,
Malaysia.
Tel: (60-4) 437-4301

Master Chim Chin Sin,
42 Taman Permai,
08100 Bedong, Kedah, Malaysia.
Tel: (60-4) 458-1729
Mobile Phone: (60) 012-552-6297

Master Morgan A/L Govindasamy,
3086 Lorong 21, Taman Ria,
08000 Sungai Petani, Kedah, Malaysia.
Tel: (60-4) 441-4198

Master Yong Peng Wah,
Shaolin Wahnam Chi Kung and Kung Fu,
181 Taman Kota Jaya,
34700 Simpang, Taiping, Perak, Malaysia.
Tel: (60-5) 847-1431

AUSTRALIA

Mr. George Howes,
33 Old Ferry Rd, Banora Point,
NSW 2486, Australia.
Tel: 00-61-7-55245751

AUSTRIA

Sylvester Lohninger,
Maitreya Institute,
Blättertal 9,
A-2770 Gutenstein.
Telephone: 0043-2634-7417
Fax: 0043-2634-74174
E-mail: sequoyah@nextra

BELGIUM

Dr. Daniel Widjaja,
Steenweg op Brussel 125,
1780 Wemmel, Belgium.
Tel: 00-32-2-4602977
Mobile Phone: 00-32-474-984739
Fax: 00-32-2-4602987
E-mails: dan widjaja@hotmail.com,
daniel.widjaja@worldonline.be

CANADA

Dr. Kay Lie,
E-mail: kayl@interlog.com

Mrs. Jean Lie,
Toronto, Ontario.
Telephone/Fax: (416) 979-0238
E-mail: kayl@interlog.com

Miss Emiko Hsuen,
67 Churchill Avenue, North York,
Ontario, M2N 1Y8, Canada.
Tel: 1-416-250-1812
Fax: 1 - 416- 221-5264
E-mail: emiko@attcanada.ca

Mr Neil Burden,
Vancouver, British Columbia.
Telephone/Fax: (250) 247-9968
E-mail: cosmicdragon108@hotmail.com

ENGLAND

Mr. Christopher Roy Leigh Jones,
9a Beach Street, Lytham, Lancashire,
FY8 5NS, United Kingdom.
Tel: 0044-1253-736278
E-mail: barbara.rawlinson@virgin.net

Mr. Dan Hartwright,
Rumpus Cottage, Church Place,
Pulborough, West Sussex RH20 1AF, UK.
Tel: 0044-7816-111007
E-mail: dhartWright@hotmail.com

GERMANY

Grandmaster Kai Uwe Jettkandt,
Ostendstr. 79,
60314 Frankfurt, Germany.
Tel: 49-69-90431678
E-mail: Kaijet@t-online.de

HOLLAND

Dr. Oetti Kwee Liang Hoo,
Tel: 31-10-5316416

IRELAND

Miss Joan Brown,
Mullin, Scatazlin, Castleisland, County,
Kerry, Ireland.
Tel: 353-66-7147545
Mobile Phone: 353-87-6668374
E-mail: djbrowne@gofree.indigo.ie

ITALY

Master Roberto Lamberti,
Hotel Punta Est Via Aurelia, 1
17024 Finale Ligure (SV), Italy.
Tel: ++39019600611
Mobile Phone: ++393393580663
E-mails: robertolamberti@libero.it

Master Attilio Podestà,
Via Aurelia 1,
17024 Finale Ligure (Savona), Italy.
Tel/Fax: +39 019 600 611
E-mail: attiliopodesta@libero.it
OR
Hotel Punta Est Via Aurelia 1,
17024 Finale Ligure (Savona), Italy.
E-mail: info@puntaest.com
Web-site: www.puntaest.com

Mr. Riccardo Puleo,
via don Gnocchi, 28,
20148 Milano, Italy.
Tel: 0039-02-4078250
E-mail: rpuleo@efficient-finance.com

LITHUANIA

Mr. Arunas Krisiunas,
Sauletekio al.53-9,
2040 Vilnius, Lithuania.
Tel: +3702-700-237
Mobile Phone: +370-9887353
E-mail: induva@iti.lt

PANAMA

Mr. Raúl A. López R.,
16, "B" st., Panama City,
Republic of Panama.
OR
P.O. Box 1433, Panama 9A-1433.
Tel: (507) 618-1836
E-mail: raullopez@cwpanama.net
taiko@hotmail.com

PORTUGAL

Dr Riccardo Salvatore,
Tel: 351-218478713

SCOTLAND

Mr. Darryl Collett,
c/o 19A London Street, Edinburgh,
EH3 6LY, United Kingdom.
Mobile phone: 0790-454-7538
E-mail: CollDod@aol.com

SPAIN

Master Laura Fernández,
C/ Madre Antonia de París, 2 esc. izq. 4° A,
Madrid - 28027 – Spain.
Tel: 34-91-6386270

Javier Galve,
Tai Chi Chuan and Chi Kung Instructor
of the Shaolin Wahnam Institute
C/Guadarrama 3-2°A-28011-Madrid,
Spain.
Phone: 34-91-4640578
Mobile Phone: 34-656669790
E-mail: shaolin@inicia.es

Master Adalia Iglesias,
calle Cometa, n° 3, atico,
08002 Barcelona, Spain.
Tel: 0034-93-3104956
E-mail: adalia@xenoid.com

Master Román Garcia Lampaya,
71, Av. Antonio Machad,
Santa Cruz del Valle,
05411 Avila, Spain.
Tel: 34-920-386717, 34-915-360702
Mobile Phone : 34-656-612608
E-mail: romangarcia@wanadoo.es

Master José Díaz Marqués,
C/. del Teatro, 13
41927 Mairena del Aljarafe / Sevilla,
Spain.
Tel: + 34-954-183-917
Mobile Phone: 34-656-756214
Fax: + 34-955-609-354
E-mail: transpersonal@infotelmultimedia.es

Dr. Inaki Rivero Urdiain,
Aguirre Miramon, 6 – 4° dch.,
20002 San Sebastian, Spain.
Tel: + 34-943-360213
Mobile Phone: 34-656-756214
E-mail: psiconet@euskalnet.net
Web-site: www.euskalnet.net/psicosalud

Master Douglas Wiesenthal,
C/ Almirante Cadarso 26, P-14
46005 Valencia, Spain
Tel/Fax: +34 96-320-8433
E-mail: dwiesenthal@yahoo.com

Master Trini
Ms Trinidad Parreno,
E-mail: trinipar@wanadoo.es

SOUTH AFRICA

Grandmaster Leslie James Reed,
312 Garensville, 285 Beach Road, Sea Point,
Cape Town, 8000 South Africa.
Tel/Fax: 0927-21-4391373
E-mail: itswasa@mweb.co.za

SWITZERLAND

Mr. Andrew Barnett,
Bildweg 34, 7250 Klosters,
Switzerland.
Tel/Fax: +41-81-422-5235
Mobile Phone: +41-79-610-3781
E-mail: andrew.barnett@bluewin.ch

USA

Mr. Anthony Korahais,
546 W147th Street, Apt. 2-DR,
New York, New York, 10031, USA.
Tel: 917-270-4310, 212-854-0201
E-mails: anthony@korahais.com,
anthony@arch.columbia.edu

Mr. Eugene Siterman,
299 Carroll St., Brooklyn,
New York,11231.
Tel: 718-8555785
E-mail: qipaco@hotmail.com

Index